THE OLD GUILDHALL, NEWBURY. REMOVED 1828.
FROM AN ETCHING BY BLANDFORD FLETCHER.

A HISTORY OF NEWBURY

WALTER MONEY, F.S.A.

Introduction by
Helen M. Purvis, F.L.A.

NEWBURY BOOKSHOP
11 OXFORD STREET, NEWBURY
1972
&
THAMES VALLEY PRESS
MAIDENHEAD

First edition published in 1905 by
W. J. Blackett, Newbury, as The Popular History of Newbury.
This edition published 1972 for
Newbury Bookshop in conjunction with
Thames Valley Press, Maidenhead.

ISBN 0 90029 405 1

Printed in Great Britain by
Redwood Press Limited
Trowbridge, Wiltshire

FOREWORD

Money's much sought-after History of Newbury has for some time been in very short supply, and even if he has been able to track down a copy, the would-be purchaser has often had to pay a high price. I hope that by making it available in the present form a new generation may enjoy reading about the making of this English town, and that the book may again reach the wide audience it had when it was published, and which it richly deserves. It is not only a valuable history, it is a most readable story, and I hope that others may find the same pleasure in it that I found when I first read it.

I am most grateful to Miss Purvis, Newbury's Librarian and herself most knowledgeable on Newbury's history, for writing the new Introduction.

Newbury Bookshop 1972 — Nicholas Scarf, Bookseller.

INTRODUCTION TO THE 1972 EDITION

We of Newbury are eternally grateful for the works of Mr. Walter Money, for many towns have no such comprehensive histories to consult. Newbury Public Library is literally built on Money's HISTORY OF NEWBURY, for a copy was placed beneath the foundation stone, which was laid in 1905, the year of the original publication of the volume reprinted here. Money's History was also the first book borrowed from the library, and since then several generations have worn out numerous copies, which are in constant use, and have been lent far afield. A resident in America once wrote applying to become a member of the library in order to "borrow Money", but as there are known to be copies in Newbury's daughter-town of Newburyport, Mass., he was referred to sources nearer home.

The first Newbury history published by Walter Money was "THE FIRST AND SECOND BATTLES OF NEWBURY AND THE SIEGE OF DONNINGTON CASTLE" which appeared in 1881, a second edition following in 1884. Years of painstaking research, as well as prodigious local knowledge must have gone into this minutely detailed and colourful chronicle, in which the author overlooks no item of fact or legend. The book was highly praised by the historian S. R. Gardiner, and a copy was accepted by Queen Victoria. Modern historians have sometimes critized its military history, but it nevertheless remains an outstanding achievement.

In 1887 came the monumental "HISTORY OF THE ANCIENT TOWN AND BOROUGH OF NEWBURY IN THE COUNTY OF BERKS.", which is virtually a work of reference, and which includes a series of chronological notes, lists of Mayors and Rectors, extracts from the Churchwardens' Accounts, and copies of inscriptions. Nearly twenty years later there appeared the "POPULAR HISTORY OF NEWBURY", which may be read as an engrossing narrative. With illustrations and material on the surrounding district not included in the earlier work, it has a wide appeal to the reader who is not a student of history, but who enjoys stories of the past, especially when associated with familiar places.

Mr. Walter Money was born at Donnington in 1836, into a family which had been connected with the district for three hundred years. He received some architectural training, and his brother Mr. J. H. Money was a practising architect, who lived at Speenhamland, and who designed part of the Municipal Buildings, the former cattle market, and the Falkland Memorial on Wash Common. Mr. Walter Money married Miss C. A. Gilmore, whose parents lived in Herborough House in Bartholemew Street. The remains of this substantial brick house, which once stood in a pleasant garden, have recently been demolished for the widening of Market Street corner. When the motor showrooms of Messrs. Nias occupied the site, which they did until a few years ago, there was a plaque on the wall commemorating the Money family's association with the premises. In his later years he lived at Shaw Dene, keeping in touch with current affairs by means of that most modern invention, the wireless. He was a Fellow of the Society of Antiquaries, a founder member of the Newbury Field Club, and local secretary of the National Trust. His interests were varied, for he was also a promoter of the Didcot to Southampton railway line, a member of the Town Council, as well as designing the coat of arms then used by the Berkshire County Council. He gives the impression of having been a modest man, who would not object if a brief reference were made to one or two other Newbury writers whose works stand beside his on our shelves, and form a treasure-house of Newbury lore.

In 1839, when Walter Money was three years old, "THE HISTORY AND ANTIQUITIES OF NEWBURY AND ITS ENVIRONS" was published anonymously, printed by Hall and Marsh of Speenhamland. The original intention was to publish it in parts, but after part one the idea was abandoned, and it appeared as a complete work. The author, or perhaps one should say, compiler, since he acknowledges assistance from several other persons, was established as Mr. Edward Whitaker Gray, a gentleman of considerable influence in the town, Born in 1787, he died at Woodspeen in 1860, and is buried at Enborne. The Dictionary of National Biography describes him as a cheese-factor and mealman of Bartholemew Street. The "HISTORY AND ANTIQUITIES" is an attractive book, illustrated with several engravings, and it includes notes on twenty-eight local parishes, and a botanical catalogue. Mr. Gray is the first to record some of those little human anecdotes through which the past becomes very much alive for us. Some of these appear again in Money's histories, notably that of the roast pig in Lushy Gully, intended as supper for a group of hungry Parliamentarians, but inconsiderately carried off by a Royalist cannonball. This story was told to Mr. Gray by a friend of his who farmed at Enborne and whose great-grandfather was present at the scene; so close are we to past events.

In 1859, Mr. Henry Godwin, another F.S.A., who, though a native, lived for many years at The Lawn, Speen, and was a local solicitor, published a slim volume in yellow boards entitled "THE WORTHIES AND CELEBRITIES OF NEWBURY." Here we can read the history behind many great names, among which are some that grace our streets today: Pembroke, Dolman, Winchcombe, Packer. Mr. Godwin, like Walter Money, was a constant contributor of papers to Newbury Field Club, whose proceedings fortunately continue to this day and contain an invaluable fund of information on the town and its surroundings.

In recent years, local history and environmental studies have played an increasing part in teaching and learning, with a consequent demand for local sourcebooks. To satisfy this need, Miss Vera M. Garlick, M.A., formerly archivist of Newbury, published her modestly priced "NEWBURY SCRAPBOOK" designed for students and newcomers. This brings the history of the town up to date and emphasises aspects not previously covered, such as the development of industry and commerce in the area.

Money's "HISTORY" was originally published at 21s., the "BATTLES" at 7s. 6d., and the "POPULAR HISTORY" at 6s., figures which sound ludicrous in view of the price which one would have to pay today in the rare event of finding a secondhand copy of any of them.

Walter Money's tangible monument in the town is the gallery in the Borough Museum dedicated to his memory, but his name is a household word. It is a delight to see a reprint of this book, and to know that it is again available to a new generation of Newburians. It is a privilege to introduce to new readers this History, which is no dry-as-dust textbook, but the story of ordinary townspeople who lived here before us, and shaped, or were shaped by, events in that microcosm of English History—our home town.

Helen M. Purvis, F.L.A.,
Librarian.

Table of Contents.

CHAPTER XVII.

CHAPTER XVIII.

CHAPTER XIX.

CHAPTER XX.

CHAPTER XXI.

Table of Illustrations.

GEOLOGICAL PLATES AND DIAGRAMS.

A

POPULAR HISTORY

OF

NEWBURY.

CHAPTER I.

INTRODUCTORY—THE TOWN OF NEWBURY—ITS SITUATION—RAILWAY COMMUNICATION—MUNICIPAL BOROUGH—POPULATION—ITS SANITATION—ECCLESIASTICAL STATUS—ITS STREETS AND OLD HOUSES—SCOPE OF THE WORK.

Introductory. The bright and flourishing town of Newbury is an ancient and interesting place, whose annals bring prominently into relief many of the remarkable events of former times, and its neighbourhood is rich in historical associations.

Lying as it does in one of the most beautiful portions of the fertile valley of the swift-flowing Kennet, which winds gracefully through the rich and verdant meadows which gird its margin, it would seem to have always been the home of peace and tranquillity, and yet few towns in our island have seen more of the war and turmoil which in times past devastated our land. We know how its old castle valiantly stood out for the proud Empress Matilda, and the graphic story of its siege by King Stephen constitutes one of the most dramatic episodes in this contest between the two competitors for the crown. The Wars of the Roses, and the Civil War of the seventeenth century, in their turn raged around the old town, and the two memorable battles of Newbury, fought in its immediate neighbourhood, have obtained for it historical, if melancholy renown.

Its situation on the great high-road from London to Bath, from which places it is about equi-distant, gave it in times past a share in almost all that was going on, and thus it has been the scene of events at least as interesting and prominent as those associated with many other towns of far larger population and more extended celebrity. Besides this road, it is also traversed due north and south by the main road from Southampton and Winchester to Oxford, and it is also readily accessible by road or rail to all the leading towns in the vicinity.

At the time when the Great Western Railway was constructed, the projected line ought to have run through Newbury—its natural course—but was literally driven off by the senseless opposition of the bigoted proprietors of several large ancestral estates, through which the line was proposed to be carried. The doom of the business element of the place was, for a time, as good as sealed, but this has been in a great measure remedied by the construction of the existing line, by which the metropolis is reached at nearly any time of the day in a little over an hour. When the connections now in progress between Westbury and Taunton are completed, the route through Newbury will once more become the main line from the Metropolis to the West of England. A great advance in improved railway facilities was effected by the construction of the Didcot, Newbury, and Southampton Railway, an independent line as far as Winchester; and the completion of direct communication between Southampton and the manufacturing districts of the North may ultimately do much to stimulate the industrial and commercial resources of the town and neighbourhood.

Newbury is the post and market town for a considerable out-lying district. It is also a Municipal Borough with a Commission of the Peace, and a separate Court of Quarter Sessions. It is not a Parliamentary Borough, but gives its name to the Newbury or Southern Division of the County of Berks.

The entire area of the Newbury Urban District is 1,828 acres, inclusive of twenty-four of inland water. At the census of 1901, it contained 2,580 houses and a population of 11,061—males, 5,083, females, 6,008. In the ten years' interval between the censuses of 1891 and 1901, the number of inhabited houses increased by 195, but the increase of the population in the same period was only 59, there being a decrease of 43 in the number of males, which was rather more than balanced by an increase of 102 females. From the figures of the last census, it appears that the females out-numbered the males by no less than 955, or nearly one-eleventh of the whole. This disparity runs through each age group above 15 years, and it will also be seen that there is a deficiency of the younger and more vigorous members of the community, with a corresponding excess of old persons, as compared with the averages of the whole combined district.

The town is provided with an excellent system of sanitation, and every house is connected with the sewers, which have recently been extended so as to take the drainage of the out-lying village of Donnington in the Rural District. The outfall and works are on the outskirts of Thatcham, where the sewage is successfully treated in bacteria tanks. The scavenging of the town is systematic and satisfactory. The Birth Rate was 23·5, and the nett Death Rate 15·1 per thousand of the estimated population, half of the number of deaths being persons above 65 years of age.

Ecclesiastically, Newbury is in the Diocese of Oxford and Archdeaconry of Berks.

The town comprises three principal streets, placed somewhat in the form of the letter Y—Northbrook Street, so called from the brook which traverses its course northwards; Bartholomew Street, from the ancient hospital of St. Bartholomew; and Cheap Street, the "Chepe" or Market Street. The Market Place, which is almost in the centre of the town, is spacious, and was formerly occupied by the picturesque old Guildhall, which has as its successor, on a part of the site, a modern terra-cotta statue of Her late Majesty Queen Victoria.

No one who is a lover of antiquity can fail to walk through Newbury without noticing its ancient gabled houses, too few, alas, but still a sufficient number are left to show us how quaint the old town must have looked before the advent of the many pretentious modern buildings we now see around us. Some of the more noticeable specimens of "Old Newbury" will be found in Northbrook Street, where the remains of the house occupied by "Jack of Newbury" still bear the impress of the fifteenth century. Another house, nearer the bridge, with projecting gables is also a prominent feature in the street, and there is too a fine Georgian house on the other side of the way, built by one of the Head family, with seven pilasters and handsome cornice. Nearer Speenhamland there is a very quaint hostelry, known as the "Monument," and there are several other old buildings at this end of the town that give a peculiar character to the place, and contribute at the same time to the attractive appearance of the street. Amongst these may be mentioned the old Elizabethan house with pointed gables, in the Broadway, which was formerly the manor-house of Speenhamland, and was for many years occupied as a hatter's shop by the Croft family. The house in Cheap Street in which Lord Falkland received his last Communion the night before the First Battle of Newbury, is still standing, and the room little changed, structurally, since that eventful period. The Litten Chapel, where Jack of Newbury was married, and St. Bartholomew's Almshouses in the "City," are also worth a visit.

It is not an easy matter to compress within a comparatively small space the chronicles of a town which has played such a conspicuous part for so many centuries in our national life, but our object will be first of all to give in brief a general history of Newbury from earliest times to the present, and this, as far as possible, in chronological order. We propose afterwards to treat of the municipal, ecclesiastical, and other institutions of the town; and further, to deal with its geology and natural history, and other local matters of interest, as fully as our space will permit.

CHAPTER II.

EARLY EXISTENCE OF NEWBURY—THE RIVER-DRIFT MEN—NEOLITHIC, OR SECOND STONE AGE—PILE STRUCTURES—THE CELTS—THE BRONZE AGE—OCCUPATION BY ROMANS—THE STATION OF "SPINÆ"—THE ANGLO-SAXON PERIOD—NAMES OF PLACES—LOT MEAD—THE ROADS—THE SETTLEMENT ON THE KENNET—THE NEW-BOURG—THE DOMESDAY SURVEY.

The Early Period. It is clear from the investigations of the archæologist that Newbury did not, as the old history books allege, arise out of the ruins of the Roman station of "Spinæ," but that, undoubtedly, the site of the present town was occupied by men of the Palæolothic or First Stone Age—the "river-drift men," who existed in Europe during the long series of ages represented by the Pleistocene period, numerous stone implements, generally known as "celts," showing no marks of rubbing or polishing, hammer-stones and cores, also implements from the older gravels, of a very primitive type, having been found in the town during the course of modern excavations.

The river-drift men certainly claim by far the highest antiquity of the inhabitants of Europe, and probably lived for countless generations before the arrival of their successors of the later Stone Age. These river-drift men were contemporary with the mammoth or woolly elephant *(elephas primigenius)*, a tusk of which animal was found in the bed of the Kennet at Newbury, in 1886, and measures 6 feet by 22 inches round at the thick end, and 9 inches at the other, and when entire must have been 10 or 13 feet in length. Bones of the *Bos Primigenius* or huge pre-historic ox, have also been found in the Old-River Terrace gravels on the south side of the town, of Pleistocene age. In the year 1888, there was found in the gravel near the Goods Station at Newbury, at a depth of between 18 and 20 feet, a tibia of the *Bos*, 19 inches in length with a circumference at the joint of 16 inches. It was associated with portions of a shed antler, of what is probably reindeer, on account of length of beam. A piece of leg bone of another species of deer was also found in the same spot.

From the elder of these primitive inhabitants of the early settlement on the banks of the Kennet, whose shadowy outline is all we can indistinctly trace in the dim distance of remote ages, we pass on to the Neolithic or Second Stone Age, though it is to be noted that between the earliest traces of this and the latest relics of the Palæolithic period, a very long interval of time must have elapsed. This is generally understood as the Neolithic Age of antiquaries, as immediately preceding the Bronze Age, which, in turn, was followed by the Iron Age, but each of which in most localities over-lapped its successor, so that there was no hard and fast line of separation between them, but each only very gradually and in process of time gave way to the more useful material which arose, and in the end supplanted it.

It is with all these periods that we have to do in considering the early inhabitants of Newbury, but more especially with the Neolithic Age, a vast number of flint implements of various kinds having been found in the peat and white marl during the drainage operations in 1894. With these were associated bone-drills, sun-dried pottery, and other traces of the race of men who inhabited the district in pre-historic times, and co-existed here with several animals which lived and died on the banks of the wide river, which once filled the valley.

The typical strata of the Neolithic lake-basins are well illustrated in sections opened out during the progress of the above-named works, when a pile dwelling was unearthed in Bartholomew Street, about six or seven feet under the roadway. It was constructed of fir poles, about 6 inches in diameter, driven into the peat, with numerous parallel timbers crossing the pile-tops. The surface of the platform was at the surfacc of the peat. As only a very small portion of the structure was exposed, the method of affixing the horizontal timbers was unable to be determined. They must have been fixed, otherwise when the lake covered them they would have floated, for the marl covered the platform. Considerable portions of other pile structures were met with in the Market Place in 1876, also in Cheap Street, and it was apparent in these instances that the vertical piles had been roughly morticed to receive the tenons of the cross beams.

After the lapse of unknown ages, came the Celts, who are generally allowed to have their origin among those Eastern hordes, which, from the earliest period, were continually pressing on towards the West, driven further and further by the pressure of the swarms behind them, though at what particular date they crossed over to Britain must be a mere matter of conjecture. They are described as tall and light-haired, of fair complexion, and with skulls of a round or broad shape, hence they are termed *brachycephalic* ; and armed with weapons of bronze they easily overpowered the tribes they found in possession, who were only armed with weapons of stone. Thus they soon over-ran and conquered almost every part of the British Isles.

Of the Bronze Age, Newbury has furnished several good examples. Perhaps the most noteworthy were two bronze spear-heads, discovered in the turbary at Speen Moors in 1825, one of which is of great interest and rarity, and described as being the second example of its kind that has been brought to light. Near the spear-head was also found a human skull at the contact of the peat with a substratum of shell marl. This skull is in the Oxford University Museum, together with another found in the peat opposite Benham House.

As to the chronology of the Bronze Period, we are, to a great extent, at fault. We know that when this country was first invaded by the Romans, iron was in use, and, probably, had been for some centuries, as we know to have been the case in Gaul and Germany. But though at the time of the Roman invasion, the Bronze Period may be said to have ceased in this country, it is almost impossible to say at what date it may have commenced, nor, indeed, at what date it ceased. No doubt there was an over-lapping of the Bronze with the Iron Period. Still it does appear by no means improbable that bronze may have remained in use in this country, down to, at all events, within a century or two of the invasion of Cæsar.

It is probable at the time of, and a long period before the first Roman Invasion in B.C. 55, that this district formed part of the territory of a tribe powerful, though not, perhaps, amongst the very foremost of the British tribes—the Atrebatii or Atrebates, whose chief town was Calleva or Silchester; the Bibroci occupying the south-eastern, and the Segontiaci, a portion of the southern side of the county.

The Roman Period. We are not without clear proof that during a part, at least, of those three centuries-and-a-half during which they held Britain, the Romans were settled in this locality, and although no foundations of buildings have been disclosed, nor any definite outline of a Roman camp can be traced, yet numerous relics of this period have been discovered in various parts of the town from time to time. In 1827, a Samian Vase, in perfect condition, was discovered near Stroud Green, on the southern outskirts of the town, with the letters D.O.M. impressed in one line and S.M.L. in another below it, that is extended,

DEO OPTIMO MAXIMO
SOLVIT MERITO LVBENS

which may be ascribed to the Second or Third Century, A.D. In the vase was a deposit of light coloured ashes, which had evidently been calcined; a small piece of iron or steel about two inches long, fixed in a sort of handle of horn, on which were the letters P.R.M., was also found some 10 feet below the surface in excellent preservation. Some Roman coins, not described, were also found with the vase. In 1830, a coin of Galba (A.D. 68), also one of Trajan (A.D. 98—117), were found in the town; and in 1839 a bronze steelyard was dug out of the peat. Numbers of Roman coins were also found in the "City" when the Grammar School was built at the Litten in 1848. Roman pottery and coins were also found on the site of the London and County Bank in the Market Place. Coins of Diocletian (A.D. 284—313), and Probus (A.D. 276—282), have also been found on the south side of the town.

But the most important evidence of Roman occupation was brought to light in 1856, when a Romano-British Cemetery was discovered in digging for ballast near the Great Western Railway Goods Station. The gravel bed at this spot reached up to within a foot of the outer surface of the earth, and appeared never to have been disturbed since its first deposit, except here and there, with streaks downwards of one to five feet of black soil, lying nearly due north. In and around this black soil were found nearly 100 human skeletons, together with a terra-cotta amphora, a cinerary urn of black clay, two stands of cinerary vases, two moulded glass vessels or unguentaria, one of which has inscribed on the bottom, S.P.S.; a small red clay vase of tazza form, five glazed pateras, two Samian cups or bowls, and other sepulchral vessels, some showing what the contents had been, viz., calcined bones and ashes, and that the custom of disposing of the dead by cremation had not been entirely abandoned.

From the localities where Roman coins have been found in Newbury, we may gather the following probable inferences:—

That in the neighbouring suburb of Speen we have the Roman *Spinæ* or *Spinis*,* one of the earliest of those military stations by which Rome at once curbed and civilised her conquered provinces. That *Spinæ* was one of the earliest of these stations we know, as we find it mentioned by name, and the leading roads connected with it, in the *Antonine Itinerary*, compiled between A.D. 125 and A.D. 140, during the reign, if not under the special instructions, of Hadrian.

That this defensible and well-watered spur of the Speen plateau, commanding the ford or passage of the river, was in,

* With regard to the name of *Spinæ* or *Spinis*, as it occurs in the Roman Itinerary, it has been generally assumed that this appellation is derived from the country hereabouts being covered with thorns, but as a result of further investigation it appears highly probable that it is a legacy of a still earlier date. The Romans, as we know, only latinized the British name of places; and the British or Celtic names were universally formed from local characteristics, that is from the situation of the settlements, either on the hills or in the valleys, near the fords of the rivers, the sea, or the coast, as connected with the public roads passing through the country. In reference to the "Rose Briar" theory, it must be remembered that the British name for thorns was very different from the Latin or Saxon names for the same thing, and as the primitive names of places given by the first settlers underwent but very little change either from the Romans or Saxons who succeeded them, we must apply to the Celts for our vocabulary.

Speen Hill, as it is now spelt, which in all probability was the site of the station denominated *Spinis*, rising a headland above the flat through which the Kennet flows, might have been called *ijspen*, that is the height above the *ijs* or water; the same as Penard in Somerset, and Penarth in Wales, imply the height above the *ar ed* or settlement near the *ar* or water. Penhill in Mendip is so denoted because it is the highest point on the line of the country, also Penarth in Cumberland implies the height above the rhydd or ford. By dropping the *ij* in *ijspen*, it becomes Spen, or as it is now pronounced, Speen.

if not all through British times, a fortified post, for security and observation, to secure which was but the outcome of the keen military instincts of the Roman invaders.

That being situated on an eminence at the intersection of the great Roman roads from London to Bath and Cirencester, at which places we know the Romans clustered in great numbers, it would be a useful and safe halting and directing place for travellers, such as the *mansiones* and *mutationes* common all along the principal Roman highways.

That the use of a station for the troops at this point would, no doubt, immediately arise by the large amount of traffic concentrated here by the great roads which converged at Speen.

That it by no means follows that there were permanent buildings on the hill-top at Speen, but that the camp may not only have been used for the purposes indicated, but as a "Specula" or Watch-tower for the protection of the ford-way of the Kennet, and the town then springing up on its banks, and afterwards called the New-bourg, or the New-borough.

That the Romans began to visit our locality soon after the final subjugation of Britain by Claudius; that the period when they were most numerous here was from about A.D. 250 to within some thirty years of their leaving Britain altogether; and that about the end of the fourth century, they began to leave our immediate neighbourhood.*

That as the Cemetery and most of the coins were found on the south side of the town, and right bank of the Kennet, the Roman settlement was there.

The Anglo-Saxon Period.

We pass on to Saxon times. Berkshire formed part during the Heptarchy, of the kingdom of the West Saxons. The *Chronicle of Abingdon*, preserved among the Cottonian Manuscripts in the British Museum, imparts to us the earliest authentic historical notice in relation to this county. It is to the effect that Offa, King of the Mercians, whose reign commenced A.D. 758, having conquered Kinewulf, King of the West Saxons, seized upon the country from Wallingford to Ashbury, which lay between the Ickeneld-street and the Thames. In the succeeding century, the irruption of the Danes constitutes the most remarkable incident, and their defeat by Ethelred, assisted by Alfred, at Æcesdune or Ashdown, on the Berkshire hills, has invested this district with considerable interest, and renders it a favourite resort of the antiquary and the tourist.

* The *Saxon Chronicle* says, under the year 418 A.D., "The Romans collected all the treasures there were in Britain, and some they hid in the earth, so that no one has since been able to find them; and some they carried with them into Gaul." But this withdrawal was rather a gradual process than a single act, and the Roman occupation, which had lasted for 350 years, and conferred incalculable benefit on Britain, came to an end.

NEWBURY FROM WEST MILLS.

Berkshire had always a palace in the time of the Saxon Kings; and Faringdon, Wantage, and Lambourn (King Alfred's own demesne), had also royal residences, but whether we were ever favoured with a visit from this greatest of English Kings, the chroniclers do not inform us.

Few districts in England were more connected with the long and confused struggle between the Romano-British population and the Saxon and Danish raiders than this, but we find no mention of the new-bourg on the banks of the Kennet—(*Cyneta*)—so we can only consider it was, in all probability, too small and thinly populated a place to attract much attention. Neither have we any Saxon Charters to assist us in our investigations. There is, however, scarcely a local name that does not proclaim the traces of these Teutonic immigrants, who, establishing their homes on the soil, have bequeathed to us the names of their farms and villages, which attest the wide extent of country once occupied by one or other of the great divisions of the Saxon race.

The idea uppermost in the English mind seems to have been the importance of property, and the necessity of enclosing it. The names of Green*ham*, Ben*ham*, Crook*ham*, Midg*ham*, Wool*ham*pton, *Ham* Mills, *Ham*stead, Leck*ham*stead, and Speen*ham*land, may be given as a few examples, all of which convey the notion of something walled in or protected, a house or dwelling, *ham* and *home* being English forms of *heim*, which we meet with in many German names. Differing little in meaning is *ton*, which we find in Donning*ton*, Aving*ton*, Brimp*ton*, Comp*ton*, Eas*ton*, Wes*ton*, East Gars*ton*, etc. *Burn* or *bourn*—a brook—is represented in Winter*bourn*, En*bourn*, and Lam*bourn*. *Ford*—a crossing—in Box*ford*, Wel*ford*, Shef*ford*, Sandle*ford*, etc. *Stræt*—a road, the *via strata* of the Romans— in High *Street* lane, Boxford; Enborne *Street*; West *Street*, Burghclere, etc.

These few instances are enough to show how abundant in the names of places are the traces of the Anglo-Saxon occupation of the immediate neighbourhood, while in the town itself we have the familiar local appellation of Saxon derivation in the word *Litten*—a churchyard or burial place, on the site of the ancient Hospital of St. Bartholomew. This name is significant of the possible existence of a still earlier religious building on this spot, the name alone furnishing positive proof of its Saxon origin.

Another interesting survival of Anglo-Saxon times is the name of "Lot Mead," a field on the north-west side of the Lammas Land in Northcroft, which, probably, represents a portion of the original partition of lands, under the Anglo-Saxon government, which, when cleared, were divided by *lot* to individuals according to their rank and dignity. Or it may be a portion of the old Common Meadows, divided into acres, or equal-sized pieces, the property to the hay upon it being determined yearly by lot. Speaking of these "Lot Meads," Aubrey, the Wiltshire antiquary, says :—

"Here is a Lot Mead celebrated yearly with great ceremony. The Lord weareth a garland of flowers, the mowers at one house have always a pound of beefe and a head of garlick every man, according to that of Horace, 'O dura messorum ilia!' with many other old customs still retayned."

There are, however, no traditions of such festivities in connection with Newbury "Lot Mead," and the name of the allotment alone survives.

Our extensive Common-lands are distinctly of Anglo-Saxon origin, and a survival of the establised principle of associated agricultural life in this country, and are but a remnant of those extensive areas which the town and village communities once possessed in common.

But of all the antiquities of a country, the *roads* are necessarily the oldest. We know nothing of the fate of the public buildings in the towns, but we have ample proof that the Anglo-Saxons were not road-makers, and adopted the Roman roads and bridges which they found in every part of the island. Of these primary local roads, it has hitherto been a question whether in Roman times there was not another route from London to Bath, following very much the same track along the valley as the present old coaching road to Reading, its direct course, instead of following the somewhat circuitous route *via* Silchester. That this was the case, seems pretty evident from the record of a Manor Court held at Aldermaston, in 1550, when the road is incidentally referred to as *the King's high waye, called Harrowe Waye, leading from Newbury to Reddinge*, and is described as crossing the Holy Brook at Beenham, bordering on the property of Edward Hildesly, or Ilsley, thus giving its locality much where it now passes along the valley.

In this name of "Harrowe Waye," we have a designation clearly of Saxon origin, and of considerable historical importance in dealing with the perplexing question of the identity of the roads which traversed the Roman colony of Britain. The Saxon *Here-path* or *Here-way*,* signified one of the great military roads of the Roman Empire, of which we have another survival in the "Harroway," an ancient trackway, which passes near Whitchurch and St. Mary Bourn, and forms a direct line of communication between London and Exeter, so much so, in fact, that the telegraph poles are now fixed along its course, as affording a shorter route than the famous turnpike road leading from the Metropolis to the West.

---

* The name Harrow-way may possibly be derived from the A.S. *har*—hoar or ancient—Hoarway.

To return again to the more general subject, in the absence of any explicit evidence, we can only surmise that after the Saxons became established in this district, they occupied that portion of the site of the present town which lies on the south bank of the Kennet, which was here crossed by a ford at a broad shallow just above (west of) the present bridge.* The oldest bridge (wooden) was, probably, thrown over the narrower part of the river below the ford, and, subsequently, when the river was made navigable, a portion only of the ford was left, banked off from the other half of the stream, which was deepened, and, an old timber bridge, having houses on either side,† replaced by the structure now standing.

At this early period in the history of the Germanic settlers, the town of Newbury, in a true sense, cannot be said to have as yet existed. The few nameless Romano-British habitations, in time, may have been displaced by the followers of Cerdic and Cynric. It was probably not until some years after the Conquest, that, the country being settled, there grew up on the south side of the river a number of houses which came to be called the New-bourg. The time when these houses were sufficient in number to claim a name, is practically proved by the name itself. The word "burh" had not, until the eleventh or twelfth century, completely lost the meaning of a fortress, and came to signify that of a "town," and the Latin *burgus* seems to have gone through much the same stages. On the Continent, however, the meaning of the "bourg" seems to have come in very soon, and to have acquired a special signification; that is, the bourg of a town was the bourg outside a town, the "forbourg" or "faubourg,"‡ as it is called. This was the special meaning here of the "borough," *i.e.*, the other side of the river from London, and the New-borough, Neuf-bourg; but we only get it in the Latinised form of *Nubiria* or *Nuburia*. The town thus sprung up during the close of the eleventh century, when it had its name.

Of Speen, however, or "Spinæ," though all trace is for a time lost, we find a wood called "Spene" in a Saxon charter of the date of A.D. 821, and no more than this dim and uncertain light is thrown on this period of our history by documents.

---

* Formerly the only way to West Mills was along the course of the shallow water of the Mill tail, which was entered just below the old "Globe" stables, on the north side of the church. This ford was pitched with cobbles similar to the Roman roadways. From the north side of the town there was an entrance to the ford-way by what is now the Conservative Club.

† Referred to in a survey of 1608, as "Certain houses called the shops lying upon the Bridge in Newberye."

‡ *Apropos* of "Forbourg" it is a bit of comparative topography that both at Reading, a Benedictine Abbey, founded by Henry I., and at Leominster, an off-shoot of the same monastery, the name of the "Forbury" is still given to an enclosure which formerly contained the outer court of the abbey or priory. The name also occurs at East Garston in the Lambourn Valley, where it is applied to a grass enclosure near the church.

We may reasonably conclude, therefore, that the Romans occupying the British hill-station with Spinæ, had already extended it to the holding of the ford-way over the Kennet. The Saxons burnt and plundered both, and held the passage over the river by the "New-bourg" only. If the supplanted Spinæ was really deserted, when the hamlet again rose can never be determined, and it is not surprising that historical evidence of its having again risen into notice should not be forthcoming until a much later date.

The New-bourg, with its water supply and water communication situated on a ford-way of the Kennet, where the neighbouring roads must always have converged, had in it the elements of commercial prosperity, such as the smaller villages of Speen and the like could never possess. If Spinæ was originally important as occupying the commanding hill-land of Speen at a time when the defensive capabilities of a site were all-important, its direct descendant, Newbury, took its position of superiority from its better suitability both for the purposes of commerce and of peace.

Hitherto we have been almost entirely in the region of conjecture. We now come to a period in which we can, with certainty trace our town, though even as yet we have but *glimpses* of its history.

The first historical reference to the name of Newbury, occurs in the "Ecclesiastical History of England and Normandy," by Ordericus Vilalis, the Norman-English chronicler, who entered as a monk at St. Evroult in 1085, and died in 1141. In recounting the founding of the priory of Aufay, about the year 1079, from documents which were handed over to his monastery when the property bestowed on this priory or dependency was transferred to St. Evroult, Orderic records the gift by Bernard, of Neufmarché, of the church of Speen (de Speinis), and the tithes, together with twenty shillings of the manor of Newbury (de censu Neoburia), in exchange for the churches of Burghill and Brinsop, two parishes in Herefordshire.

From these records it is certainly evident that Newbury was in existence at that time as a *vill*, and known by its present name, though not being a separate manor the name does not occur in Domesday Book.

Much has been said in the larger work, which provides materials for this shorter history, to show the intimate manorial connection that at this time existed between the ancient settlement of Speen, with its more opulent offspring—Newbury, which may here be briefly summarised. The manor of Newbury was originally in the manor of Speen, and the first documentary evidence, therefore, deals with the connection between the borough and the present village. That is to say, the revenue or tithes of a certain portion of the town which had grown up within the ancient manor, were, with the church of Speen, first appropriated by the Lord of the Manor, Bernard of Neufmarché, to Aufay. The manor itself afterwards appears to have been taken from Bernard of Neumarché's control, and bestowed on Humphrey Vis-de-Lu, by whom it was held at the time of taking the Domesday Survey. Finally, when Bernard of Neumarché regained the favour of his sovereign, William II., he recovered the manor of Speen, and with it part of the revenue of the town of Newbury.

Domesday Book. The name of Newbury does not, as we have said, occur in Domesday Book, but the absence of the name of the town is no more unaccountable than the omission of several equally important places in other parts of England, which were undoubtedly of sufficient consideration to be entitled to a separate and distinct notice.

Many reasons have been assigned for what may appear discrepancies in the Domesday record, but none of these explanations exactly apply to Newbury, which, though not specifically mentioned, appears to have been represented in the new-bourg, which grew up partly within the manor of Speen, and partly within the manor of *Ulvritone*, described as being in the Hundred of Thatcham, and which in the reign of Edward the Confessor, belonged to a Saxon thegn named Ulward.

In the absence of materials for the exact definition of the area of the manor of Ulvritone, it is probable that the portion lying between Enbourn and Greenham, occupying part of the old parish of Newbury, so far as it lies on the south side of the Kennet, was the Ulvritone which Ernulf de Hesding, the Domesday lord, possessed some time after the Conquest; and that the parish of Newbury as it now stands, is half in the old Ulvritone manor, and half in that of Speen. On that part of Newbury lying on the south bank of the Kennet, the tithes were appropriated by the lord of Speen, and that is why Bernard of Neufmarché, or his successor Vis-de-lu (the Domesday owner of Speen) could give them to the monastery of Aufay, without asking the consent of any of the then existing authorities, not even that of the priest of Newbury, nor that of the lord of the manor in which the other half of Newbury was situated. The twenty shillings from the manor of Newbury, previously mentioned as being paid to the Speen lord, doubtless was in proportion to what the south part of Newbury paid to the Hesding lord.

There is also collateral evidence of the relationship between Ulvritone and Newbury in the circumstance that the Domesday owner of Ulvritone, Ernulf de Hesding, gave to the Abbey of St. Peter of Préaux, the Church of Newbury, and the tithe of the whole rent or assize of the vill, and, moreover, of anything from which a tithe could be taken. He appointed also one hide of land and a priest's house, free from any toll, or customs, or service.

In 1086, when Domesday Book was completed, there were fifty-one houses in Ulvritone, while the Survey mentions only twenty-eight in Reading. Probably, however, the small number of hagæ in Reading is to be accounted for by the town having been attacked by the Danes in 1006, on the invasion of Sweyn, King of Denmark, when the place was almost entirely destroyed. Be this as it may, Ulvritone, or the modern Newbury, appears to have been a more important place as regards population than its neighbour Reading.

Few of the followers of the Conqueror appear as tenants *in capite* of so many estates in England at the time of the Domesday Survey, as Ernulf de Hesding, who held no fewer than forty-eight manors, but who, being unjustly accused by William Rufus, of treason, and put to the "wager of battle," left the country in disgust, resigning all the lands he held into the King's hands. Though the King was unwilling and opposed him, Ernulf departed on a pilgrimage to the Holy Land. He travelled as far as Antioch, where he died in or about the year 1095. The lands he held in England, or the chief portion of them, were subsequently held in three parts. The family of Cadurcis or Chaworth held those in Gloucestershire, which were nearly half the whole. The Chaworths and the Counts of Perche, those in Berks and Beds ; the Fitz Alans, Earls of Arundel, those in Oxon and Wilts. But whether they were held by them as heirs of Ernulf, or whether they were a regrant of the confiscated lands by King William to three other families, there is nothing to show.

CHAPTER III.

THE MEDIÆVAL PERIOD—SANDLEFORD PRIORY—THE SIEGE OF THE CASTLE OF NEWBURY—HENRY II. AT NEWBURY—THE BURGESSES OF NEWBURY—KING JOHN AND NEWBURY—DESCENT OF THE MANOR—THE PROTECTOR MARSHAL—HENRY III. AT NEWBURY—TOURNAMENT AT NEWBURY—INTENDED NUNNERY AT SANDLEFORD—PARLIAMENTARY REPRESENTATIVES—ROYAL VISITS—THE SHOOTING BUTTS—THE TOWN GATES—THE BLACK DEATH—DESCENT OF THE MANOR—WARS OF THE ROSES—INSURRECTION OF THE DUKE OF BUCKINGHAM.

Sandleford Priory. Some time between the years 1193 and 1202—but the evidence is not sufficient to fix the exact date—Geoffrey, the fourth Count of Perche, and Matilda, his wife, founded on some land about a mile south of the Kennet, and between that and the Enbourn river, at a place already called Sandleford, a priory for Canons Regular of the Order of St. Augustine.*

* It appears probable that previous to the foundation of the priory by the Count of Perche and his wife Matilda, a small community of secular Canons or Recluses dwelt here, as the "Recluses of Sandleford" are referred to in the Pipe Roll, 26 Hen. II., 1180.

It has already been shown how the Norman owner of Speen Church, and by implication of Speen manor, had assisted in the endowment of the Church of Aufay, with part of the revenue of the town of Newbury. Similarly in this case we find Geoffrey of Perche granting certain revenues from the mills in Newbury to his newly-founded church at Sandleford. The two circumstances thus connected with Newbury, allow us to realise that the part of the "vill" on the north bank or Speen side of the Kennet, belonged to the then lord of the manor of Speen, Bernard of Neufmarché; while that on the south bank or Greenham side, was the property of Geoffrey, Count of Perche.

The Siege of the Castle of Newbury. During the war between Stephen, Matilda, and the Church party, the town of Newbury came into considerable prominence in connection with the siege of its Castle, which is thus referred to by Henry of Huntington:—

> "The King, in the same year (1152), made an attack on the Castle of Newbury, which is not far from Winchester, and at length carried it by storm."

The event is also alluded to in the Chronicle of Gervase of Canterbury, who thus briefly summarises Stephen's operations before Newbury:—

> "The King then besieged the Castle of Newbury, and having created a fort there [at Wallingford], deprived the besieged of any opportunity of going out."

Another allusion to the siege of the Castle is to be found in the Cartulary of Bermondsey Abbey, where the names of the witnesses to a charter are given as being present at the siege of Newbury:—

> "William, Earl of Chichester; Richard de Lucy, William Martel, Richard de Camvil,* Roger de Fraxino, Jordan de Pod, witnesses of King Stephen's charter *at the siege of Newbury.*"

The Castle, no trace of which now remains, was probably erected early in the reign of Stephen, when a multitude of unlicensed castles were constructed (*castra adulterina*), and employed not merely for the security of the builders, but to enable them to prey upon their neighbours with impunity. It would seem that these castles were built with great rapidity, and with but little expenditure of labour upon earthworks, for in the next reign they were destroyed without difficulty, and scarcely any of their sites are now to be recognised. They were the work of the lesser barons, probably with the connivance of their chief lords, or even of Stephen and Matilda, who were little scrupulous as to the terms on which they

* In 1189, King Richard I. gave the manor of Benham-Valence, in Speen, to Richard de Camville, son of this Richard, who was a staunch adherent of Stephen all through his wars with the Empress. He followed Richard I. in the first Crusade, and like so many other noble English soldiers, left his bones before the walls of Acre.

accepted assistance. It is, therefore, highly probable, for we have no authentic history, that the Castle of Newbury was erected by one of the Counts of Perche, early in the reign of Stephen, one of whose first acts on coming to the throne was to give licence to all lords who chose to build castles on their own land.

Beyond the incidental references we have given as to the siege of the Castle, we were fortunate to discover in the National Library at Paris, a contemporary narrative of the proceedings of the opposing forces, in "L'Historie de Guillaume Le Marechal," which constitutes the most interesting historical episode in connection with the history of the town at this obscure period that has recently been acquired. The manuscript gives the detailed history of William Marshal, Earl of Pembroke, Marshal of England, who, in his old age, was Regent of England during the first three years of the boy-king, Henry III. The author was one John of Erlegh, or de Erlega, so-called from a lordship at Early, near Reading, who was one of the Marshal's most trusted servants and companions in the war.

From the poem, which practically stands alone, so that its accuracy cannot be tested by reference to other authorities, it appears that the siege must have lasted more than two months, and was signalised by many notable exploits, of which the following is a short summary:—

The King summoned the Constable to deliver up the castle, which he refused to do; an assault was then made on the garrison, and repulsed. The royalists thereupon blockaded the town, upon which the defenders of the castle requested a truce to consult their commander John Marshal. It was granted for one day only, but an extension was demanded of the King, in order that the Marshal might communicate with the Empress. Stephen then consents on the condition that one of the sons of the Marshal is surrendered as an hostage. They, therefore, sent the Marshal's second son, William, to whom the poem chiefly relates, and the interest is henceforward centred in this youth, who becomes the hero of the story. The quarrel between Stephen and Matilda, and the narrative of the siege being but accessories surrounding this event. John Marshal having yielded his son to Stephen, hastens to make Newbury a strong garrison, and when the time of the truce expired he refused to deliver up the castle, and is represented to have risked the life of his son. Stephen decided that the boy should be hung, and for fear that someone might be tempted to save him, he accompanied the lad to the place of execution. On the way, the boy, who knew nothing about the treatment they were preparing for him, seeing the Earl of Arundel hold a bright javelin in his hand, said to him, "Sire, give me that javelin!" The King, touched by the prattling innocence of the child, had him taken back to the camp. But sometime after, the King was persuaded to have the child thrown from a military sling for throwing stone balls, when the boy's childish innocence again saved his life. "God," says he, "What a beautiful swing; it is just my size." "Take him away," says the King, "one would have a heart of iron to see such a child perish." One sees that Stephen was sensible to the graces of infancy. Further on we see him to still better advantage, when engaged in playing a childish game, *aux chevaliers*, with his young prisoner, that is to say, with the blooms of a plant which grew in the open land around the castle, and is described as having a broad and pointed leaf. It was probably the common plantain (*plantana lanceolata*), with which children still amuse themselves in the manner described in the poem, and the game is called "Playing at Soldiers" to this day.

Some remains of the castle were existing in 1627, when a portion of the timber work was used for making an outer door or "grate" at the Church; and it is also referred to in 1644. The formation, however, of the wharf, with a basin or wet dock on or near the space the castle is supposed to have occupied, completely obliterated all traces of the remnants of any ancient buildings which might have furnished indications of the Norman fortress so inseparably bound up with the early history of Newbury.

Henry II. at Newbury. Two years after, the treaty of Wallingford was concluded, by which Stephen was to hold the Kingdom for life, and Henry was to be his successor, Newbury was honoured by a visit from the young King, as shown by a charter witnessed here in 1155.

The Burgesses of Newbury, 1189. The few glimpses that we have been able to gain of Newbury in these early days, troublous as the times were, seem to imply increasing wealth and population, and a comparative immunity from those desolating scourges with which other parts of the country were visited. This, to some extent, is borne out by the Pipe Rolls of the first year of Richard I.—1189—in a return relating to the tallages of the demesnes and lands then in the King's hands. In this return, out of 19 entries relating to Berkshire, Newbury is the only town in which the term "Burgesses" is used, the others being simply "Homines" of Wallingford, Windsor, Wantage, and other places—thus showing that Newbury had probably been more or less a "corporate" town since Anglo-Saxon times; and had enjoyed some, if not all, of such rights as those of managing its own affairs, and of jurisdiction within its boundaries. We also find in the earliest record of the Perche estates, references to the fulling mills in the town, besides corn mills, showing that the clothing industry was carried on in Newbury at this early date, and that it was a time of considerable commercial activity, wherein guilds, fairs, and traffic generally flourished.

King John, 1199—1216. The reign of King John is interesting to us here on account of his being the reputed founder of St. Bartholomew's Hospital, and as having instituted the annual fair, which is still kept up. He was probably well acquainted with this place from his frequent visits to the town, and to his favourite hunting seat at Freemantle Park, Kingsclere. It is difficult to realise at the present day, but at this time the whole district was apparently little more than a continuous woodland, and as such, appealed to the sporting instincts of the Norman and early Plantagenet Kings. The chief part of the southern portion of Berkshire was occupied by the great forest of Windsor, which extended in one direction into Buckinghamshire, and in another into Surrey as far as Chertsey, Cobham, and even Guildford; and reached westward as far as Hungerford along the vale of the Kennet, which was disforested in 1226.

King John was at Newbury in 1200, 1203, 1204, 1210, 1214, and 1215, the date of the grant of the fair, as shown by his "itinerary" and other confirmatory evidence.

Descent of the Manor. On the death of the last Count of Perche at the Battle of Lincoln, in 1217, where he fought against the young King Henry III.,* the manor was forfeited to the Crown as an escheat, but was soon afterwards granted to his nephew and heir, William, Bishop of Chalons-sur-Marne, who subsequently sold his interest in this and the other Berkshire estates to William Marshal the younger, son of the Protector Marshal, who succeeded his father as second Earl of Pembroke in 1219, and to whom the manor was confirmed in 1220.

William Marshal, the Protector, the hero of the poem on the siege of the Castle of Newbury, had left ten children—five sons, and five daughters. Each of the sons in turn were Earls of Pembroke, and Marshals of England, and all died without issue. When the male line became extinct, their vast estates descended to the heirs of the five daughters, Matilda, who married first Hugh Bigot, and secondly John de Warren, Earl of Surrey; Johanna, who

---

* The Count of Perche was one of the confederate barons who adhered to Prince Louis, the Dauphin, son of the King of France, and commanded a band of 20,000 "wicked French freebooters," who, after the relief of Mountsorel, marched to besiege the Castle of Lincoln in 1217. The royal army stormed the great gates of the city, of which they soon became masters, while Fulk de Breaute with his followers, made a sally upon the French troops within the town. The Count of Perche, though aware of his double attack, was unable to resist the impetuosity of his assailants. The cavalry in which his army abounded, were of no service, and his troops which were attacked before and behind in the narrow streets, were quickly slain or put to confusion. The Count of Perche was slain in the cathedral by Randulf, Earl of Chester, who instantly proclaimed King Henry; and the young king was carried in triumph in the arms of the principal royal leaders, and homage was done him by the barons present, amid the shouts of the victorious soldiery.

married William de Munchensey, whose daughter carried the Earldom of Pembroke to her husband, William de Valence, half-brother to Henry III.; Isabella, married first Gilbert de Clare, Earl of Gloucester; and secondly, Richard, Earl of Cornwall, King of the Romans; Sybil or Sybilla, married William de Ferrers, Earl of Derby; and Eve or Eva, who married William de Braose.

On the partition of the estates of Walter Marshal, Earl of Pembroke, in 1249—he died in 1245—the revenue from the manor of Newbury was divided in moieties between Roger Bigot, Earl of Norfolk; the heirs of William de Ferrers, and the heirs of William de Braose. William de Ferrers left his share of the inheritance between the two families of Mohun and Mortimer, who with their descendants, thus obtained an interest in the manorial revenue of Newbury.

Henry III. at Newbury.

King Henry III. was at Newbury in the years 1222, 1223, 1226, and 1228, when, it appears, he lodged at an hostelry or guest-house then existing in the town, and apparently used for the lodging and entertainment of the Court when travelling or engaged in hunting expeditions in this neighbourhood. There is a record of an hostelry of this character in 1444, on the west side of Bartholomew Street, which belonged to Winchester College, and was used for the convenience of the students and others journeying between Wykeham's famous foundation at Winchester, and New College, Oxford.

Tournaments in Newbury, 1248.

On Ash Wednesday, 1248, a gathering took place in Newbury, which must have caused much excitement and interest amongst the quiet burghers of the town in those days, graced, as it seems to have been, by the presence of the King (Henry III.), namely, a great tournament in which young William de Valence, the King's half-brother, rashly tried his immature strength against his sturdy peers, and being overthrown more than once, is soundly beaten into the bargain "to teach him the first steps in knighthood."

These passages of arms were often productive of grave breaches of the peace, besides causing the death of a certain number of distinguished jousters occasionally, and they had fallen under the ban of the church, and been especially anathematized. But in spite of such condemnation, the King found reason to continue tournaments, and there is no doubt the custom was a very popular one. The ostensible object was to instruct the nobility in the management of their horses and lances; they also encouraged a military spirit, and an emulation for martial glory in time of peace. But a more cogent motive was, perhaps, to be found in the revenues which accrued to the King's private purse, what we should now call the "entrance fees," being very heavy.

Two years after the tournament at Newbury, William de Valence received at the King's hands the manor of Benham, hence called "Benham Valence," which keeps the name of this early owner green in the neighbourhood to this day.*

There was another important assemblage at Newbury at the close of the same year, between the King's nobles and Richard, Earl of Gloucester, but the annalist does not record the occasion.

Sandleford Priory, 1274. On the partition of the vast domains of the Marshals, Earls of Pembroke, a moiety of the revenues of the Manor of Newbury became vested in the Clares, Earls of Gloucester and Hertford, a name not hitherto brought into association with the interesting monastic foundation at Sandleford, whose history is so interwoven with that of the mother parish of Newbury. But it appears from an entry in the Papal Records, that in 1274, Matilda, Dowager Countess of Gloucester and Hertford, resolved to establish at Sandleford a foundation for 40 enclosed nuns, under the rule of St. Augustin, and also a place apart for 10 priests of the Order of Fonterraud. The necessary preliminaries having been completed, a mandate was issued by the Pope to the Archbishop of Canterbury, and John de Derlington, of the Order of Friars, to carry out the pious intentions of Matilda de Clare. The priory is reported to have been then occupied by three Augustin Canons only, without Abbot or Prior, and while imperfectly obeying their rule, had an income of £100 a year—a considerable sum in 1274. This endowment the Countess proposed to augment to £200 a year. A clause was also inserted in the mandate that all existing rights should be preserved, and a fitting pension assigned to the three occupying Canons, either at Sandleford or at some other place of their Order. Some unforeseen and unrecorded circumstance seems to have occurred and prevented the completion of the design. It is probable she was called to her rest before the completion of the work, or there may have been some dispute between the papal authorities and the Bishop of Salisbury, Sandleford being in his diocese. There is certainly no record of the existence of a Nunnery at Sandleford in addition to the Priory, the names of whose priors are to be found in deeds and other documents relating to the monastery.

---

* It is to be regretted in the interests of local topography that the historic name of "Valence" has been of late years ignorantly tacked on to that of Beenham, near Reading, with which parish it has no connection. Its adoption arose from an evident blunder in Ashmole's "Antiquities of Berkshire," published by the notorious Curll, in 1719, where the documents quoted, clearly appertain to the manor of Benham-Valence in Speen. This work was not published for some years after Ashmole's death, and the "abominable impudence, ignorance, and carelessness of the publisher" is referred to by Hearne in his "Reliquiæ Hearnianæ."

Newbury sends Members to Parliament, 1302—1337.

In the year 1302—30th of Edward I.—Newbury, then termed a "Burgus" or Borough, was called upon to send two representatives to Parliament. The names of the representatives were Nicholas de Everyntone, and John Goldsmith. Our town again exercised this right in 1337—11th Edward III.—when three representatives were sent to Westminster, viz: Thomas de Chadyndon, Philip Ryce, and William Anselin.

Why Newbury discontinued to send members to Parliament, we are not told, though a tolerable conjecture may be formed. In these early days it was not considered a privilege, but a burden, because it was a question of expense, the boroughs having to pay the wages of their representatives. It was really a costly luxury to the good burghers of Newbury, and no doubt here as elsewhere, the sum necessary was raised with reluctance by men little solicitous about the political franchise.

Royal Visits, 1308—1321.

King Edward II. paid a visit to Newbury in 1308 and in 1320, when he lodged at Sandleford Priory. Another visit to Newbury is recorded in the progresses of 1321.

The "Buttes" of Newbury, 1319.

If we may rely on tradition, the Archers of Newbury did good service in many a stricken field, and excelled in the use of the long bow—a weapon so familiar in the "happy hitting hands" of our ancestors. Like other towns, Newbury had its "Buttes," consisting of hillocks or banks of earth provided for practice. These, it appears from a document preserved among the archives of St. Mary's College, Winchester, were situated on the south side of the Enborne Road, on or near the site of the present Grammar School, known as "The Buttes," but even the name has long since disappeared from the local records.

The "Gates" of Newbury, 1329—1336.

There is a local tradition that in mediæval times, Newbury was surrounded with walls and gates, but whether these supposed mural fortifications formed part of the outer defences of the Castle, which withstood the famous siege by King Stephen, or that there were "gates" only, used for purposes of a pacific character, like the *octroi*, we have no records or existing evidences remaining to enlighten us. The only records we have been able to find bearing on the subject are two documents belonging to Winchester College, dated 1329 and 1336 respectively. In the first of these, a piece of land at Newbury "without the East Gate," is referred to; and in the other, a piece "without the South Gate." There is no doubt that the use of these gates or barriers in places like Newbury, was that they afforded facilities for the collection of tolls on merchandise and agricultural produce entering the town, which were held of the

Crown by a succession of manorial lords, who rigidly enforced on the bailiffs and other officials the duty of accounting for these imposts, from which their chief income in such large market towns as Newbury was derivable. In the case of Newbury, such gateways at the entrances to the town were of the first importance, as the governing body formerly claimed the right of *toll traverse*, or a toll on all corn brought into the borough over the streets and highways thereof, which produced a very considerable revenue.

The Black Death, 1347—9.

The Black Death, that terrible scourge which visited England this century, after beginning at Southampton, laid its hand upon Newbury and other towns, and is said to have swept away a great part of the inhabitants. For three years it interrupted all business, and led to a great decline of prosperity. So large, indeed, was the mortality, which extended to the cattle, that there were no shepherds and no flocks, and it is recorded the plague was so disastrous at Crookham that the labourers had all died, and the lands had, in consequence, gone out of cultivation. This was the case in many other neighbouring places.

Descent of the Manor.

On the death of Edmund Mortimer, in 1303, the connection of this remarkable family with Newbury was continued by his son Roger Mortimer, created Earl of March, 1328, who was executed and attainted in 1330, when all his honours became forfeited. This sentence was twenty-four years afterwards reversed by Parliament in favour of Mortimer's grandson, Roger Mortimer, son and heir of Edmund Mortimer, his eldest son, who in 1353 obtained the reversal of his grandfather's attainder, the reason assigned being the illegal manner of the proceedings. Roger Mortimer, second Earl of March, died in 1360, when Edmund Mortimer, third Earl of March, acquired with his other estates, the Manor of Newbury. He died in 1381. Roger, who succeeded his father as fourth Earl of March, was slain at Kenles in Ireland, in 1398. Edmund, eldest son and heir of Roger Mortimer, was the fifth and last Earl of March. He died in 1424, whereupon Richard Plantagenet, Duke of York, son of Anne Mortimer, Countess of Cambridge, sister of the last Earl, became his heir, and here ended the male line of the family of Mortimer, Earls of March, but whose heir female carried all the great estates, and the best title to the throne, to the said Richard, Duke of York, whose son and heir Edward, became, afterwards, King of England, by the title of Edward IV. Thus the vast possessions and the honours of the house of Mortimer, including the Manor of Newbury, passed into the hands of the Crown.

The Wars of the Roses, 1460.

During the weary struggle between the houses of York and Lancaster, known as the "Wars of the Roses," in which feudalism perished by its own hand, the town of Newbury was the scene of important transactions, and its inhabitants were conspicuous for the part they played in support of what they considered the rightful cause. The townspeople of Newbury had throughout the contest between the contending factions shown a steady attachment to the House of York, and the Lancastrians, alarmed at the activity of Warwick, appointed commissioners to search throughout England for the adherents of the Duke of York, and in pursuance of their orders

> "The Erlle of Wylshire, tresuer of England, the lorde Scales, and the lorde Hungreford, went to the towne of Newbury, the whyche belonged to the Duk of York, and there made inquysycione of alle thayme that in any wyse had shewed any fauore or benyuolence or frendshyppe to the sayde Duk, or to any of hys: whereof some were found gylty and were drawne, hanged, and quartered, and alle other inhabitantes of the forseyde toune were spoyled of alle theyre goodes."

So far from being cowed into submission by these stern measures, the men of Newbury remained loyal to the banished duke, and the ghastly sight of one of the quarters of a partisan of Jack Cade, seems rather to have inflamed than discouraged the townsmen, who were opposed to the obnoxious administration of the country.

The Insurrection of the Duke of Buckingham, 1483.

Twenty-three years after the rigorous proceedings of the Lancastrian Commissioners at Newbury, the town was the scene of an armed insurrection, the object being to bring about the deposition of the usurper, Richard III., and the adoption of Henry Tudor, Earl of Richmond, as their King. Plots against Richard were formed in various parts of the kingdom, and Henry Stafford, Duke of Buckingham, who considered he had a claim to the crown as the descendant of Thomas, Duke of Gloucester, took up arms, and raised the standard of revolt in various parts of England. Buckingham raised forces in Wales; the Marquis of Dorset, the Bishop of Exeter (Peter Courteney), and others in Devonshire; Sir Richard Woodville, and his brother, the Bishop of Salisbury, in Wiltshire; Sir John Fogge and Sir George Browne, in Kent; and Sir William Norris, of Yattendon, and Sir Thomas de la Mare, of Aldermaston, in Berkshire.

The Berkshire men with their leaders and other supporters of Buckingham, assembled at Newbury on St. Luke's Day, 18th October, 1483, and proclaimed Richmond King of England, and further West there were musters at Salisbury and at Exeter.

Buckingham, being prevented by a flood in the Severn from joining his confederates, sought shelter with one of his dependents, but was betrayed by him, and carried to Salisbury, where he was beheaded,* and the enterprise utterly failed.† Two years later, Richard perished on the field of Bosworth, and in 1487 the last hope of the Yorkists was extinguished at Stoke, in the rout of those who had rallied round the Pretender, Lambert Simnel.

CHAPTER IV.

"BOUNTEOUS BUCKINGHAM"—NEWBURY AND THE CLOTH TRADE—"JACK OF NEWBURY"—FLODDEN FIELD—HENRY VIII. AT NEWBURY—WINCHCOMBE'S WILL—HIS HOUSE AND FAMILY—THE DOLMANS—DESCENT OF THE MANOR.

"Bounteous Buckingham" at Newbury, 1507.

"Bounteous Buckingham, the mirrour of all courtesy"–Edward Stafford, son of Henry Stafford, executed at Salisbury in 1483, by Katherine Woodville, sister to the Queen of Edward IV.—was at Newbury in 1507, on his way from Thornbury to Richmond, and the description of his escort conveys some idea of the cavalcade which accompanied the progress of one of the nobility in those days. He was attended by 20 gentry, 14 valets, and 29 grooms; and had 59 horses used by his household, and 28 for his own personal use.

In 1521, the Duke of Buckingham was accused of high treason "for certain words spoken," which were taken as evidence of disloyal views, and the principal witness against him was his cousin and steward, Charles Knyvett. The Duke fell by the hand of the executioner on Tower Hill, and was the fourth of the family in succession who had met with a violent death.

The Duke is made by Shakespeare to say, after his arraignment:

"I had my trial,
And must needs say a noble one; which makes me
Happier than my wretched father.
Yet thus far we are one in fortunes—Both
Fell by our servants, by those men we lov'd most;
A most unnatural and faithless service."

---

* It may not be generally known that the celebrated line, "Off with his head; so much for Buckingham," pronounced with so much effect by our stage Richards, is not in Shakespere, but is believed to have been one of Colley Cibber's innovations.

† Large sums were offered for the capture of the leaders, many of whom found refuge in sanctuaries, others repairing to Brittany. Sir Thomas de la Mare, of Aldermaston, one of the Berkshire insurgents, took shelter at Sion Monastery, where he appears to have taken up his abode. By his will, dated 1490, he refers to his great sorrows and losses, and also as to the possibility of being unable to pay his debtors in full, which he deplores, and begs to be leniently dealt with. He directs his body to be buried in the church at Sion, before the Crucifix, or where it may please the Abbess and Master Confessor.

Newbury and the Cloth Trade. The sixteenth century was one of increasing importance and prosperity for Newbury, and a notable era in the history of the town. For many centuries the principal inhabitants had been engaged in the cloth trade—then the staple manufacture of England, and the means, in fact, by which the town was chiefly supported. It was by the energy and efforts of the clothiers at this period that Newbury advanced to a very great degree the extent of its manufactures. Houses sprung up in every quarter, each one furnished with its loom, and there was plenty of work to keep the industrious poor, both male and female, in constant employment. The town, in fact, became a steady-going, business-like place. Cloth-working was lucrative, and so a large amount of capital was year by year invested in it. So abundant, indeed, was the employment that the wool, after having undergone various processes to fit it to be spun into yarn, was carried for that purpose to spinners residing not only in the surrounding villages, but to some of the neighbouring towns.

Jack of Newbury. It was the cloth trade of Newbury which produced its popular hero, the prosperous clothier, who for so long a period has been widely known by the familiar appellation of Jack of Newbury, described by Fuller the Church Historian, as "the most considerable clothier England ever beheld."

From Winchcombe's will we find that he is described as "John Smalwoode the elder *alias* John Winchcombe," and it is probable that on his becoming a person of importance, he dropped, as was frequently done, his proper patronymic, and assumed the name of his birthplace, Winchcombe, in Gloucestershire, a town also once known for its extensive clothing trade, and where the name of Smalwoode occurs in the registers of the parish. Respecting his character, parentage and early days, we have no information; but there is a tradition current at Winchcombe that he was a novitiate in the monastery there, and being wearied of the seclusion and restrictions of the cloister, escaped from his confinement, and made his way to Newbury. Here he was apprenticed to the wealthy clothier, whose widow he afterwards married, and became not only possessed of a wife, but of a flourishing business; from which time his life seems to have been one of uninterrupted success.

Some of the principal facts in the life of Winchcombe were in current circulation in Newbury at the close of the sixteenth century, for when that prolific pamphleteer and novelist Thomas Deloney, made him the subject of a romance, he appears to have founded his story partially on well ascertained facts, and partially on details derived from local traditional sources. Jack's chief exploit as narrated by Fuller in his "Worthies" was the active share he took in the war then raging between England and Scotland. James IV., as ally and brother-in-arms of the French King, invaded Northumberland in the summer of 1513, during the absence of a large part of the English army in France, and an order was issued for all able-bodied men throughout the country to equip themselves for war. Jack's quota was four men armed with pikes, and two horsemen for the King's service, and he answered the call by marching north at the head of fifty tall men well mounted, and fifty footmen with bow and pike, "as well armed and better clothed than any." Whether he reached Flodden is doubtful, but the following old and, probably contemporary ballad, describes the prowess of the Newbury men in glowing terms and circumstantial detail.

FLODDEN FIELD.

THE NEWBERRIE ARCHERS. AN OLD HISTORICAL SONG.*

"Come Archers learne the news I telle
To the Honoure of your Arte,
The Scottyshe Kinge at Flodden felle
Bye the poynte of an Englyshe Darte.
Though Fyre and Pyke dyd wond'rous thynges,
More wonders stylle dyd wee ;
And ev'ry Tongue with rapture syngs
Of the Laddes of Newberrie."

"The Bonnie Laddes of Westmorelande,
And the Chesshyre Laddes were there ;
With Glee theye took theyre Bows in Hande,
And wythe shoutes disturb'd the Ayre.
Awaye they sent the Grey Goose Wynge ;
Each kylled his two or three ;
Yet none so loude with fame did rynge
As the Laddes of Newberrie."

"They swore to scale the Mountayne bolde,
Where some in vayne hadde try'de ;
That theyre Toes myghte take the better holde
Theyre Bootes theye caste asyde.
Barefooted soone theye reach'd the hyghte,
'Twas a gudelie syghte to see
Howe faste the Scottes were put to flyghte
By the Laddes of Newberrie."

"Lord Stanlie sawe with much delyghte,
And loude was heard to saye,
Eche oughte, by Jove, to be a Knyghte,
For to theme wee owe the Daye.
The Chesshyre Laddes began the route,
And the Kendall Boys so free ;
But none of theme all have foughte more stoute
Than the Laddes of Newberrie."

"Now God pres'rve our Lord the Kynge,
Who travaills farre in France ;
And let us all of Bowmen synge
Whyle rounde our Cuppes we Daunce."
The Chessyre Laddes were briske and brave,
And the Kendal Laddes as free ;
But none surpass'd (or I'm a knave),
The Laddes of Newberrie."

* Printed in Armiger's "Sportsman's Vocal Cabinet," Lond., T. Griffiths, 1830.

PORTION OF "JACK OF NEWBURY'S" HOUSE IN NORTHBROOK STREET.

Although we have no actual evidence to show that the Newbury men did such special service at Flodden, a considerable number of levies were raised in the town at the time, and may have so distinguished themselves.*

On the King's return from France, Jack is said to have had the honour of entertaining him and Queen Katherine at Newbury, which he did in splendid fashion, and refused the honour of knighthood. The King and the Court were certainly at Newbury in September, 1516. On the 10th, Wolsey wrote a letter from Newbury to Sir Richard Jerningham, and it is highly probable that if the King was there, Wolsey was there also. Three days afterwards the Court removed to Ramsbury, so that there was ample time for the visit to Winchcombe.

The King was also at Newbury in 1518, the year mentioned by Deloney, when on his way from Abingdon to Southampton—the Court leaving Abingdon on the 8th June, and arriving at Southampton on the 10th, which would allow for a halt at Newbury.† But Jack's crowning work was his carrying to a successful issue the Clothiers' Petition, when, "by reason of the wars, many merchant strangers were prohibited from coming to England, and also our own merchants, in like sort, were forbidden to have dealings with France and the Low Countries," so that the cloth trade had fallen very low. The deputation seemed at first likely to miscarry, for Wolsey, to whom they were referred, put the matter off from time to time, being of opinion, as was not unlikely, that "Jack of Newbury if well examined would be found to be infected with Luther's spirit." Jack in his turn exasperated the Cardinal by saying, "If my Lord Chancellor's father had been no hastier in killing calves than he is in dispatching poor men's suits, I think he would never have worn a mitre." But the King took the matter up, and the clothiers got their order, "that merchants should freely traffic one with another, and the proclamation thereof should be made as well on the other side of the sea as the land." The Steel-yard merchants being joyful thereof, made the clothiers a great banquet, after which each man departed home,

* There is among the State documents at Loseley House, Surrey, an account of the charges of Mr. (afterwards Sir Thomas) Cawarden, Steward of the King's manor in Newbury, "for the furnyture of cxlvii persons there." The furniture being military equipment. There is no date attached, but the contents show that it is of the time of Henry VIII.

† The house of the renowned Winchcombe, which was no doubt a stately old mansion from the description given by Deloney, appears to have been always open to receive royalty and persons of distinction on their progress through Newbury, and there is no reason to discredit the old tradition that Henry VIII. and his Queen were received here by their loyal host. The Winchcombes repeatedly entertained various notabilities passing through the town, and in 1537, the Protector Somerset, brother of Lady Jane Seymour and uncle to Edward VI., with a distinguished retinue was "lodged at Master Winchcombe's house" in Newbury, and before leaving made a liberal gift to his "carders," *i.e.*, the carders of wool for spinning.

carrying tidings of their good success, so that in a short space, clothing was again very good, and poor men set to work as before. Such are the most trustworthy of the legends about this popular hero, the others, though characteristic and quaint, are too doubtful to be seriously stated.

Jack of Newbury died in 1519. By his Will, dated 4th January, 1519, he is described as residing in the parish of St. Nicholas, Newbury, and after committing his soul to "Almighty God, to our blessed Lady St. Mary, the Virgyn, and to all the holy Company of Hevyn," he directs his body to be buried in "our Lady Chauncell," in the parish church of Newbury by the side of his first wife Alice, and "a stone to be layd upon us boothe." He bequeaths to the mother church of Sarum xid., to the High Altar of the Church of Newbury "for offerings negligently forgotten" xid., and makes bequests to the several other altars in the church. To his wife Joan or Johan, he bequeaths 100 marks sterling, also his "householde stuffe," together with his cattle, wood, corn, hay, and other effects; also half his plate. He further bequeaths to her for life, and afterwards to his son John, his interest in lands and tenements he holds of the Dean and Chapter of Windsor, reserving to his said son John, the racks and tenters in a close called "Culverhouse." To the parish church of Newbury he bequeaths the sum of £10, "towards buylding and edifying the same." Then follow bequests to his friends and servants, including 40s. to William Dollman, "besides all things of his covenants." To Sir John Waite, parson of Newbury, for tithes "negligently forgotten," that is for tithes of his movable goods and chattels at the time of his death, 40s. He directs that an annual obit stall be kept for him and his friends departed at a cost of 10s., to be distributed among the officiating priests and clerks, during the term of 22 years, and that masses be sung for him "by an honest priest" for one whole year. The residue of his estate he bequeaths absolutely to his son John, whom he appoints sole executor, and as Overseers to his Will his friends, John Waite, Rector of Newbury; Sir* Robert Wright, curate; Robert Shepway, Roger Bennet, John Tunnell, and Thomas Harrison, with several others. The Will was proved by his son and Executor, at Lambeth, 24th March, 1519.

Little now remains of the ancient brick and timber abode of the princely Winchcombe, which comprised the block of buildings in Northbrook Street, now partly occupied by the "Jack of Newbury" Inn, and bounded by two lanes, each leading to the Marsh, to which place Winchcombe's factory and stores extended. The "racks" and "tenters" for drying and stretching the cloth are referred to in Winchcombe's Will, as standing within a close

* Fuller in his Church History says:—"Such priests as bore the additional Sir before their Christian name were men not graduated in the University, but being in orders, though not in degrees, whilst others entitled Masters had commenced in the Arts."

CARVED OAK PANEL, FROM "JACK OF NEWBURY'S" HOUSE, REPRESENTING THE TRINITY.

called "Culverhouse," *i.e.*, Pigeonhouse close, *Culver* being the old English name for a pigeon or dove, and was evidently part of what is now known as the Marsh, or in that locality. A fifteenth century gable with an oriel window, and carved barge-board at the north-west end of the house is still standing, and within the house a massive stone chimney piece, 7 feet wide, was discovered in 1882, and the rooms were found to have been originally panelled with oak wainscotting, considerable portions of which remain behind the modern canvas and papering.

Some interesting carvings were discovered many years since in taking down a portion of the contiguous buildings, which undoubtedly originally formed part of Winchcombe's house. On one of these, divided into ten panels is a bust, supposed to represent the renowned Winchcombe, within a raised circle, accompanied by the floriated initials I.W. The two panels on either side bear the linen pattern ornament. In the middle panel of the lower compartments is a shield, suspended by a strap and buckle with a monogram I.S. for John Smallwoode, and the panels on either side contain portrait busts supposed to represent Jack's two wives, Alice and Joan. The outer panels bear eaglets, one carrying in its beak the Tudor Rose, and with wings *closed* ; the other holding in is mouth a berry, and with wings *erect*. Another carving from the same house represents the Trinity, under the figure of a single head with three faces—an artistic "confusion of substance," which was prohibited by a Bull of Pope Urban VII.*

There is also in the neighbouring premises (No. 19, Northbrook Street), a considerable piece of oak panelling similar to that remaining in Winchcombe's house, and on one panel the I.W. and I.S. are represented in the same form as that on other portions already described, and on the brasses at the parish church ; they also occur on his monumental brass.

John Winchcombe, M.P.

John Winchcombe, the son and residuary legatee of Jack of Newbury, whose portrait in the Council Chamber is so familiar to the townsmen, appears also to have been an important and wealthy personage living at Newbury, where he continued to reside until his death. After the dissolution of Reading Abbey, King Henry VIII. in 1540, granted to the above John Winchcombe—("who had on various occasions rendered him good service,") the manors and rectories of Thatcham and Bucklebury, the consideration money being £2,619 13s. 4d., representing about twelve times that amount at the present day. He was Member of Parliament for Reading in 1552–3, and in 1556, one of the five visitors appointed to try

---

* These carvings are now at Sudeley Castle, Winchcombe, Gloucestershire. The figures are introduced in the Winchcombe Memorial Window in Newbury Church.

Julius or Joscelyn Palmer, the youthful master of Reading School, and two others, for having embraced the Reformed religion. He died on the 2nd December, 1557, and was buried in Newbury Church. The manors of Thatcham and Bucklebury were settled for the use of his eldest son, John, his wife and children, and the bulk of his other property was settled for the benefit of his other sons, Thomas and Henry.

The Dolmans. The Dolmans were another eminent family of clothiers at Newbury, who appear to have migrated from Pocklington, in Yorkshire, in the fifteenth century. The first of the name we meet with is William Dolman or Dollman, to whom Jack of Newbury bequeathed £10 by his Will, "besides all things of his Covenants," from which we may infer he was a partner, or had some interest in the business. Thomas Dolman, who is mentioned in contemporary records as an eminent clothier at Newbury, had a grant of the manor of Shaw in 1553, and his name appears in the list of gentry of Berks, 1559 to 1565. His Will, in which he is described as of Newbury, clothier, was proved by his son Thomas, 3rd December, 1576. This second Thomas completed Shaw House in 1581, and retired from trade, exciting thereby the envy of his neighbours, which has been perpetuated in the doggrel couplet :—

> "Lord have mercy upon us, miserable sinners,
> Thos. Dolman has built a new house, and turned away all his spinners."

To avenge himself of this affront, it is said, Dolman introduced the inscription still remaining over the chief entrance to the house, in Greek and Latin, which may be thus transcribed :—

> "Let no envious person enter."

> "The toothless man envies the teeth of those who eat, and
> The mole despises the eyes of the roes."

Descent of the Manor. The manor of Newbury, being retained by the Crown in its own hands, devolved on Henry VIII., who, after divorcing *one* wife and beheading a *second*, married the fair Wiltshire lady, Jane Seymour, on whom he bestowed the manor as part of her jointure. Perhaps it was fortunate for Lady Jane that she was early removed from her high yet perilous position. The King, we are told was inconsolable at the loss, and "continued in real mourning for her over the festival of Christmas." Two months, however, *before* Christmas he had offered his hand to another. On the Queen's death the manor reverted to the Crown, and was afterwards granted by Lady Jane's son, Edward VI., to the Princess Elizabeth.

OAK PANEL, WITH BUSTS OF "JACK OF NEWBURY" AND HIS TWO WIVES.

CHAPTER V.

The Martyrs of Newbury.

De Martyrio Palmeri Hexasticon.

Palmerus flammas Christi pro dogmate passus
Impositum pondus, ceu bona palma tulit,
Non retrocessit, sed contra audentior iuit,
Illæsam retinens, fortis in igne fidem,
Propterea in cælum nunc Palmifer iste receptus,
Institiæ Palmam non pereuntis habet.

Justus ut Palma florebit.

Foxe.

The Martyrs of Newbury, 1556.

Berkshire has the honour of having received the doctrines of the Reformation as early as any part of England, and Fuller says, "Let other places give the honour to the town of Newbury, because it started first in the race of the reformed religion." Whether it be literally true that Newbury was the first in that race may be doubtful, but it certainly was amongst the first, for in 1518 Christopher Shoemaker was burnt here for reading the Gospels to a disciple, one John Say. Fuller also mentions that in the beginning of the reign of Henry VIII. there was a society of "secret favourers of God's Gospel" at Newbury to the number of near two hundred, and had continued there for a space of fifteen years, when they were betrayed, and many of them "to the number of six or seven score" were arraigned, and three or four of them were burnt.

In all the histories of English martyrs there is, perhaps, none more touching than that of Julins or Joscelyn Palmer, usually written "Julius." He had been a Romanist at Oxford, and full of the zeal which urged St. Paul to hold the garments of those who stoned Stephen, had been present at the burning of the Bishops at Oxford. The spectacle of their heroic deaths led him to enquire for himself. He was soon suspected of heresy, resigned his fellowship, and became Master of Reading Grammar School. The suspicions soon followed him ; he had to fly from Reading, and went to Ensham to see his mother. Here he found no rest ; his mother cursed him for not believing as his father and she and all his forefathers had done, instead of "what was taught by the new law in King Edward's days, which is damnable heresy." "Faggots I have to burn thee," ended the old woman; "more thou gettest not from me." He departed blessing her, the tears trickling down his cheeks, whereat "she hurled an old angel* after him and said, "Take it to keep thee a true man." He then visited his friend Cope at Magdalen; went to Reading to get his arrears of salary; was there arrested, and sent with a bill of instructions to Dr. Jeffrey, who was holding a visitation for the Bishop of Salisbury at Newbury.†

He was arraigned with two other brethren, Thomas Askew and John Gwin by name,‡ in Newbury Church on the 15th July, 1556, before William Jeffrey or Geffrey, D.C.L., Chancellor of Salisbury; Sir Richard Bridges, Knight, of Great Shefford, Sheriff; Sir William Rainsford, John Winchcombe, son of Jack of Newbury, and Clement Burdett, rector of Englefield and Official Principal to the Bishop of Salisbury.

The indictment was for denying the Pope's supremacy, maintaining that the priest showeth up an idol at Mass, and other charges. At first, Palmer answered guardedly, offering to recant whatever in his teaching "will not stand with God's word," but it soon became clear to Palmer that recantation was required which he could never make. The Chancellor told Palmer that "he would wring *peccavi* out of his lying lips ere he had done with him," and the parson of Englefield called him "as forward an heretic as he had ever talked with." Rainsford appears to have taken no part in the trial, and Winchcombe acted very kindly. Sir Richard Bridges

---

* Angel, a gold coin varying in value from about six shillings and eight pence to ten shillings.

† Fuller in his Church History says :—"More sparks of persecutions flew into the diocese of Salisbury under John Capon, the Bishop, and Dr. Jeffray, the Chancellor, for this *Doeg* was worse than *Saul* himself. At Newbury he sent three martyrs to heaven in the same chariot of fire, Julius Palmer, John Gwin, and Thomas Atkin. However, this was a light flourish in respect of that great blow he received when Queen Mary died." John Capon, alias Salcot, the Bishop referred to, was successively Abbot of St. Benet Holme, and of Hyde by Winchester, and was made Bishop of Bangor, 1533, and of Salisbury, 1539. He died, 1557.

‡ The story of John Gwin, or Gwynn, a Spitalfields weaver, and the second of the three martyrs at Newbury, is made the basis of a historical tale, entitled "The Secret Room," published by the Religious Tract Society, the principal scene of the story being laid at an old manor house at Chastleton, in Oxfordshire, where Gwynn lies concealed in the "secret room," and wherefrom he is dragged forth to trial and execution at Newbury. The third martyr was Thomas Askue or Askew.

Thomas Bryce, a contemporary writer of religious poetry, thus refers to the Newbury martyrs :—

"When Askue, Palmer, and John Gwin,
Were brent with force at Newbury;
Lamenting onely for their sinne
And in the Lord were full mery:
When tyrantes merciles put them to death
We wishte for our Elizabeth."

THE MARTYRS OF NEWBURY. [From an Old Print.

the Sheriff, who had throughout the examination been trying to get fair play for Palmer, honours the youngster's courage, and for his part does not like the work he is about, and would gladly get out of it altogether. So after the first day's trial, the old Knight sends for Palmer to his lodgings, and in a friendly way exhorts him in the presence of divers persons to revoke his opinions, and spare his young years, wit, and learning :—

> "If thou wilt be conformable, and show thyself corrigible and repentant, in good faith I promise thee before this company I will give thee meat and drink, and books, and ten pounds yearly, so long as thou shalt dwell with me, and if thou shall set thy mind to marriage, I will procure thee a wife and a farm, and help to stuff and fit thy farm for thee. How sayest thou ?"

"Books ! meat and drink, and £10 a year ! a wife and a farm ! these are good things," says the author of *Tom Brown*, "but there is one thing better, Sir Richard, even the truth of Almighty God." So Sir Richard, perceiving he would not retract :—

> "Well, Palmer," saith he, "then I perceive one of us twain shall be damned, for we be of two faiths, and certain I am that there is but one faith that leadeth to life and salvation."

"Sir, I hope we both shall be saved," answers Palmer. On the Sheriff asking "How that might be ?" his prisoner answered, "Right well, sir, for as it hath pleased our merciful Saviour, according to the Gospel parable, to call me at the third hour of the day, *even in my flowers, at the age of twenty-four years*; even so I trust he hath called and will call you at the eleventh hour of this your old age, and give you everlasting life for your portion." "Sayest thou so," rejoined the Sheriff, "Well, Palmer, I would I might have thee but one month in my house, I doubt not but I would convert thee or thou should'st convert me." And now interposes the compassionate Winchcombe—"Take pity," said he "on thy golden years, and pleasant flowers of lusty youth, before it is too late." "Sir," was the young martyr's reply, "I long for those springing flowers that shall never fade away."

At the termination of the second day's examination, Dr. Jeffrey proceeded to deliver sentence of condemnation, and Palmer with his two fellow martyrs, were delivered to the secular authorities. About five o'clock in the evening, Sir Richard Bridges and the Bailiffs of the town "with a great company of harnessed and weaponed men," conducted Palmer and his brethren to the fire.

> "They put off their raiment and went to the stake, and kissed it ; and when they were bound to the post, Palmer said, 'Good people, pray for us that we may persevere unto the end, and for Christ his sake beware of Popish teachers, for they deceive you.' As he spake this, a servant of one of the Bailiffs threw a faggot at his face, that the blood gushed out in divers

places. For the which fact the Sheriff broke his head, that the blood likewise ran about his ears. When the fire was kindled and began to take hold of their bodies, they lift their hands towards heaven, and quietly and cheerfully, as though they felt no smart, they cried, 'Lord Jesu, strengthen us; Lord Jesu, assist us; Lord Jesu, receive our souls.' And so they continued, without any struggling, holding up their hands and knocking their hearts, and calling upon Jesu until they had ended their mortal lives."

The place where the martyrs were burnt was called the "Sandpits" in the Enbourn Road, but the exact spot is not known. It is, however, generally supposed to have been near the site of the pond near the Lamb Inn.*

CHAPTER VI.

THE REIGN OF ELIZABETH: ROYAL VISITS—DESCENT OF THE MANOR—KING JAMES I. AND HIS QUEEN AT NEWBURY—ANOTHER VISIT OF THE QUEEN—FALL OF NEWBURY BRIDGE—TRADE OF THE TOWN.

The Reign of Elizabeth. Royal Visits.

We gladly pass away from these odious transactions to the brighter days of the greatest of our Tudor Sovereigns. The reign of Queen Elizabeth, which witnessed the beginnings of two of the most wonderful empires of the world, the English East India Company and the United States of America, was an important era in the history of Newbury as for other places engaged widely in commercial enterprise. At this time cloth making was very general here, the means in fact by which the people were chiefly supported, and the history of the town in these golden days of "Good Queen Bess" is little more than a record of large fortunes made in trade—almshouses and other charitable institutions every way around us testifying to the generosity and piety of the old worthies of Newbury dealing with "the principal and noblest staple of all these islands, woollen cloth."

The long line of royal visits to Newbury was continued by Queen Elizabeth, who appears to have had a special partiality for

* Near the spot where the martyrdom is supposed to have taken place, on the south side of the Enbourn Road, a charred oak stake to which was affixed a long chain, was found many years since. This significant relic of a reign of sad bigotry was seen by the writer's informant, Charles Knight, of Raymond's Almshouses, now ninety-five years of age, and shown to several persons, he says, at the Black Boys Inn, the chain being afterwards sold for old iron.

the town of which she was the Lady of the Manor, and also for her castle of Donnington, and when a prisoner she begged she might be sent here in preference to any other place of captivity.

Great were the preparations made in Newbury to give the Queen a right royal reception when she visited the town in the month of September, 1568. All the highways over which Gloriana had to pass were ordered to be levelled and repaired, and the streets in the town covered with sand, probably to prevent infection, and judging from the charge for conveying the royal tent from Wallingford, it appears that some at least of the retinue lodged under canvas. There are also several entries of payments to carpenters for making presses for the robes and other necessaries, and to Mr. Polsone, the Newbury Ironmonger, for numerous locks and keys, which is suggestive of temporary accommodation. The Queen herself did not, however, lodge at Newbury on this occasion, but went with a splendid retinue to her castle at Donnington, which had been repaired and fitted up at considerable cost for her convenience and comfort, as shown in the pay book of the progress. Elizabeth had also intended to pay another visit to Newbury in 1601, when on a progress to Littlecote and Marlborough, but reached no further than Sir Humphrey Foster's, at Aldermaston, when she was recalled to Windsor to receive an embassy from the French King, Henry IV. Had the Queen been able to have come on to Newbury, the enthusiasm would possibly have been even greater than on the former occasion when she was received with great array and circumstance by the town authorities, as only a few years previously, by her "special grace and favour," the borough had received its charter of incorporation, with all its attendant "rights, privileges, and immunities."

The name of "Good Queen Bess" was not forgotten in Newbury, and it is a testimony to the lingering affection for the memory of the Virgin Queen that the day of her succession to the throne, the 17th September, was observed by ringing the bells at the Parish Church as late as the year 1739, when there occurs a payment of two shillings and sixpence for ringing on "Queen Elizabeth's Day."

Descent of the Manor.

On the death of Queen Elizabeth the manor was assigned by James I. to his Queen, Anne of Denmark, as part of her dowry, and in 1627 purchased of the Crown by the Corporation, subject to a fee-farm rent of £25 4s. 2¼d. less Land Tax, which is still paid.

King James I. and his Queen at Newbury, 1603.

In September, 1603, King James I. and his Queen visited Newbury, being on a progress, and were entertained by Sir Thomas Dolman at Shaw House. As there was not sufficient accommodation for the Queen's train, the Earl of Nottingham, Baron Howard of Effingham—who so distinguished himself as

Commander of the English Fleet, which destroyed the "Invincible Spanish Armada" in 1588,* and was rewarded by Queen Elizabeth with a grant of Donnington Castle—placed the old fortress at the disposal of the Court. A party of the Earl's workmen were consequently sent to the Castle to make the necessary arrangements. They were, however, refused admittance by order of Lady Russell, who held the appointment of Keeper of the Castle, and was at that time with her son, Lord Herbert, in Wales, and were compelled to make a forcible entry. In the meantime the vigilant Lady Russell had returned, and finding she was debarred from entering the Castle, returned to Newbury, and the next day with the Mayor and divers clothiers, all duly "weaponed," rode in the park towards the Lodge, the official residence of the keeper, which stood on the site of the present Castle House, but was forbidden by the Earl's servants to enter the Castle or the Lodge. A few days after, King James, who had been on a short visit to Winchester, returned to Sir Thomas Dolman's, when Lady Russell personally petitioned His Majesty for the restitution of her supposed rights, but the Scottish Solon judiciously referred her to the majesty of the law. The result of the action which followed was unreservedly in favour of the Earl of Nottingham, but certain questions of evidence were referred to the Judges by whom the decision was subsequently confirmed, and the part taken by Sir Thomas Dolman, who as Justice of the Peace had supported the Earl's officers, commended.

The Queen appears to have ingratiated herself with the people of Newbury by her great courtesy, as a letter from Lady Arabella Stuart to her uncle, the Earl of Shrewsbury, tells us. After much amusing comment on the journey, and alluding with great sprightliness to the chit-chat and light scandal of the day, she says :—

> "If ever thear wear such a virtu as curtsey at the court, I marvell what has become of it, for I protest I see little or none of it but in the Queene, who ever since her coming to Newbury hathe spoken to the people as she passeth, and receiveth theyr prayers wt. thanckes and thanckfull countenance barefaced,† to the great contentment of natif and forreign people, for I wod not hae you thinck the French Imbassadour wd leave that attractive vertu of oure late Queene unremembered or uncommented when he saw it imitated by our most gratious Queene."

Another visit of the Queen, 1613.

Queen Anne of Denmark was again at Newbury in 1613, and on this accasion also was the guest of Sir Thomas Dolman, at Shaw, where she remained over Sunday, and then proceeded on her way to Sir Francis Popham's at Littlecote.

* It is an interesting addition to our Municipal History to know that the Lord High Admiral of England held the appointment of High Steward of the Borough of Newbury at the time of his death in 1624

† *i.e.* without a mask. Ladies at this period usually wore masks when travelling.

Fall of Newbury Bridge, 1623. On Sunday, the 5th February, 1623. the ancient wooden bridge which spanned the Kennet, which is described as being about 30ft. in length and 20ft. wide, suddenly collapsed and fell into the river to the great consternation and inconvenience of the inhabitants. In a letter from certain authorities of the town to the Clerk of the Council to the Prince of Wales, then owner of the manor, for timber or other contribution towards repairing the bridge, the petitioners state that it is the only way by which people can get from one part of the town to the other unless they go a mile round. They further add that they have many poor people to relieve "in these hard times when clothinge, the chiefe keye of tradinge in our towne is so much decayed," and humbly crave for assistance towards the cost of repairing their bridge, which they estimate at between forty and fifty pounds.

Trade of the town. At this period the fortunes of Newbury certainly seem to have been on the decline, its trade and commerce less, and as will be seen above its chief manufacture that of woollen cloth, "much decayed." There was, indeed, a petition made about this time by the cloth-workers of Newbury and other places for the prohibition of the exportation of wool, as the dearth of wool in England had occasioned a decay of the cloth trade, and the workmen reduced to great distress.

CHAPTER VII.

The Great Civil War—The First Battle of Newbury—A Review of the Situation—'Varsity Volunteers—Newbury favours the Parliamentarians—The Disposition of the Forces—The Battle—Newbury People View the Battle—Biggs' Cottage—The Parliamentarians and Roasted Pig—The Hospital.

The Great Civil War. We now come to the period when the peaceful life of Newbury was to be rudely broken in upon by the great national revolution in the reign of Charles the First, when the struggle between the popular and monarchical principles of the constitution was soon to be decided by the terrible arbitrament of the sword.

When hostilities broke out, the chief part of the townspeople of Newbury, after failing by petitions and other means to impress upon the King and his advisers the impolicy of the course they were pursuing, openly declared their resolution to stand by the Parliament; and it is evident that their warmest sympathies were on that side throughout the war.

A very detailed history of the two battles of Newbury and the concurrent military operations which were carried on in this neighbourhood in the course of the first war has already been presented to the public. It will, therefore, be only necessary to give a brief sketch of this eventful period in our local annals.

A Review of the Situation. Before proceeding to indicate the positions occupied by the contending armies of King and Parliament, it may be well to outline the position of affairs which led up to the momentous action at Newbury in September, 1643. In the summer of that year the fortunes of the Parliamentary party were at a very low ebb, and had the King at that critical moment had the firmness of purpose to march upon London, it would probably have changed the whole fortunes of the war, but as usual on the King's side, jealousies, factions, and divided counsels prevailed, and after the surrender of Bristol to Prince Rupert, it was decided to lay siege to Gloucester, which, if it could have been recovered, was thought to have been of considerable importance from a strategical point of view, as giving the command of the Severn and the country thereabouts. This unfortunate decision was attributed to more than one of King's advisers. John Aubrey, the Wiltshire historian, asserts that it was due to Lord Falkland, and the occasion of the ultimate ruin of the King's cause, and even went so far as to say that Falkland's subsequent desperate and imprudent action at the Battle of Newbury, which led to his death was attributed "to his discontent for the unfortunate advice given to his royal master." At this juncture the City of London threw its sword into the scale, and made itself ready for a supreme effort against the King. The Trained Bands of London* were the reserve on which the Parliament relied in every emergency, and wherever the Londoners had fought they had quitted themselves like men. At Edgehill, at Brentford, and at Lansdowne they had borne the brunt of the attack, and their defeat at Roundway Down was probably due to a defect of leadership, rather than to a failure in their own courage.

Essex undertook to relieve Gloucester, and with wonderful alacrity the citizen soldiers volunteered for the service. An army of 10,000 men left London for Gloucester on the 24th August and were joined on the march by other contingents, which raised Essex's force to about 14,000 horse and foot, including a train of artillery. When the Parliamentary General set out to relieve Gloucester, he was urged for the sake of expedition to take only light field pieces with him, and to leave his heavier guns in London. This he wisely refused to do, for the King's Army was so much superior to his own in cavalry that artillery was more needed than ever. According to

* There was a local reminder of the prowess of these men in the ancient hostelry, "The Old London Apprentice," the sign at which used to be a soldier of the London Trained Bands with a wooden leg.

one account he took 40 guns with him, great and small, which did such great service at Newbury. Upon the approach of Essex the siege of Gloucester was raised, and the King and his army retreated on Painswick. Essex marched round by Tewkesbury for a feint, and then suddenly doubled back, making for the nearest way to London. His army was in a sorry plight from fatigue, and very short of provisions. Prince Rupert obtained the King's request to go in pursuit, and marched all night and next day as far as Faringdon, yet was unable to overtake the Parliamentarians. He learned, however, from Sir John Hurry's reconnoitring that Essex was passing over Aldbourne Chase, and expecting to enter Newbury that night. It was a neck-and-neck race which should reach Newbury first, this affording Essex the only clear road to London, but Rupert dashed ahead, and was in possession two hours before the Parliamentarians arrived at Enbourn.

'Varsity Volunteers. Since the publication of the second edition of the "Battles," the author has found much interesting information not mentioned by any of the later authorities. Amongst this matter is a petition presented at the Restoration by Sir John Hinton, private surgeon to the Prince of Wales, afterwards Charles II., in which it was stated that upon raising the siege of Gloucester he was commanded by the King to go to the Queen, who was then at Oxford, for recruits. He made his way through the enemy's lines unsuspected, and on arriving at Oxford some 3,000 recruits, largely composed of University students, assembled around the Royal standard, and marching with them they met the King's forces at Aldbourne Chase, and proceeded to Newbury, where they took part in the great battte. It is certainly notable that the gallant young Oxford soldier-scholars fought at Newbury, and many must lie under the green turf on the battlefield, "unwept, unhonoured, and unsung." Oxford being the headquarters of the King, was during the war little more than a great barracks; so completely did the toga yield to arms, and the rapidity with which troops are reported to have been raised at this time shows how ready volunteers were to join the King, whose fortunes were then in the ascendant. An undergraduate of the period, who wrote a history of the Civil War in verse, says:—

"When first to Oxford, fully there intent
To study learned science I went,
Instead of Logicke, Physicke, school converse
I did attend the armed troops of Mars,
Instead of books. I sword, horse, pistols bought,
And on the field I for degrees then fought.
My years had not amounted full eighteen,
Till I on field wounded three times had been,
Three times in sieges close had been immured,
Three times imprisonments' restraint endured,
In those sad times these verses rude were writ."

The University of Cambridge also furnished a strong contingent of Volunteers, who fought at Newbury. and one of these described how on being taken prisoner he was stripped, imprisoned, and almost starved to death in Newbury Church.

Newbury favours the Parliamentarians. The bulk of the people of Newbury as we have said were strong supporters of the Parliamentary party as incisively expressed by Colonel Dalbier in a communication to the House of Lords, in which he spoke of "That town (of Newbury) which hath on all occasions manifested so much affection for the Parliament." It may be remarked that the men who fought in the first war were patriotic citizens who desired constitutional government, and are not necessarily to be identified with the Republicans under Cromwell, who fought in the second war, which ultimately led to the death of the King.* An illustration of the feeling of the Newbury people may be quoted. The women of the town sat up all night cooking a good stock of provisions for the incoming Parliamentary troops, but Prince Rupert arriving first, took possession of the town, and of course utilised these provisions for his own men. When Essex sent his Quartermaster into Newbury he found the town in the possession of the Royalist forces. Therefore his men, who had marched many days and nights with little sleep or refreshment, had to remain in the low-lying fields, drenched to the skin, without food and without water, "impatient of the sloth of darkness, and wishing for the morning's light to exercise their valour."

The Disposition of the Forces. We may now proceed to indicate the position of the contending forces. The Parliamentarian army was disposed with great military skill, the right on the rising ground by Biggs Hill and Hill Farm, extending along the Enbourn Valley towards the Wash, the centre on the plateau, and the left in a more northerly direction towards Crookham Heath. The baggage, or train, was placed in "The Slings," under the shelter of Hamstead Woods. The Royalist forces were disposed on the Wash, the left wing and centre upon the brow of the hill sloping toward Newbury, his right wing resting on the low ground in front of the town. The heavy guns were planted on a roughly raised battery, remains of which existed until a short time since, extending from near the Gun public-house obliquely across the plateau, whence they could play upon any attacking column advancing up the hill. Obviously the relative positions of the two armies were greatly different. The King possessed immense advantages if they had been properly turned to account. His army was strongly posted between the enemy and London, well supplied

* "Wee stood upon our liberties for the *King's* sake, least he might be the King of meane subjects, or we the subjects of a meane King."—*Sir R. Varney's notes on Hyde's speech.*

with a great store of provisions and other necessaries both for horse and man. The King's line of retreat was safe, and he had the town of Newbury to protect him, if he found it necessary to fall back, while the Parliamentarians were in want and shelterless, and must either fight or starve. On arrival at Newbury, the King who was quartered at the residence of the Mayor, Mr. Gabriel Cox (now Mr. Plenty's house), finding Essex so close at hand, had no alternative but to prevent his further advance by taking up a hasty position extending from the town to Wash Common, and every preparation was made for a decisive battle. Wash Common then presented a more extended field of operations than now, there having been enclosures and roads constructed since. There is no doubt that the rapid movement of the Parliamentary troops led the Royalists to disregard the very common precaution of a study of the ground. They, in all probability, pushed beyond the town towards Wash Common by the main road leading south out of Newbury, but the value of the rounded spurs near Skinner's Lane which commanded the whole of the low-lying ground between the town and the Wash, had escaped their notice either through negligence or fatigue after their hasty march.

The Battle. On the 20th September, 1643, over 20,000 men were engaged from early morn till mid-night in deadly combat. At five o'clock, Sir John Byron started with a considerable body of foot and horse to attempt to gain possession of the hill at Cope Hall, which was the key to the whole position, Essex having here planted a battery, which domineered the King's guns on the Wash, and made them of little avail. Prince Rupert, unable to endure the patient waiting until the right moment came to throw himself on the Parliamentary columns at their exit from the lanes before they had time to deploy on the open ground, bore down with a numerous and imposing body of horse on the right wing of Essex's force on Enbourn Heath. To charge the Parliamentary horse and cut them off from the main body was but the work of a few minutes. In the words of the "Old Cavalier"—

"Then 'spur and sword' was the battle word, and we made their
helmets ring;
Shouting like madmen all the while, 'For God and for the King!'
And, though they snuffled psalms, to give the rebel dogs their due,
Where the roaring shot poured thick and hot, they were stalwart
men and true."

Cut off from support, with neither horse nor cannon to rely on, the two regiments of trained bands on Enbourn Heath found themselves exposed on open ground to the discharges of the enemy's artillery, and to the rush of Rupert's horse. They bore the onset nobly; closing up their ranks, the London apprentices and tradesmen stood like a wall, whilst Rupert's choicest cavalry dashed up against their pikes in vain. Many a saddle was emptied by the musketeers in the squares. It was the pikemen at Newbury who withstood the onrush of Rupert's cavalry. The muskets of the trained bands would not have stopped his charge. "His horsemen," says Clarendon, "endured their storm of small shot, but could make no impression on their stand of pikes,* and were 'forced to wheel about.'" While the right wing was thus engaged, Essex's centre had pushed up the hill. For hours there was a deadly struggle amongst the lanes and hedges. At length two regiments of Parliamentary horse, led by Sir Philip Stapleton, advanced from the end of the lane by Cope Hall, and drove back a royalist regiment by which they were assailed, but being at length outnumbered and outflanked, they were beaten back behind their own line, a temporary success that led to a phase of battle, which natural as it seems now, was then a matter of wonder, for the Roundhead horse, flying before their pursuers, found shelter and leisure to reform in rear of the infantry squares of the City Brigade, which stood "as a bulwark and a rampire." The carnage was terrible, and a tradition survives that the narrow lane leading to Skinner's Green from the Wash was so choked with the slain that a passage had to be cleared before the troops could again be moved forward. The Royalist commanders had failed to do more than keep Essex in check. Their attack on his right at Enbourn Heath had profited them little. In the afternoon, massing large forces on their own right, they directed a fresh attack on his left in the valley of the Kennet, on either side of the Enbourn Road. But the eye of the veteran Skippon, who acted that day as second in command of the Parliamentary army, caught sight of them as he was encouraging his men upon the hill. Hurrying down, he drove back the Royalists, and returned with the assurance that the army would not now be assailed in its rear, nor its baggage pillaged. But there is no evidence whatever, nor is it likely that the baggage was brigaded at Hamstead during the whole of the action. When that action was determined on and was unavoidable, no wise general would have left it there close in rear of a flank. It would have been moved somewhere. As the battle turned in favour of the Parliamentarians it would have been, probably, advanced to the centre ready for the advance the day after the battle, when it would of necessity have moved before the army left the Wash. Retreating then as Essex would have been in face of an enemy who might at any time pursue, the custom was observed even as it has been far back in Greek or Roman times, to move the baggage column first, so as to protect it from the enemy which followed it. Night was coming on, but the battle still raged along the whole line from the Kennet to the En brook. A final effort was made by the Parliamentary troops in the valley to seize a ford over the Kennet, apparently by Guyer's lane, but this was defeated by a body of the King's Life Guard with heavy loss. On the whole the Parliamentary

* The pikes mentioned had a stave of ash about 12ft. in length and a sharp steel lozenge-shaped head, and a large business in making pike handles was done at this time by the Bailys, of Thatcham, ancestors of the celebrated astronomer.

army had gained ground. The contest raged in a desultory way till midnight or thereabouts. During the night the King's troops threw back their left, which retired into Newbury, whilst the chief part of the horse crossed the river into the fields on the Speen side, and quartered in detachments in the neighbouring villages. Doubtless in the first exhaustion of both armies when the battle ceased, the Royalists still barred the way to London, though to a far less degree than when the morning of the 20th September dawned. The whole result of the day must be taken into account in assessing the crown of victory. There is the strongest circumstantial and presumptive evidence that the King's troops when rested abandoned the actual battle-field to their antagonists. Such a course has always been deemed decisive as far as any particular contest goes. A renewal of the fight would have compelled the King to make that dangerous movement, a frontal attack, against a victorious—or at least not unsuccessful army—holding high ground of the Common land from Cope Hall towards Sandleford, and which was so posted from Cope Hall to the Kennet as to threaten in flank such an attempt. That such an attack was never even dreamt of is proved by the speedy retreat of Charles' troops to get to the shelter, not of Newbury, but of the river Kennet. The way to London was open at last, and the next day Essex and his troops proceeded on their march to London by way of Greenham Common, Brimpton, and Aldermaston. No sooner had they entered the deep lane between the latter place and Padworth than a sudden attack was made on their rearguard by a body of cavalry under Prince Rupert. After a sharp encounter and heavy loss, the Royalists retired, and Essex crossed the Kennet at Padworth, and pushed on to Theale, where he quartered for the night. Between 5,000 and 6,000 men were killed and wounded on both sides. The Parliamentarians proceeded on their way to London, where the citizen soldiers made a triumphal entry, being welcomed by the Lord Mayor and Corporation, and banqueted at the Guildhall, after the manner of the City Imperial Volunteers in recent days. The King, after throwing a garrison into Donnington Castle, retired to Oxford.

Newbury People view the Battle. We gain some curious information concerning the interest in the battle taken by the people of Newbury from an autograph letter, belonging to the Priory of the Annunciation, Woodchester, written by Sir Edmund Southcote (who belonged to an old Catholic family seated in Devonshire, descended from John Southcote, Chief Justice of the Common Pleas), relating in the form of a narrative, addressed to his son Philip, the story of the military experiences of his father (Philip's grandfather), Sir John Southcote, Knight, during the Civil Wars, particularly alluding to the part he took in the first action at Newbury. From his account it will be seen that as soon as the unwonted and solemn sound of battle had reached the ears of the inhabitants of Newbury, instead of as we might have supposed, shutting themselves up in their houses, they actually went out to the high ground at the rear of the King's army, which commanded a view of the field of battle, and watched the various changes of the fight, amid the deafening roar of cannon, the sustained fusilade of the infantry, and the dashing charges of the opposing cavalry. But there is something mysterious in the stirring and irresistible appeal that the magic music of the trumpet and the drum makes to the heart, and it is, therefore, no wonder that the citizens of Newbury, accompanied by their good wives and the youths and maidens of the town, went forth with their King to the battle-field, and as the writer of the narrative observes—"to wish success to the King's friends." This opinion is, however, but natural to a partisan and stranger to Newbury, and the remark in no way qualifies the view that the town as a whole was favourable to the Parliamentary cause.

Biggs' Cottage. Biggs' Cottage, where Essex rested on the night preceding the fight, is an old-world tenement, near Enbourn Street, and it was on Biggs' Hill—the rising ground close by—that, Lord Clarendon states, he drew up the right wing of his army in order of battle. The place is noted on contemporary maps, and a study of the locality helps to an understanding of the reason why Essex dominated the King's guns on the Wash. Coins of the period were found some years ago in an old well here, also a diamond ring. Lord Craven is the owner of the cottage, which we hope may long be preserved as an historic landmark.

The Parliamentarians and Roasted Pig. As any little incident which marks locality becomes interesting and important in ascertaining with correctness the position of the opposing forces, an anecdote may be related. It is told in "The History of Newbury," published in 1839, and chiefly compiled by Mr. Alderman Edward William Gray, whose family resided at Enbourn for many generations, and were buried in the old churchyard. The story goes that a party of Parliamentarians were regaling themselves in Lushy Gulley, on the south side of the residence built by Colonel Burslem at Enbourn, now the residence of Mr. Valpy, thinking they were out of danger. when to their great consternation, a cannon ball passed between the party, fortunately without further injury than carrying away a roasted pig which they were eating. This story was told by the late Mr. John Matthews, whose ancestor fought with the Trained Bands, and the sword worn by him on the occasion of the battle, with an elaborately worked pair of pistol holsters—part of his equipment—are now in the possession of Mrs. Heath, of Faccombe Manor.

The Hospital. This is a picturesque old house now occupied by Mr. Whitington, nurseryman, and since the First Battle has always been known as "The Hospital." After the battle, the King issued a Proclamation that the wounded Parliamentarians, "though they be rebels and deserve the punishment of traitors, yet

BIGGS' COTTAGE.

out of your tender compassion upon them as being our subjects, our will and pleasure is that you carefully provide for their recovery as well as for those of our own army, and then send them on to Oxford." There was no distinction on either side if suffering was to be relieved, and it is recorded that the King offered any of his surgeons to Hampden in his last extremity. The army doctors in general are distinguished in the public records by their exertions. They moved from place to place wherever the calls of humanity were brought to bear upon them, through a country disturbed by armed men, with passes, but still in peril. They were arrayed on opposite sides, and few on the Royalist side escaped persecution and confiscation. Amongst these officers may be mentioned Dr. Thomas Baily, of Newbury, a very eminent physician in history, whose estate was sequestered on a charge brought against him that by his persuasions he induced Prince Rupert and the rest of the King's army to take Reading, in 1643, and seize the Parliamentary Committee then sitting there, for which service he was made M.D. at Oxford. He died at Newbury, of an infectious disorder, the following year, 1644, in the prime of life. This Dr. Baily was the son of Dr. Ralph Baily, Fellow of New College, and afterwards a physician of note at Bath. Sir John Hinton, previously mentioned, who brought up the Queen's Volunteers from Oxford, and whose family were connected with Newbury and Welford, was another sufferer. He was private physician to the Prince of Wales, afterwards Charles II., and was also sequestrated for his adherence to the King. The wounded on both sides were collected by their comrades, and this old house which is still known as the Hospital, and every neighbouring building was filled with friend and foe who had been struck down in the fight,

"The weary to rest, and the wounded to die,"

while, it is said, 60 cartloads were taken into Newbury to be treated by the regimental surgeons and their assistants, and others sent to the neighbouring villages. Newbury Church was used as a hospital after both the first and second battles, as were also the old Grammar School Chapel and buildings, and in the accounts of St. Bartholomew's Hospital there are charges, in 1645, for making clean the school after the soldiery, and for "woode and tarr to aire the schole."

The sick and wounded of the trained bands, such as could travel, were sent to London to be treated there. The four great hospitals of St. Bartholomew, Bridewell, St. Thomas, and Bethlehem were freed by Parliamentary ordinance in 1644 from all taxes and assessments on the ground that "great numbers of sick, wounded, and other soldiers have for the time of 20 months past been constantly kept in the said hospitals at very great and extraordinary charges, especially for their keep and diet." Barber-Surgeons are mentioned among the forces of the Parliament, and an interesting seal, probably used by a guild or fraternity of Surgeons, members of the Barber-Surgeons Company attached to the City Trained Bands, was found near the spot where the Falkland Memorial stands, a few years since, inscribed, "The Sosciety and Loyalty of Chyrvrgeons Hall, London," and is now in the British Museum. Of the local doctors practising at Newbury, at this time, Dr. Hugh Barker was of great repute. In the first battle it is mentioned that the Parliamentary army left behind them many surgeon's chests full of medicaments. One of these chests was supplied by the Government to each surgeon on the staff, and at the beginning of hostilities was valued at £25. In the armies raised by the Parliament there were usually two or three medical officers attached to the staff of the General, who supervised and controlled the medical administration of the whole army. There were also regimental surgeons and assistants who were attached to each particular regiment. The pay was about 4s. a day, equal to a little over 12s. of our money. When more medical stores were needed the practice seems to have been to issue warrants to the Apothecary-General for the supply of internal medicaments, and to the Surgeon-General for external medicaments, or frequently a more summary mode was adopted, as we gather from a warrant dated at Marlborough, in 1644, empowering the officers to seize all "Physick and Chirurgery" in the town for the use of the army, the owners to be paid out of the contributions raised from the inhabitants of the district. Besides these arrangements for the cure of wounded soldiers, there was an effort made to provide some support outside the hospitals, both for disabled soldiers and for the widows and orphans of the dead. An Act passed in the 43rd year of Elizabeth's reign had imposed the duty of maintaining disabled soldiers upon the parishes to which they belonged, and it was this Act, no doubt, which gave Elizabeth the undeserved reputation she enjoys in the old ballad :—

"To the soldiers that were maimed
And wounded in the fray,
The Queen allowed a pension
Of fifteenpence a day.
And from all costs and charges,
She quit and set them free ;
And this she did all for the sake
Of brave Lord Willoughby."

In consequence of this Act, the Parliament passed an ordinance ordering the constables and churchwardens of every parish to levy a rate for its disabled soldiers, and for the widows and orphans of those who had fallen. As the parishes showed no great alacrity to assess themselves, Parliament went a step further, and shortly after the first battle of Newbury ordered a special tax of about £4,000 a month to be levied on the counties in its power for the next six months. Through all these stormy times the heroic character of the English nature nobly manifested itself, both on the side of the

Cavalier and Roundhead. Terrible and unsparing on the battlefield, steadfast in purpose, these sturdy English hearts

> "revered the claim
> Of every unprotected name;
> And spared, amid its fiercest rage,
> Childhood, and womanhood, and age."

It is also worth noting that independently of the care of the sick and wounded in the neighbouring houses, many of the disabled officers remained on the battlefield for several days after the action, and it is mentioned of Sir William Springett, a Parliamentary officer, whose mother married as her second husband the famous Quaker, Isaac Pennington, that "he lay for some nights on the field in Lord Roberts' coach, there being neither time nor convenience to pitch his own tent which he had brought with him. For some days he lived on candied citron and biscuit, until he was able to go back to his regiment in Kent." The Lord Roberts referred to was the Parliamentary General, Lord Robartes, of Truro.

The Death of Falkland. The tradition as to the spot where Lord Falkland fell, indicated until recently by a poplar tree in front of Falkland Farm, must be regarded as extremely doubtful. Falkland was killed as the royal cavalry were advancing towards the body of the Parliamentarians, who were endeavouring to gain the hill in front of Skinner's Green lane, above Cope Hall, but at this early period of the fight Essex had not gained a footing on the Wash, Byron advanced at five in the morning, and Lord Falkland rode in the first rank as a trooper. In those days the cavalry charged three deep, and at a trot, each rank in succession discharging their long pistols into the serried mass of pikemen till an entrance was made. Byron took his cavalry round the flank of the line of battle, until he came to the first open ground admitting of a charge. The fields were full of enclosures, the hedges being lined on both sides with musketeers. Byron gave orders to make an opening through the hedge, when Falkland, more gallantly than advisedly, spurred his horse through the gap, where he and his horse were immediately killed. The body was not discovered until the day after the battle, when it was found "stript, trod upon, and mangled, and could only be identified by one who waited upon him in his chamber by a certain mole his lordship had upon his neck." Lord Falkland, having a presentiment that he would not return alive, the night before requested the attendance of Dr. Twisse, rector of Newbury, and at his lodgings in Cheap Street received the Sacrament. In the house is now to be seen a cupboard fitted into a recess, concealed by a panel. Falkland Farm is traditionally pointed out as the place where a party of Royalist officers had a high carousal the night before the battle. The dead bodies were principally buried in several tumuli on the Common, some of which have become nearly obliterated. At this point was the thickest part of the fight, and here they were buried where they fell. When one of these mounds was cut through in making a road, many skeleletons were discovered, together with portions of accoutrements, and buttons identifying several of the regiments engaged.

THE FALKLAND MEMORIAL.

The Falkland Memorial, of which a view appears on an opposite page, was inaugurated with public formality in 1878. The author of this work purchased the piece of ground andpresented it, and collected the whole of the subscriptions, the total cost being about £1,000. His idea was to commemorate Falkland and the whole of those who fell, Royalist and Parliamentarian alike, but the late Earl of Carnarvon, who took an active part in the matter, and the other members of the committee were strongly of opinion that it should only commemorate Falkland and the Royalist officers, although Falkland's sympathies at first were in the opposite direction.

The Memorial consists entirely of Cornish granite, the base being formed of a series of rock-faced steps, from the Lamorna quarries; upon these rests a block of Penryn stone, weighing twelve tons, on which the four inscriptions are cut in lead characters. The superstructure comprises an octagonal plinth with gablets on four sides, having sunk panels filled in with a cross on the front face, and coronets and ciphers of Lords Carnarvon, Sunderland, and Falkland carved on the other panels. The octagonal shaft which surmounts this is a monolith, 17 feet in height, the total height of the Memorial being about 33 feet, and about 40 tons of granite were used in the work.

The Memorial bears appropriate inscriptions on its four sides; on the east side being a quotation from Thucydides, in Greek characters, on the west side from the Latin author Livy, and on the south side from Edmund Burke. For the north side, the inscription is as follows:—

"IN MEMORY OF THOSE
WHO, ON THE 20TH SEPTEMBER, 1643,
FELL FIGHTING IN THE ARMY OF KING CHARLES I.,
ON THE FIELD OF NEWBURY, AND ESPECIALLY OF
LUCIUS CARY, VISCOUNT FALKLAND,
WHO DIED HERE IN THE 34TH YEAR OF HIS AGE,
THIS MONUMENT IS SET UP BY THOSE TO WHOM
THE MAJESTY OF THE CROWN AND
THE LIBERTIES OF THEIR COUNTRY ARE DEAR."

Mr. J. H. Money, architect, of Newbury, furnished the design, and the work was executed by Messrs. W. and J. R. Freeman, of Westminster and Penryn.

THE FALKLAND MEMORIAL.

SHAW HOUSE.

CHAPTER VIII.

THE SECOND BATTLE OF NEWBURY—THE RIVAL ARMIES—THE FIELD OF BATTLE—THE FLANK MARCH.

The Rival Armies. This engagement took place on October 27th, 1644. After the defeat of Essex in Cornwall, the King marched eastward, meaning to relieve Donnington Castle, held by Sir John Boys, and also Basing House, each of which was strictly invested ; his Majesty then intended to press on towards Oxford. This the Parliamentary forces attempted to prevent, and Manchester, Waller, and Essex had in all about 11,000 foot and 8,000 horse. They effected a junction at Basingstoke, and marched on to Newbury. To the chief command of this army of nearly 20,000 men, the Earl of Manchester was nominated, in the absence of the Earl of Essex through illness. Cromwell retained as before the rank of General of the Horse. The whole body, wound up to the highest pitch of enthusiasm, then prepared to advance against the King. Charles having relieved Donnington Castle, had ill-advisedly despatched the Earl of Northampton with 1,500 of his best horse for the relief of Banbury, and had so weakened his forces that they did not exceed 10,000 all told, when he was forced to fight. The combined Parliamentary army was determined on a supreme effort to crush the King, and end the war. Having encamped in Aldermaston Park, they came on to Newbury by way of Bucklebury Common, and took up a position with every advantage locality could confer, on the plateau extending from Clay Hill to Cold Ash Common, thus commanding the whole of the surrounding country.

Charles, owing to his inferiority in point of numbers, did not venture to risk a battle in the open field, but took up a strong defensive position in Newbury, between the rivers Kennet and Lambourn. On the south, the town was protected by the Kennet. On the north-east, troops were quartered in the village of Shaw, which was strengthened with a breastwork and in Shaw House, a little in advance of the village on the northern bank of the Lamboun—" a strong stone house," which obtained celebrity as the scene of the deadliest struggle in the ensuing fight.

Every house or other building in the village of Donnington that offered shelter or cover to the besiegers during the investment of the Castle was burnt or otherwise destroyed by order of Sir John Boys, the damage done being assessed at £5,283 18s. At Shaw, the old Rectory, which stood on the north-west side of Shaw House, was also burnt, and in a brief for the Rector, the Rev. John Royston, the loss incurred is stated to have been over £2,000. These sums were equivalent to very much larger amounts according to the present value of money.

On the west, Prince Maurice with his brigade of Cornish horse and the Duke of York's regiment with five pieces of artillery, was posted, their front being strengthened by a breastwork extending across the heath to wards the swampy valley below, known as Speen Moors. In the two large fields lying north of Newbury, between the rivers Kennet and the Lambourn, was stationed a large body of horse, together with a train of artillery. Approach to this quarter was rendered the more difficult by the neighbourhood of Donnington Castle, which was held for the King by a strong garrison of horse, foot, and artillery, under the intrepid Governor, Sir John Boys. Strong guards were placed on the south of the town, and detachments of horse guarded the out-lying passages of the Lambourn at Bagnor and Boxford to check any advance upon the fords.

The Field of Battle. The plan of the Parliamentarians, when they found Charles so strongly placed, was at once to attempt both of the principal Royalist positions at Shaw and Speen, and thus if both sides succeeded they would completely surround the King. For this purpose it was decided at a Council of War that the greater part of Manchester's horse, with all the horse and foot which had lately been under the leadership of Essex, and almost all the forces under Waller and Hesilrige, together with the London brigade, should separate from Manchester, and by a flank march surprise the Royalist's position at Speen Hill. Manchester and Crawford meanwhile remaining with the other portion of the troops on the hill at Shaw. It being agreed between Manchester and Waller that as soon as the sound of cannon should be heard at Speen, the former should advance with his forces upon the Royalist quarters at Shaw.

Acting on this decision, the right wing of the Parliamentary army, under Waller, Cromwell, and Skippon, marched by way of Hermitage and Chieveley to North Heath, where they halted for the night (Saturday, 26th October), when, local tradition says, the future Protector slept at the Blue Boar Inn. The next morning they were early on the move, and having crossed the Lambourn stream at Boxford with but slight opposition from the Royalist outpost, here stationed to defend the passage, proceeded by High Street Lane to Wickham Heath, thence to Speen Hill.

As soon as it was daylight on the morning of the battle, Sunday, 27th October, Manchester commenced the attack on the Royalist post at Shaw by dispatching a body of 400 musqueteers to force the entrenched position at the south-east angle of the park. Being without adequate support, the Parliamentarians were driven back in confusion, and in attempting to gain a passage by a temporary bridge thrown over the Lambourn, many fell by the swords of the pursuing Cavaliers, and numbers were drowned in endeavouring to reach the opposite bank.

After this unsuccessful attempt to pierce the Royalist line at Shaw, no further effort was made by Manchester, who seems to have manifested great indifference throughout the day, until the preconcerted signal informed him that the right wing had fallen on at Speen Hill.

The Royalist reserve of cavalry at Speen being absent on a foraging expedition, the enemy easily got possession of a neighbouring wood, and after an hour's hard fighting dislodged the Cornish horse and foot, and drove in and dispersed the force of Prince Maurice in the valley below. Many of the King's troops, outnumbered to a great degree and already demoralised by increasing panic, fled for protection to Donnington Castle, and others into Newbury, followed by Cromwell's victorious horse. The King, who was present in person, could not altogether prevent this flight of some of his force, and at one time found himself in imminent danger. At this crisis, Sir John Cansfield, a worthy Lancashire cavalier, gallantly galloped forward with his troop to the support of the King, and succeeded in driving back the Parliamentary squadrons. A fierce three hours' contest followed in the fields lying between Donnington and Newbury; the Royalists, however, succeeded in holding their own till night, and Waller retired into Speen.

Meanwhile on the other side of the town, the second column, which comprised Manchester's battalions, having heard the distant firing at Speen Hill, prepared to essay the more difficult task of forcing the King's position at Shaw House. "It was about four o'clock in the afternoon," says an eye witness, "we heard the cannon begin to play, and saw the fiering of the muskiteers on Speene Hill, which discovered the service to be very hot; and not long after, with joy and thankfulness, we beheld the hasty disorderly retreat of the enemy towards Newbery." Whereupon, Manchester "animated by this encouraging sight," led 3,000 foot and 1,200 horse with some guns down Clay Hill, singing a psalm as they went to storm the defences of the Royalists at Shaw House, and if succeeding, to effect a junction with their friends in the fields lying between Newbury and Donnington. Charging with great impetuosity, the Parliamentarians were met by the Prince of Wales' regiment of horse, who, having received and returned the fire of the advancing column, were forced back into the gardens of "Doleman's House." Here in the garden at the east side of the house the severest conflict and most terrible struggle took place. Again and again Manchester's men strove to carry this well defended post, but were driven back, leaving the gardens and breastworks covered with dead and wounded. For four hours, while the infantry of the Parliament were thus engaged, the cavalry were drawn up for their support barely beyond the range of the enemy's pistols, and being thus fully exposed to their fire, suffered most severely. At length, a reserve of the Royalists coming up, the Parliamentarians retreated to Clay Hill, to the top of which they were pursued by the enraged Cavaliers, who had with them two light field guns. One more attempt was made by Manchester with a strong body of cavalry to force the position at Shaw, but it was foiled by the pluck of the Royalists, who stood their ground and compelled their assailants to retire.

It was now ten o'clock, and a clear moonlight night. The King, who had been a personal witness to that part of the conflict in which his army had suffered most, and unaware that at Shaw the tide of war had turned in his favour, resolved not to expose himself to a second encounter with a force so superior until he had reinforced his own ranks, He had utterly lost his left position, and, therefore, determined to act on the resolution he had taken in the morning in case of an unfavourable issue, namely to retreat to Wallingford and thence to Oxford. Orders were accordingly issued to the officers at once to draw off their men, artillery, and military stores to Donnington Castle, and make what haste they could to get beyond the reach of pursuit.

These movements were not unobserved by the enemy, who evidently also fancied itself worsted on this side, as they also drew off from all parts of the field in the night, and offered no opposition to the withdrawal of the Royalists. Charles himself with his immediate attendants and a squadron of life-guards, made good his escape to Bath, where he met his nephew, Prince Rupert, who was engaged in getting together the Welsh and northern reinforcements, whose expected junction had so long detained the Prince in the West, and deprived Charles of his assistance at Newbury. Prince Maurice ably conducted the retreat, and the next morning discovered the Royalists far advanced on their way to Oxford.

Here began the famous quarrel between Manchester and Cromwell, which ended in the charges brought by Cromwell against the Earl, the Self-denying Ordinance, the re-modelling of the Army, and thence through successive stages came the rest of Cromwell's career, ending in his Protectorship of the United Commonwealth of England, Scotland, and Ireland, with their Colonies and Dominions.

The famous Flank March. The story of the remarkable flank march of some fifteen miles in the presence of the enemy by the main force of the Parliamentary army, which was first related in detail in the "Battles of Newbury," has excited widespread interest and criticism. Many of the most distinguished military authorities being of opinion that the conception of this flanking movement originated in divided counsels and personal differences among the Parliamentary commanders, and was not due to any tactical value such a proceeding may have possessed. Further, that if the flank march was expedient, such a detour was perfectly unnecessary. On this question it may be submitted that like the previous battle the actions that took place round Newbury from the 26th to the 28th October, were the results of an attempt to make a flank march in the presence of the enemy. But there is a great difference between the two cases. The first battle was the natural consequence of an effort to force a way past the Royalist forces, who blocked the best road to the Parliamentary troops on their return march to London, and this could not be done without collision. The second battle was also accompanied by a flank march, but this was the result of a preconceived plan. In the former case success mainly depended on bringing all the available forces of the Parliament to bear on an important point—the high road on the Wash—that is, to strike the heaviest possible blow at the barrier opposed to the Parliamentary troops by the King's army. In the latter case such concentration was not necessary, for the Royalists were not now to be pushed past, but were to be beaten by a decisive action. Glance for a moment at the battlefield. Its western side was singularly strong. The high land of Clay Hill which the Parliamentarians first gained, gave them, it is true, a command of fire and observation over the low land at its foot, but beyond that it had no tactical value. The attack from this point must pass from ground tactically strong for defence over low-lying water meadows or open fields against the strongest of all field defences—fortified posts and villages. As we have seen, the right flank of the Royalists on this side rested on the Kennet. It was further intersected at right angles, roughly speaking, to this portion of the line of defence by the Lambourn, which passed within their position, and all the permanent bridges were in their hands and guarded—that is to say, any attack delivered here by Manchester must be either limited in front or dislocated and split in two parts by the tributary stream. Thus the first assault took place between the Kennet and the Lambourn, giving the Royalists an opportunity of concentrating all their force in that area for the defence of the narrow strip of land. The second attack was delivered north of the Lambourn, again giving the King an opportunity of almost neglecting the scene of the last fight, and concentrating his defence against the other half of the severed portion. No combined attack could be effected, as for such a purpose the passage of the Lambourn was impossible, and many bridges would have had to be thrown over in order to bring about unity of action and facility of lateral communication, so as to render an attack along the whole right front at all practicable. Physically, therefore, or naturally, the decisive blow could not be struck here, the bravery of the troops and the military skill on both sides being equal. But there was yet another consideration. The old Elizabethan mansion at Shaw with its outworks, natural and artificial, and the village itself flanked on its right by entrenchments reaching certainly as far as the present London Road, if not further, together with the entrenchments on the Marsh fields echelloned in rear of the former, and therefore again flanking them, offered an entrenched position of very considerable strength. To turn the right flank of this line would have been a matter of grave difficulty. To attempt a turning movement on the left of Shaw House would have been equally doubtful, for the ruins of Donnington village which had been burnt, if held by Royalist troops and supported by the Castle, which stretched out as a commanding outwork overlooking the fields by which the attacking troops must move, could not be passed, and the line of battle must have therefore embraced the entire area from Donnington Castle to the Lambourn at Shaw Bridge. But on the left side of the three-fronted position of the King the conditions were somewhat different. There were fewer villages or points upon which a line of troops could be formed. The Castle was less effective in affording assistance to the defence on this side. If the heights above Speen could be gained, the advance could be made over gentle slopes, over ground offering no particular advantage to the Royalist troops, for it was open and unsupported, and when the assailants descended from the hill they would be on equal terms with the defenders as far as the ground was concerned. Again, on this side at least there was full space for the development of force.

The area between the Lambourn and Kennet was here wide and clear. If a large force could be brought there it would have ample room for free and uninterrupted action, while if the King's troops could be forced from the Speen hills, all the commanding artillery positions, combining range with security and view, and domineering the town of Newbury, would be at the disposal of the Parliamentarians, leaving their opponents no corresponding advantages. The King's Generals seem to have been either ignorant of or indifferent to this weakness. The entrenchment on Speen Hill, then open common ground—the " narrow heath " referred to by Waller and Hesilrige —was but restricted, it did not even extend so far across the high land as to completely close the plateau; and it is a matter of no wonder, therefore, that when the attack was made the advance turned without difficulty the left of the entrenchment, and compelled its early abandonment. To summarise the tactical features of the Royalist position, the right was, owing to the defensive posts and field works, and the natural configuration of the ground, very strong. It was practically unassailable in those days, for the feeble artillery of the time could make but little impression on stout houses and earthen parapets. Unless the villages, etc., could be burnt and rendered untenable by shell-fire, their capture could only occur after terrible loss, even if it occurred at all. But the left was naturally weak, and was not " improved " by artificial means. The possibility of a sudden blow here seems never to have seriously crossed the mind of the Royalist Generals. The centre, Donnington Castle, may be left out of the question. A central attack there would be actually limited to the area from Bagnor round the front of the Castle to Donnington village or at the most Shaw House, that is, against the strongest part of the position, and against the powerful redoubt formed by the field works of Sir John Boys. If delivered here, ample time would be given to the Royalists to concentrate all their strength and meet the foe on equal terms with the enormous additional advantages of a powerful line of artificial defence.

The conception, therefore, of the flank march evinced great military ability, and was skilful in the extreme. It aimed at the weakest part of the enemy's line, it possessed the element of surprise by taking such a route as to conceal its movement from all possible inspection by the enemy until too late to avert the blow, it covered the movement by a series of false attacks by the detachment left at Clay Hill, which fully performed the duty of a "containing" force by disguising its own weakness, and so deceiving the enemy as to compel him to keep his order of battle unaltered until the "turning detachment" had arrived on its proper field of operations. There is but one extraordinary point in connection with it, and that is the ignorance displayed by the King of the proposed combination. No sound of movement of troops during the day or night seems to have reached the ears of his outposts; no spy or informer gave him any intimation of it; even the patrolling party from Donnington, which tried to molest the march on the plateau above Boxford, does not appear to have sent back news of the approach of so large a body of men; or even if it did, was any idea apparently formed of strengthening the left to meet the attack. Either the Generals could not or would not believe, or the mobility of the troops was of so inferior a character as to render an alteration in the array impossible, except after long delay and preparation. Still more remarkable, perhaps, is the indecisive result of the battle. Naturally the "containing" force at Clay Hill was decisively checked; they could expect no more, and their duty so far was well performed. But the main attack was never fully pushed home, or it must have resulted in the rout of the King's troops. That it did not do so can only be due to supineness on the part of the Parliamentarians, for the King was able to withdraw his troops past Donnington Castle by a road which passed across the very battlefield that should practically have been in Parliamentary hands.

Possibly fear of the redoubtable Castle of Donnington and the garrison of Shaw may have led the Roundhead leaders to consider that discretion was the better part of valour. Be this as it may, it is very evident that they started on this flank march with a definite system of tactics in view, of which we have sufficient evidence in the depositions submitted to the Parliamentary Committee appointed to investigate the quarrel between Manchester and Cromwell. For instance, Colonel Hooper, who was with Balfour and Skippon at Speen, states that if Manchester had fallen on the enemy as soon as the other forces at Speen had delivered their attack, "the King's army could not possibly have escaped, being then encompassed between the two bodies of the Parliament's army at Speen and Shaw." General Watson, Scout-Master-General, also says that if Manchester had done his part "it would in all probability have ruined not only the King's army in Newbury Field, but also put that part of it which was located at Shaw and in Dolman's house past a possibility of retreat." Cromwell testifies to the same effect; as also does Colonel "Dick Norton," who affirms that if Manchester's forces had engaged as arranged "it might have given the enemy an utter overthrow." The late Professor Rawson Gardiner has accepted the writer's narrative with very little variation, and makes but little comment on this important incident, beyond stating that the Parliamentary commanders came to the conclusion after reconnoitring the Royalist position that it was useless to attempt to make a frontal attack.

CHAPTER IX.

THE SIEGE OF DONNINGTON CASTLE.

In 1643, shortly after the First Battle of Newbury, the Castle, being then the property of John Packer, one of the clerks of the Privy Seal, and Secretary to George Villiers, Duke of Buckingham, was garrisoned by order of the King on account of its commanding the great road by which the western trade was carried to London. The following Commission is without subscription, but undoubtedly refers to the appointment of that staunch supporter of the royal cause, Sir John Boys,* to the command of the fortress :—

"Charles R. Trusty and well-beloved, we greet you well. Whereas we "have thought fit for the defence of this part of our County of Berks, to leave "a sufficient number of soldiers in Donnington Castle, we have made choice of "your foot and of the dragooners of Sir Robert Howard. Wherefore our will "and pleasure is that you forthwith repair with the said forces unto the said "Castle, there to continue and keep the same for our use, and to command all "the officers and soldiers therein as you shall find fit for our service. And for "your so doing, these shall be your sufficient warrant. Given under our "sign-manual at our Court at Newbury, this 22nd Sept., 1643."

Sir John Boys lost no time in putting his commission into execution, and on assuming the Governorship of the Castle entered heartily upon the service, not omitting the least thing that might contribute to the defence of the place entrusted to his keeping with the best advantage, taking particular care, as will be seen, to have the fortifications in good condition, clearing the country round of all hedges, trees, or other shelter within the reach of cannon shot, and not suffering any houses or buildings to remain that might favour the approach of the enemy. It must, however, have been very discouraging to Boys to receive a warrant soon after he had taken over the Castle, to deliver up what appears to have been the only two pieces of ordnance in the place, for the service of Lord Hopton, who was advancing to the relief of the Marquis of

---

* Sir John Boys was the son of Edward Boys, gent of Bonnington, Kent, and was baptised at Chillinden in the same county, 5 April, 1607. He was, therefore, 36 years of age at this time.

Winchester at Basing. But the following characteristic letter from the brave faithful soldier shows his readiness to obey orders, and at the same time the great advantage the absence of artillery might give the enemy, who were hovering round the scantily furnished garrison.

This letter also indicates from a reliable source the disposition of "the factious Towne of Newbury"—

"Right Honble

"I received a warrant under yor Lopps hand this day for the delivery of "the two peeces which are in the Castle vpon demand of the Lord Hopton, "which I intend to obey and performe, yet I thought good to acquaint "yor Lopp of the want of two peeces, two Cannoners and two Matroses* more "in this place, for I expect the enemy every day here, they scouting continually "neere vs, giving out words they will shortly roote vs out, yett what they "expresse I can neither feare nor believe, but 'tis not good to dwell in too "much security, hauinge such ill Neighbours as the factious Towne of "Newbury, which lately betrayed some of his Maties friends, not so much as "giving mee notice that I might in time have relieved them. This I thought "good to declare vnto yor Lopps that I might be freed from the Accusation of "not giving timely notice of the want of peeces in this place, which shall be "maintained soe longe as I am able to subscribe my selfe,

Yor Lopps most faithful servant,

"Denington Castle, CASIMIRUS STURT,†

"12th of October, 1643. [JOHN BOYS.]

"Right Honble I forgott to mention yor Lopps order concerning the "Amunition which was goeing for Basing, which shall Accordingly [be] "performed.

"To the Right Honourable
"the Lord Percy Generall
"of his Maties Traine of Artillery
"att his Lodgings in Christ Church in Oxford
"present wth my service
"These.

This letter is endorsed by Lord Percy, younger son of Henry, 9th Earl of Northumberland, created Baron Percy of Alnwick, 28 June, 1643, and who was Lord Chamberlain of His Majesty's Household,

"Gounr. Donington."‡

The ammunition for the garrison at Basing referred to in the postscript of Sir John Boys' letter could not be delivered there by reason of Waller being at this time "before the house" with a force of about 7,000 horse and foot, as mentioned in the subjoined extract from the accounts of Capt. Henry Stevens,|| Commissary General of the King's Army.

The main element of defence of this little fortress was its massive gate-house, with barbican and portcullis, and the extensive

---

* "Matroses"—Assistant Gunners.

† The reason of this *nom de plume* is not apparent, as Sir John Boys does not seek to hide his identity, but when great secrecy was needed we may suppose that this was the war name by which he was known.

‡ Rawlinson MS. D. 395, fol. 141, Bod. Lib.

|| "1643, Nov. 6, Pd. for three loads of ammunition carried from Oxford "toward Basing House, but by reason of the enemy's being there brought back "and delivered to Dennington Castle—the carts went 32 miles wch at ye rate "of 6d. a mile for each cart amounts to £02. 08. 00."

series of earthworks constructed by Boys, and thickly planted with the heaviest guns he was subsequently able to obtain. His lines of circumvallation were further strengthened by palisades, or stakes of strong split wood, about nine feet long, six or seven inches squaré, three feet deep in the ground, in rows about two and a half or three inches apart, placed on the covert-way, at about 3ft. from and parallel to the parapet, or side of the glacis, to secure it from surprise. He was, in fact, indefatigable in fortifying the whole line of his position, and strengthening his entrenchments wherever the ground would allow an enemy to approach. The remainder or domestic part of the Castle with its subordinate towers and curtain walls was incapable of withstanding an artillery attack at a short range. At the same time, standing as it did on an elevated mound, it was difficult of access on every side. It was, however, more especially owing to the brilliant heroism, skill, and dash, displayed by Sir John Boys and his small garrison, whose daring deeds and chivalrous adventures appear almost incredible, that the old Castle became a post of such strategic value, and was so obstinately maintained against the almost overwhelming numbers and organised efforts of their powerful but unsuccessful antagonists.

In the spring of 1644, the Royalists were quartered for a month at Newbury, and then marched to Reading. Leaving that town, which they dismantled of its fortifications, they remained at Wantage and the neighbourhood for some days. The King intended to make a stand at Abingdon, but on the approach of the Parliamentary army under Essex, Abingdon was evacuated without firing a shot, and occupied by the enemy, who also threw troops into Newbury, so that before the end of May the Parliament became masters of all the south and east of Berks, except Donnington Castle; Colonel Boys, however, confident in his cause, held his own, and made daring excursions in gathering stores and provisions, and fought many desperate skirmishes with the Parliamentary forces. But in the month of July he drew on himself the wrath of Waller by an audacious attempt to seize the Mayor and some of the principal citizens of Newbury belonging to the Presbyterian party "on the Lord's day," and Lieut.-General Middleton was sent with a body of between 3,000 and 4,000 horse and foot to reduce the Castle. On Wednesday morning, July 14th, Middleton cannonaded the Castle in the regular way, and captured several musqueteers which had been placed in a barn, part of which still stands on the south-west side of the Castle farm-yard. When ready for the assault he summoned John Boys in these terms:—"Sir, I demand you to render me Donnington Castle for the use of the king and Parliament. If you please to entertain a present treaty you shall have honourable terms. My desire to spare blood makes me propose this. I desire your answer.—John Middleton." "Sir," answers Boys, "I am entrusted by His Majesty's express command, and have not yet learned to obey any other than my Sovereign. To spare blood, do as you please, but myself and those who are with me are fully resolved to venture ours in maintaining what we are entrusted with, which is the answer of—John Boys. Donnington Castle, July 31, 1644." The assault lasted six hours, and the assailants then drew off with a loss, according to the Royalist accounts, of 100 men, a Colonel, a Major, and several other officers killed.

On the following Monday morning the Castle being "recommended" by the Parliament to Major-General Brown, Governor of Abingdon and Commander of the Forces of the Associated Counties of Oxon, Berks, and Bucks, Middleton proceeded to join Essex in the West. After his departure the siege was continued, and it was decided that each line of defence in succession should be taken by assault. But although the Castle was a weak fortress on which Boys' ingenuity had done wonders in rendering it defensible at all, the commander did not despair, and all that science and determination could effect were vainly tried against the skill and activity of this redoubtable garrison.

The *True Informer*, a Parliamentary Journal, from Saturday, August 21st to Saturday, August 24th, thus describes the progress of affairs :—

> "By Letters from our Forces before Denington Castle it is understood that "the Castle cannot, in all probability, hold out but one week more if ever the "battering pieces are come, which are designed for that service ; there are at "present but 200 foote and two troopes of Horse before it, that they have "slaine Captayne Taylor the grand Papist,* and two or three of their men, and "have lost three Troopers and eight or nine foot souldiers, which were surprised "by them in the Castle. Lieutenant-Colonell Boys, sonne to that Boys who "wrote the Postills† is now Governour of the Castle."

The same week *Mercurius Aulicus* informs its readers that Capt. Lamb, of Col. Welding's regiment, was killed at Donnington Castle. Meanwhile, after the departure of Middleton, Colonel Jeremy Horton‡ (Lieut.-Col. of Lord Wharton's regiment), who is described as Adjutant-General to Major-General Brown, was instructed to blockade the Castle. Accordingly, having received reinforcements from Abingdon, Windsor, and Reading, he began to lay close siege to the place and raised a battery in the meadows on the south side of the road leading from Donnington to Speen, whence he beat down three of the towers and part of the curtain-wall in a twelve days' cannonade. He then sent a summons to surrender, which favour, if not accepted, he declared "in the presence of God, there should no man amongst them have his life spared." John Boys replied "that he would keep the place, and neither give nor take quarter." That night he made a sally, beat

* Captain Taylor was buried at Speen Church, 10th August, 1644.

† This is an error. The Governor was the son of Edward Boys, and it was his ancestor, Dr. John Boys, who wrote the "Postills," or commentaries.

‡ Col. Horton was half-brother to Sir John Horton, of Broughton-Gifford, Wilts, and Elston, co. Gloucester, Sheriff of Wilts, 1617. He died in 1647, leaving his claims on the Parliament, amounting to £4,000, to his three nephews, Sir John's younger sons.

the besiegers who had removed their guns to the Snelsmore side of the Castle, out of their trenches, killing a colonel, the chief cannoneer, and many soldiers, and captured a large quantity of arms and ammunition. In a bombardment of nineteen days, twelve at Speen, and seven at Snelsmore, the besiegers had spent over 1,000 rounds on the Castle, but Boys still stood his ground.

Before the Parliament men had well recovered themselves, the King marched into Newbury, on his way from the West, relieved the Castle, and knighted John Boys. After the action of the 27th October, when the King's army was fairly gone, the Parliament forces marched into Newbury, and in full force surrounded Donnington Castle. They again summoned the indomitable Boys to surrender, assuring him this time "they would not leave one stone upon another." "If so, I am not bound to repair it," was the Governor's scornful reply. Being urged a second and a third time, with the offer that he should be permitted to march out with all the arms, ammunition, and stores deposited in the Castle,—"Carry away," he said, "the Castle walls themselves, if you can; but by God's help, I am resolved to keep the ground they stand on till I have orders from the King, my master, to quit it, or will die upon the spot." An assault was consequently determined on, but the officer who led the storming party having fallen at their head, and differences prevailing among the Generals, nothing further was done at this time. Boys though not entirely unaware of the dissensions which, after the battle of the 27th, raged throughout the Parliamentary camp, while the Castle for a time remained practically unmolested, wrote to Secretary Nicholas on the 31st October, informing him of his pressing necessities, and that he could no longer hold out if not relieved. This requisition could not, however, be complied with till the King had been reinforced by Rupert, as any attempt to succour the beleaguered Cavaliers without the relieving party being secured by a sufficient force was utterly impracticable. The town of Newbury was at this time occupied by a large body of horse and foot under Manchester and Waller; and it was a fortunate circumstance for the Royalist commandant that this inaction should have occurred; by which Charles was afforded an opportunity of getting together an adequate number of troops with which to relieve the harassed and starving garrison.

It will be seen by the letter referred to, addressed by Colonel Boys to Sir Edward Nicholas, that the besiegers had some 8,000 foot, in addition to a body of horse, and a good town at their back providing them with ample food and quarters. And it is a remarkable episode in military history, which few occurrences in modern times can parallel, that the loyal governor of the Castle should have been able to defy a force so immensely superior in numbers. But the letter also shows how easily this feeble fortress might have been secured, had there been anything like unanimity among the Parliamentary leaders.

THE KING'S CAMP AT DONNINGTON CASTLE,
1644.

From a drawing by Cattermole.

Colonel Boys wrote thus to Nicholas :—

"Sir,—I am very glad his Mat's Army is safe and well, and shall heartily "pray that Prince Rupert may speedily joyne with ye King's army that soe "there may be an imediate course taken for my reliefe."

"Sr I know it is ye usual manner for men in my condition to p'tend more "want than indeed they are in ; but I doe here faithfully assure you that if I "be not relieved wthin six days I must be enforc'd to do what my "heart bleeds to think on ; it is now too late to say how much this poore "place hath been neglected, wth now nothing but speedily expedic'on must "make good. Manchester and Waller are both in Newbury—it is said they "are neere 8,000 foot wth I am apt to believe, they have but few horse wth "them, those things I am here intrusted wth * makes ye enemy lie close to "mee but wth small guards. I desire I may be informed when reliefe shall "come that I may be in readiness.

"Donnington Castle, Yrs etc.,
"October last, 1644. JOHN BOYS."

"My Lord Cleveland † is very well in Newbury. I have here above 250 "men and officers wth of necessity I must support with releefe or perish, wth "were left behind." ‡

It was at this time that the famous quarrel between Manchester and Cromwell began, which ended in the charge brought by Cromwell against the Earl—the Self-denying Ordinance—and the remodelling of the army. In the midst of their quarrel, thirteen days after the battle, the King led his army back, relieved Donnington Castle, carried off all his artillery and baggage, marched down the hill, through the village of Donnington, and across the front of the enemy's position, with drums beating and colours flying.

Bright were the breast-plates and the head-pieces there,
And buff-suits laced
Half the Cavaliers graced,
And scarves of silk tissue those gallants did wear.
They follow the course of the Lambourn down,
And flaunt all their banners in sight of the town ;
The Roundhead men may come on if they choose,
The Royalists will not the combat refuse. ‖

Manchester declined the challenge, and the King returned with his army to the Castle, where he lay that night—Saturday, November 9th, 1644.

A correspondent of a London Diurnal communicates the following intelligence from the Parliamentary army in connection with the return of the King to Donnington Castle :—

"Friday, Nov. 8th.—This day the King designed a partie of 6 or 7,000 "horse and foot to relieve Dennington Castle and to fetch away such things "out of the Castle as were most materiall, vizt.—

"1. The King's Crown, which His Majesty wore on some high dayes, and "had carried and brought back from Exeter.

"2. The Great Seale and other Seales which the Lord Keeper had left "also in the said Castle.

---

* The King's Artillery and personal baggage is apparently referred to.

† Lord Cleveland was wounded in the battle on the 27th.

‡ The writer is indebted for the above interesting letter to C. H. Firth, Esq., M.A., Balliol Coll., Oxford.

‖ "Donnington Castle"—A Royalist Story by Col. Columb.

"3. The King's Writings and divers Writs of great consequence, which "were also carried thither.

"4. Divers Jewells, much gould, silver, and other treasure, which was "also in the said Castle.

"5. That they should endeavour to bring away what artillery and "ammunition they could.

"6. To carry relief with them to the Castle."

On Sunday morning, November 10th, the King's troops were drawn up in marching order on the heath adjoining Donnington Castle, with so many of the light field guns which had been left behind on the retreat after the battle as they could conveniently attach to their train, the "great pieces" of ordnance that were planted on the works below, about eighteen smaller pieces of artillery and a good store of ammunition being left with the garrison, which was well supplied with provisions. From Snelsmore Heath the army marched to Winterbourn, where the troops were halted, and the King and his staff, it is said, attended divine service at the Parish Church. The route was then by Boxford, Shefford, and Lambourn to Marlborough, whence the King relieved Basing, and then, visiting Faringdon on his way, arrived at Oxford on the 23rd of November. Essex soon after put his troops into quarters at Reading, Newbury, and Abingdon, and the year 1644 closed. In the following June, Naseby was fought, and the First Civil War was virtually at an end.

Late in October, 1645, Cromwell and Colonel Dalbier were near Newbury after the storming of Basing. The Parliament had ordered that Donnington Castle should be taken, and had sent letters to the three Committees in Oxford, Berks, and Bucks, to join forces for this purpose. Cromwell, aware of the character of the royalist governor and garrison at Donnington, seems to have considered the chances of an assault and to have decided against it, for he marched into Devonshire to join Fairfax, leaving Dalbier to accomplish the reduction of a stronghold which, like Basing House, had been such an eyesore to the Parliament. On the 6th November, 1645, Dalbier marched with the forces of the three associated counties to Newbury to meet a contingent from Hampshire of 500 foot and 200 horse, which had been ordered to join him there. Dalbier's force was subsequently further augmented by 200 foot, furnished by the committee of the county of Sussex, and five companies of foot and a troop of horse by the County of Surrey. A troop of horse, which had been engaged at Basing, was also sent by the County of Kent, together with 200 foot from Windsor and Henley, and 300 foot and 100 horse from Reading. Notwithstanding all these reinforcements, Dalbier did not apply himself to reduce the Castle, and intelligence having reached him that the King had returned to Oxford, he at once postponed the siege and retired with his force to Aldermaston. He was aware of the temper of the fearless commander of the Castle, Sir John Boys, who had bade defiance to Cromwell, Manchester, Waller, and the whole Parliamentary army; he, therefore, thought it prudent to collect all his available strength before he ventured to approach the little fortress whose active and spirited defender had so often defied the forces of the Parliament and beaten them off.

Meanwhile the King's affairs were daily becoming more disastrous. While Fairfax was obtaining success after success in the West, the royal forces were everywhere being defeated and dispersed. It was not until December that Dalbier again returned to Newbury, when, much to his chagrin, he found on his arrival at Donnington that the whole of the houses in the village and adjacent places had been burned by order of Sir John Boys; consequently he withdrew his infantry into Newbury and quartered the horse in the immediate neighbourhood. The season of the year was very unfavourable for military operations, "the winter being very rude and violente"; and as every place affording shelter or protection had been burnt or otherwise destroyed, Dalbier could not lay close siege to the Castle as he had intended. Meanwhile the Parliament were asking what was being done before Donnington. and it is evident that they were not satisfied with the progress of affairs and Dalbier's lingering proceedings. Early in December a report was ordered to be made concerning Donnington Castle, and shortly afterwards the whole business was referred to the committees of Hants, Surrey, Sussex, and Kent, and the committees of the three associated counties of Oxon, Berks, and Bucks, with a request that they would represent their opinions to the House of Commons. These joint committees presented their report on the 9th January following, and a letter was also read from Colonel Dalbier; both of these were recommitted for further consideration.

Nothing of moment or of military interest occurred for some little time in connection with the siege of the the Castle, Dalbier remaining quiet in his quarters at Newbury, and postponing his intended operations against the threatened fortress until the spring. Sir John Boys in the interval was vigilantly on the watch against any surprise from Dalbier's force, whose movements from his position at Donnington he could clearly observe. He therefore made every preparation against the inevitable assault, knowing full well that all depended on his own exertions, that no aid could be expected, and that the calamity which he had so long and honourably striven to avert, must necessarily soon follow. But this did not discourage the gallant governor, who laboured vigorously in restoring and enlarging the defences, provisioning his little garrison and securing forage for the horses of his trusty band of forty troopers. "Such gallants were they," says Captain Knight, a Royalist officer of the garrison, "that the enemy's horse never faced the Castle, but they received some loss."

Although the investment of the Castle had not yet actually commenced, the two parties were not inactive, there being frequent "beating up of quarters" and daring sallies by Sir John Boys on the Parliamentary troops lying at Burghclere, Woodhay, Balsdon

House, Kintbury, and Greenham Manor-house, all of which are fully narrated in the author's work on this subject.

In the month of March, 1646, Dalbier resolved to take more active measures, and commenced a regular investment of the place. Having advanced his force to the hill facing the Castle "towards Shaw," Dalbier sent a final summons to Boys to surrender, who desired three days' respite in order that he might acquaint the King then at Oxford with the condition of the garrison, and receive his

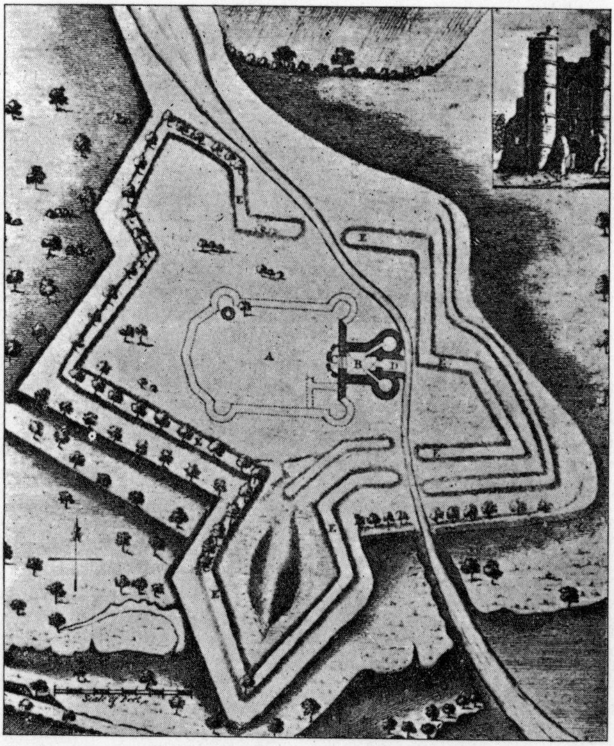

OUTWORKS OF DEFENCE.

instructions before surrendering what had been committed to his charge. This was looked upon by Dalbier as an excuse for delay, and the same night he commenced the siege in earnest by raising a redoubt and temporary works on the east side of the park, commanding a clear range to the south side of the gateway. Sir John, who could not digest such rough proceedings of the enemy, commanded a sally with horse and foot from the Castle on Dalbier's men, who, seeing the palisaded gate which closed the passage through the earthworks shut, and the bridge that crossed the ditch at the field-work of the battered building drawn, were lying carelessly in their trenches, and little suspected an attack. But in this they were deceived, for Sir John had had a private sallyport made within the bulwark trench, and palisades filled up with earth. These he now cleared, and passed his party of horse and foot through undiscovered, led by Captain Donne, who suddenly fell upon the enemy and beat them out of their works, killing about eighty of the Parliament men, and taking back with them to the Castle above 63 prisoners, four colours, and many hundred arms, besides some of the spades and pick-axes of the working party. Dalbier, enraged at the loss, marched with all his forces, horse and foot, to regain his trenches, which he did without dispute; and the next day planted a huge "Mortar Piece*" on his works, the shells from which fell upon the ancient masonry with destructive effect, and in a few hours it came down in such masses that the old place was well nigh shattered to pieces. Dalbier also fired the barn and some of the other out-buildings of the Castle.

Like a true soldier, Dalbier, knowing he had a brave enemy to deal with, and admiring his pluck and determination to fight to the last for the King, at this juncture wrote to Sir John Boys, again suggesting a treaty, and informing him that Lord Hopton had given up his army in the West to General Fairfax; that Lord Astley was lately routed at Stow-on-the-Wold; that Chester had surrendered, and that he could expect no relief. Therefore he advised him to yield the Castle betimes, while he was able to offer him favourable conditions, "which advice proceeded from him of mere love as to himself and so many gallant men with him, to whom he bore much honour and love, and finally that this was done against most of the will of his officers." Upon this Boys called a Council of War of his officers, to whom he communicated Dalbier's letter. The result of this Council was not to believe Dalbier upon his bare word, but if the King's affairs were as he represented them to be, he (Dalbier) should be asked to grant a pass to two of themselves, Royalist officers of the garrison, to go to Oxford and have an interview with the King, to acquaint him with the condition of the Castle, and to learn his Majesty's determination. This request Dalbier courteously granted, and Captain Donne, who as we have mentioned, commanded the last sortie from the Castle, and Captain Osborne, were there-

* The bore of this formidable piece of artillery must have been more than fifteen inches in diameter, judging from portions of the projectiles which have been found near the Castle wall. From the correspondence of the Derby House Committee, we learn that the name of the "Firemaster," an artillery officer selected for the express purpose of directing the use of this "Great Mortar Piece" was *Roberts.* He is reported to have done good service to the Parliament on a former occasion "with but little encouragement." His pay was 10s. a day, and that of his men 2s. When the Castle was "taken in," orders were sent for the Mortar and its "equipage" to be forwarded under a sufficient convoy for the use at the siege of Banbury. Particular instructions were given that "Firemaster" Roberts should accompany this heavy piece of ordnance, which threw hollow shells filled with powder, grape-shot, and other combustibles with deadly effect to everything within reach, and gave the *coup de grâce* to the Castle.

upon sent to the King at Oxford, who returned answer to Sir John Boys that he should get the best terms for himself and his garrison he possibly could, and, if permitted, he should march oft to Oxford and bring off all the artillery of the Castle with him.

At the time of the surrender there were in the Castle six pieces of ordnance, about twenty barrels of gunpowder, with a proportionable quantity of match and other ammunition, and from 140 to 200 men, together with a good store of baggage.

The field which tradition points out as that in which Dalbier was encamped and where the treaty for the surrender of the Castle was negotiated, is still called "Dalbier's Mead." It lies on the eastern side of the Castle, and near the gardens and park of Donnington Castle House.*

CHAPTER X.

State of Newbury and the Country-side—Dutch Prisoners—Newbury Tokens—Distinguished Commonwealth Visitors—The Restoration—The Plague—Visit of Pepys, the Diarist, to Newbury—"Strange and Wonderful News from Newbury"—and other Historical Notes.

State of Newbury and the Country-side, 1645.

The state of the town of Newbury and the surrounding villages at this time of civil discord, when authority and law in some sense were for awhile inverted, and misrule on all sides appeared to be gaining the ascendancy, can to some extent be gathered from the local records.

As to the place itself, it had been universally agreed that though but a town of second class, it was one of great importance to whichever party could occupy it—the storehouse of merchandise, ammunition, and arms; the key of the river Kennet and of the high road to London—and so its geographical position had rendered it the theatre of distraction and confusion.

The clothing trade had for some time continued to languish, for inland communication was interrupted by serious embarrassments, and enough had occurred to shake public and private confidence. Not only had the town been the place where two bloody battles had been fought, but it had been stormed and sacked, and laid under contributions by both the conflicting parties. The outlook got increasingly alarming day by day, and those who ventured to travel for commercial purposes might hazard their property or their lives. The Civil War, of course, gave a sort of licence to marauders, who, under pretence of fighting on one side,

---

* For a more detailed account of the events in the great Civil War, described in this and the two previous chapters, the reader is referred to the "Battles of Newbury, and the Siege of Donnington Castle," published by W. J. Blacket, Newbury.

plundered both. Experience had shown that neither the road, the river, nor even the town itself was sufficiently secure, and the commonalty were, of course, victimised as usual, without relief or reparation of any kind.

An insight into the condition of the town and immediate neighbourhood at this time (1645), is obtained from a report of the proceedings at a meeting of all classes of the people, knights, gentlemen, freeholders, and other inhabitants of the county, held on Compton Downs, wherein their grievances under military tyranny, to be embodied in a petition to the King and both Houses of Parliament, are pathetically set forth. For a long time they say they have been "overpressed with insupportable burthens and contrary commands of many garrisons, and armies on either side" to the utter ruin of themselves and families. Further, that "by these unnatural wars the true worship of God and their religion are almost forgotten, and that their ancient laws and liberties are altogether swallowed up in the arbitrary power of the sword."

Another illustration is obtained from a letter written by a tenant farmer in the neighbourhood, who had been put in prison at Reading, presumably for not complying with the exactions of one party or the other. "We cannot," he says, "enjoy our land because the armies of both sides be so near to us, consuming the profit of our grounds. Besides, taxes are so hard we are not able to pay them." He goes on to say that in his parish there are but sixty-eight yard-lands, which at ten pounds a yard-land comes to six hundred and eighty pounds a year, and the taxes laid upon them by both armies was twelve hundred pounds a year besides free quarter. The relator adds that he had 11 horses taken by the King's soldiers, and bought nine of them back again, which he brought home to the farm. While trying to find the other two, the other nine were again taken and never recovered. This did not end his troubles, for in going to market with a load of corn, some of the Earl of Manchester's soldiers (Parliamentary) met with his men and took away his team of horses, which he never had back. This reminds us of the old song :—

"I had six oxen t'other day,
And them the Roundheads got away;
A mischief be their speed.
I had six horses in a hole,
And them the Cavaliers stole,
I think they be agreed."

Such was the demoralisation of the soldiery that they did not hesitate to shed blood when engaged in their looting expeditions. For instance, a body of soldiers from the Parliamentary garrison at Reading made a foray on the farm of a well-known yeoman at Woolhampton, named Andrew Pottinger, who, while endeavouring to save his sheep from being taken, was struck on the head by one of the soldiers and killed on the spot.

Many other occurrences of this kind are reported, characteristic of the heat and temper of the times. But without descending much into particulars, it is evident that principle, where any had existed, had now degenerated into a love of gain, and the root of all evil, combined with the unlicensed extravagance of other passions. While the country-side suffered and yearned for rest and reconciliation, the poor clothiers of Newbury were in quite as bad a plight. They had to pay the most extortionate assessments, and yet could not send their goods to London for fear of being plundered on the way. Much of the traffic was managed on pack horses, but these might be the bearers of ammunition, and when the packages of cloth were stopped and opened on the road, they became the property of the greedy soldier. An instance of this may be given in the case of John Cooke, a well-known Newbury clothier and benefactor to the town, who was plundered of cloth valued at £1,000, representing four or five times that sum at the present day.

Sir John Boys, Governor of Donnington Castle, was the terror of the western road, and in January, 1645, a large company of Wiltshire clothiers and carriers, knowing what to expect, had entered into a composition with Sir John that they should be unmolested on the route by paying £3 for each waggon. On their way they were met by a body of cavalry from Basing House, and the whole convoy was captured; but staying too long at Marlborough with their booty, were surprised by a party of Roundhead horse, and lost the spoil and many of their men. In the month of May following, a party of west country clothiers obtained from the Royalist Governor of Devizes a pass for London, and entered into a bond to pay £400 excise on the cloth they were carrying. As they approached Newbury, Sir John Boys sallied out and demanded the full amount in the King's name. No expostulations could save the poor clothiers, and they were forced to raise the money in Newbury. They had not gone far before some Royalist troops from Wallingford pounced upon them, and in the end they only obtained their final discharge by consenting to pay an additional £10 on every pack of cloth, or leaving an equivalent in value.

There was not much to choose between either party—religion and manners were alike violated—and the Parliamentary force, in spite of the claims of its leaders to religious superiority, had by this time grievously degenerated, and it required the stringent pressure found in the final exertions of Cromwell and Fairfax to reduce it to order.

That many of the houses in the town were more or less damaged during the war is evident from the fact that in almost every instance the more ancient buildings appear to have been reconstructed with old oak timbers, which have previously been displaced and re-converted for the same purpose.

The Dutch Prisoners, 1653.

Although Newbury was now quiet as far as national affairs went, being sheltered from further troubles by powerful friends among the Parliamentary party, yet about this time there was much complaint of the fresh burden cast upon the town by having to support 100 prisoners

THE OLD CLOTH HALL, NEWBURY.

captured by the Admirals of the Commonwealth, Blake, Deane, Monk, and Popham, in the course of the Dutch War.

The Newbury Tokens. During the Commonwealth and the early part of the reign of Charles II., many tradesmen for convenience, and owing to the scarcity of the current coins of small amount, were allowed to make their own pence, half-pence, and farthings. The earliest private token in brass or copper bears date 1648, and in such large quantities and varieties were these pieces issued, particularly half-pence, that the country was swamped with pence and half-pence of the most varied description. Newbury was not behindhand in availing itself of the opportunity of doing a little coining. The Corporation struck a piece for general use, and several traders made others for themselves and their customers. Nine varieties are recognised, and it is curious that they are all farthings. The Corporation piece bore on one side the borough arms, and the inscription "Borough of Newbery," and on the other or obverse, "In County of Berks, B.N. 1657." In another issue the name of the town is spelt "Newbry." One of the Newbury tokens is of exceptional interest, and very rare. It was issued by the Rev. Joseph Sayer, rector of the town, and bears on the obverse, "Joseph Sayer, Rector," and the Borough Arms; on the reverse the appropriate device of an open Bible in the field, as it is heraldically termed. It is possible that this particular token was connected with the celebration of the Holy Communion. At this period, each intending communicant on some day in the week preceding the celebration, notified his or her intention to the clerk, and received a metal token. There is a charge entered in the Churchwardens' accounts for 300 tokens for a preceding Rector, the Rev. Benjamin Woodbridge. The other known brass tokens in connection with the Borough are as follows:

Obverse. Thomas Cowslade—A lion rampant.
Reverse. Grocer in Newbury. T.C.C.

O. William Harrison—The Grocers' Arms.
R. Of Newbery, 1657. W.S.H

O. John Hill—A Scull.
R. Of Newbury. J.S.H.

O. John Naish—in—The Grocer's Arms.
R. Grocer, Newbury. J.S.N., 1652.

O. Thomas Younge—The Mercers' Arms.
R. Junier in Newbury—His Farthinge.

O. Jonas Noroway, Junior—The Grocers' Arms.
R. Grocer in Newbury. J.S.N.

The custom of issuing tokens was continued until the year 1672, when the Goverment struck a sufficient quantity of half-pence and farthings for the exigencies of trade, and the further circulation of private tokens was prohibited by Proclamation.

Distinguished Commonwealth Visitors. In the summer of 1654, John Evelyn records a visit he paid to Newbury, he being then on his way to his wife's relations in Wiltshire. The celebrated diarist describes Newbury as a "considerable town," and Donnington as "famous for its battle, siege, and castle; this last had been in the possession of old Geoffrey Chaucer."

The following year, Major-General Disbrowe, brother-in-law to Cromwell, arrived at Newbury with troops advancing to suppress the rising in the West, under Penruddock, Grove, and other Cavalier officers, in which one, John Kensey, described as a surgeon of Newbury, was engaged, and executed at Salisbury.

The Lord Protector himself passed through Newbury in 1650 on his way from Bristol to London, after his campaign in Ireland. His progress was a sort of triumph, and all ranks of people contended, either from regard or fear, who should show him the most respect. The Newbury ringers gave him a peal, and were paid half-a-crown for this compliment to "General Crumbwell."

The Restoration. Notwithstanding the Puritan element that prevailed in Newbury during the period of the Commonwealth, there were few towns in England where the day of the Restoration of Charles II. (29th May), was celebrated with more enthusiasm. The bells were rung for two days, bonfires were made, and the jollity continued till the next morning. The Corporation feasted and distributed wine, ale, and cakes to the people; the soldiers fired volleys, and companies of apprentices roistered through the streets. The emblems of royalty that had been obliterated were furbished up once more, the royal arms set up again in the Church, together with a "Deske" for the Bishop, and all rejoiced to see the King enjoy his own again.

Royalty again looked favourably upon Newbury, and a few years after his restoration (in August, 1663), the King, accompanied by the Queen, his brother James, Duke of York, and the Duchess, together with Prince Rupert and a distinguished party, paid a visit to the town. The royalties were received by the Mayor and other authorities with great array and circumstance, and after an address of congratulation "on ascending the throne of his ancestors," the "Merrie Monarch" was presented with a purse of gold. Charles and his court then adjourned to Shaw House, where they were splendidly entertained by Sir Thomas Dolman. After dinner the King and the Duke of York, accompanied by Prince Rupert, renewed his acquaintance with the fields of battle. Queen Catherine of Braganza, again visited the town in 1678.

The Plague. The year 1665 will always be memorable as the year when the plague, which had been known here before at the early part of the century, raged so fearfully in London and elsewhere. The authorities at Newbury had, indeed, tried to insist upon the inhabitants removing all rubbish and dirt from their houses for avoiding infectious diseases, yet notwithstanding these well-directed efforts, the streets and ways remained in a filthy and ruinous condition from the negligent manner in which they were generally repaired. There was, of course, no system of proper sanitation, and the kennel or ditch in front of each house served for all drainage purposes. We do not possess any information as to the extent to which our town suffered by this terrible scourge, but there is a tradition that the bodies of persons from Newbury who died of this epidemic were taken by night and buried on the open downs round Blewbury, a horn or trumpet being sounded to let the people of the village know that the bearers of the dead were approaching, and that they should keep within doors. That victims of the plague were buried in orchards, the open commons, and downs, we have evidence in more than one local parish register. If the Newbury dead were carted off to the downs for burial, it would account for the absence of registration, the panic being so intense.

Visit of Pepys, the Diarist, to Newbury.

Pepys, the famous Diarist, and Secretary to the Admiralty in the reign of Charles II. and James II., paid a visit to Newbury in June, 1668:

"Come to Newbery," he says, "and there dined; and musick; a song of the old Cavalier of Queen Elizabeth's, and how he was changed upon coming in of the King, did please me mightily; and I did cause W. Hewer to write it out. Then comes the reckoning (forced to change gold), 8s. 7d., servants and poor, 1s. 6d. So out and lost our way, but come into it again, and in the evening betimes came to Reading."

The Great Frost, 1683-4.

The frost this year was terrible. It began in the beginning of December, 1683; there was then a constant frost for seven weeks, producing ice eighteen inches thick. Many parks of deer were destroyed, and flocks of sheep, the forest trees, and even the oaks were split by the frost; most of the hollies were killed, and nearly all the birds perished. The Kennet was frozen over, and when the thaw came the greater part of the town was flooded; the town bridge was considerably damaged, and had to be temporarily secured by shores and props, while the Marsh bridge was bodily carried away, and landed in a neighbouring meadow. The flood of waters made a breach in the river bank at the bridge and in other places, so that great fears were entertained that the whole town would be inundated, but this was happily averted by the prompt measures adopted.

"Strange and Wonderful News from Newberry."

In the Bagford collection there is a curious old black-letter ballad, printed from an Ashmolean broadside, entitled "Strange and wonderful news from Newberry," with the imprint of Charles Corbet, 1684, which appears to be a literal version put into rhyme of an incident concerning a youth named Shuff, of Newbury, who was choked by eating custard. The subject is also treated in the same collection under the title of "A Ballad on the renowned Shuff of Newbury." The first of these is unique, and of the other only two exemplars remain. Many opinions have been expressed as to what kind of delicacy is referred to, but we may suppose it to have been what used to be called in London "Pudding-Pies," and are still known by that name in the East Riding of Yorkshire and elsewhere. As a specimen of the humour of the period we give the first of these ballads, which is entitled "A Warning to all Custard Eaters," and consists of fifteen stanzas, to the tune of *Whittington's Bells*:—

Let *Totman Court* and *Islington*
And *Paddington* also*
Attend with Lamentation
Unto a Tale of woe.

Although 'tis strange 'tis true no doubt, of it you may be sure,
It is in the News-books put, there's nothing can be truer.

Of many several kinds of Deaths I oft have heard, I wis;
But never knew any lose his Life by such a Cause as this.

At *Newberry*, that fatal place, where many a Man was muster'd
And lost his life, oh! there it was a Youth was slain with *Custard*.

In that same Myrish, bloody Fenn as once it did appear;
Or *Essex* and his Custard-Men† did choak the Cavalier.

There liv'd this pretty dapper Youth, who was of little stature;
Shuff was his name, in very truth, and tender was his nature.

He with a Boy a Wager laid, a *Custard* he would Eat
Before the Boy should run so far, and back again retreat.

The people all assembled were to see this piece of Wit;
They were agreed, and started fair, this ran, the other bit.

The nimble Lad did run and laugh, so through the way he scour'd;
That he was coming back ere half the *Custard* was devour'd.

The eating Champion seeing that, much like Jack Pudding's Bastard,
Clapt t'other half into his throat, and choak'd himself with *Custard*.

This suffocating *Custard* wrought within his gullet so,
That on the ground he tumbled down, ah, woful overthrow!

Two-pence in *Custard* did him choak, and brought his courage down,
When Death struck him 'twas thought he took the Cream of all the Town.

One spark of Fire consumes a House, small Prison makes one pant,
The Sword-fish mortifies the Whale, the Mouse the Elephant.

But never did I see the Throat under my Lord Mayor's roof,‡
Unless they brought it scalding hot it was not *Custard* proof.

---

* "Totnam" or Tottenham Court, "a Mansion in the fields," was formerly celebrated for its tea gardens, and at the tower end of Islington, in 1611, were eight inns principally supported by summer visitors:—

"Hogsdone, *Islington*, and Totnam Court,
For cakes and creame had then no small resort."
Wither's *Britain's Remembrancer*, 1628.

Paddington was also famous for its tea gardens, much frequented by the citizens for curds and whey.

† The City Trained Bands.

‡ A very large *Custard* was formerly annually prepared for the Lord Mayor's feast:—

Now May'rs and Shrieves all satiate lay;
Yet eat, in dreams, the *custard* of the day.

Let this a warning be to those that go to *Islington* ;
Custard will kill, Experience shows, as soon as any Gun.

Beware how you on Holidays abroad do feast your Wives ;
For they that feed on *Custard* go in danger of their lives.

The other ballad, consisting of nine stanzas, was sung to the tune of *Chevy Chase*, and has a full title as follows :—

"On this Tragical occasion a Courier was immediately dispatch'd to His Majesty's Almonder at Christ Church in Oxford, whose office it was to act as Coroner in that Ancient Borough ; who, having made all the Expedition so weighty an Affair required, upon his arrival summoned a very Wise Jury no doubt, who, having examin'd all Witnesses and maturely weigh'd the most minute circumstances, found as a Deodand* due to the King that part of the Custard which remain'd uneaten. If anyone desires to be further informed in this Matter, let them consult the Records of that Ancient Burrough, or that Living Oracle, the Recorder thereof."

The Duke of Monmouth's Rebellion.

In 1685, a certain amount of excitement must have been caused in the town by the arrival of the Earl of Faversham, Lieutenant-General of the forces of King James II. with 150 Life Guards, then known as Lord Oxford's Horse or the Oxford Blues, with a body of Foot Guards on their way to join the other forces engaged in putting down the Rebellion of the Duke of Monmouth. A few days after took place the last fight deserving the name of a battle that has been fought on English ground—that of Sedgmoor.

The name of one Newbury man only who joined the partisans of the ill-fated Monmouth has been handed down to us, namely, William Marshall, who was convicted at the Quarter Sessions of the Borough, in August, 1686 "for being in the Rebellion in the West Country," and committed to Reading gaol.

"Est-il-possible."

In the Spring of 1687, George, Prince of Denmark, accompanied by his Consort the Princess Anne, daughter of James II. arrived at Newbury *en route* for Bath, where the Prince was to drink the waters for his asthma, and as the Princess was known as a decided champion of the Protestant faith, she received a hearty welcome from the town authorities and inhabitants. Prince George, who is described as a heavy, uninteresting man, was in the habit when any news was told him, to exclaim in French "Est-il-possible ?" "Is it possible ?" and hence he acquired this nick-name. When James II. was lingering at Andover on his return from Salisbury, after the successful landing of the Prince of Orange, he was deserted by his son-in-law with Lords Ormond and Drumlanrig. The trio had supped with him the night before, and when the King heard of the Prince's defection, he said bitterly, "What ! Is Est-il-possible gone too ? After all, a good trooper would have been a greater loss."

---

* Deodand—anything forfeited to the Crown when a person came to a violent end without the fault of any responsible individual.

King James II. at Newbury. King James arrived at Newbury in 1686 when on a progress, and was received by the Mayor and Corporation in all their "formalities," but either from the borough coffers being quite empty or the King's profession of Romanism, he does not appear to have been presented with anything more material than an address, so far as we can judge from the Municipal records and journalism of the day.

The Prince of Orange. Although Newbury did not play an important rôle in martial affairs after the Civil Wars, there was a slight revival of the old military fever when drums beat for volunteers to rally round the standard of William, Prince of Orange, who was then on his march from Torbay towards London.

Newbury itself was strong in support of the "champion of the Protestant religion and liberties of England," and if we may judge from the old ballad of the "Couragious Soldiers of the West," they warmly espoused his cause.

The Prince with his Dutch troops and adherents, marched into Newbury on Sunday, the 9th December, 1688, and lodged at Sir Thomas Dolman's at Shaw House, who "kept up his old mansion at a bountiful old rate," and lived in a style of even greater magnificence and open-handedness than his father; the old banquetting hall, it is said, being filled to overflowing every day by retainers and guests. The following morning the Prince took leave of his host, and proceeded on his way towards Abingdon.

The Battle of the Boyne. In the month of June, 1690, King William III. passed through Newbury on his way to Bristol, where he embarked for Ireland, and after his successful campaign– the battle of the Boyne was fought the 1st July—he again entered the town on his return to London. So warm was the popular sympathy shown him on all hands, that his journey became a triumphal procession. The townspeople of Newbury "testifyed their duty and affection with all possible demonstrations," and the Corporation presented the hero of the Boyne with a purse of fifty guineas. and an address of welcome.

Queen Anne at Newbury. Queen Anne was at Newbury in 1703, and was received by the borough authorities and the inhabitants "with all imaginable joy, honour and triumph." The royal party then proceeded to Shaw House, where they were magnificently entertained by the then owner, Thomas Dolman. As a recognition of the manner in which he had received the Queen, Mr. Dolman was knighted at St. James's the following 11th November.

Riot at Newbury. In 1706, a riot occurred in the town, described in a broadside of the period as the "Newbury Skirmish" between a military press-gang and a number of the townspeople, in which one of the soldiers, a sergeant, was killed, and on the other hand several of the mutineers were wounded by their opponents.

Accession of George I.

After the death of Queen Anne, in 1714, George I. peacefully succeeded, and as Newbury was strongly in favour of the Hanoverian succession, the Jacobite risings which soon followed in other places in no way affected the town. The King was proclaimed by the Mayor at the Market Cross in the Market Place, with the usual formalities, and as the majority of the townsmen were attached to the Whig interest, they commemorated the event by founding a political organisation known as the Constitutional Club, which, as a social convivial fraternity, lingered on until recent times.

George the First displayed a great partiality for Hanover, and we are unable to connect him personally with Newbury. His inability to write or speak our language interposed to prevent much sympathy between himself and his subjects.

Daniel Defoe's description of Newbury in 1724.

The author of "Robinson Crusoe" in his "Tour through Great Britain," published in 1724, thus refers to the manufacturing interests of Newbury at that time:—"The town of Nubery is an ancient cloathing town, though now little of that remains to it, but it still retains a manufacturing Genius, and the people are greatly employed in making Shalloons, a kind of stuff, which though it be used only for the Lining and Insides of our Cloaths—for Women use but little of it—nor the men for anything but as above, yet it becomes so greatly worn both at home and abroad, that it has increased to a manufacture of itself, and is more considerable than any single manufacture of Stuffs in the Nation. This employs the town of Nubery, as also Andover, and abundance of other towns in other centres."

Great Flood at Newbury.

One of the worst floods ever known in Newbury occurred in the year 1726, when one of the side arches of the old wooden bridge over the Kennet was thrown down by the rush of the waters, and much damage done in other parts of the town.

The Jacobite Rising of 1745.

Although the cause of the Stuarts had extremely declined by the middle of the eighteenth century, and the nation was turning its thoughts to improved industry in peaceful submission to the Brunswick dynasty, yet great alarm seems to have been felt when the romantic enterprise of Prince Charles and his Highland Clans first became known, and which came upon the country very much like a thunder cloud in a summer sky.

Newbury was once again to be connected with the national history, and was selected as a central position as a depôt for despatching troops to the north. A permanent camp of some 5,000 or 6,000 men was maintained on Greenham Common for a considerable time at this period. Troops were also encamped on the Wash and quartered in the town.

On the 16th April, 1746, was fought the battle of Culloden, insignificant in comparison with many other battles, but important as finally setting at rest the claims of the expatriated house of Stuart to the British throne. The Duke of Cumberland, who commanded the army of the Government, and used his victory with notable harshness and cruelty, was closely associated with this neighbourhood, as he spent a considerable portion of his early years at Midgham House, where his Preceptor and Governor, the Right Hon. Stephen Poyntz resided. Shortly after Culloden, the Duke paid a visit to Midgham, and presented his old tutor (Mr. Poyntz) with the sword he used at the battle, and also the bullet with which he had been wounded. These relics were preserved at Midgham House until the estate passed into other hands. The Duke, who was the founder of the Ascot race meeting, trained his horses at Keat's Gore, East Ilsley, where a fine old mansion formerly stood, and it was here the celebrated horse "Eclipse" is said to have been foaled and trained.

The Great Heat of 1747. The heat in the summer of 1747 was of great intensity, and is thus alluded to in a letter written from Newbury by Dr. Thomas Sherlock, Bishop of Salisbury, to his friend, Edward Weston :—

"We suffer by the great heat, but as the visitation work is divided between me and the Bishop of L [ondon], we have got through it with great ease. The general distemper that we and our servts are subject to is a Great Thirst, wch wou'd be more tolerable, hast not the hot weather spoiled all the drink of the country."*

The Small Pox. The Small Pox was very prevalent in Newbury in 1753, and "in order to encourage the laudable practice of innoculation," the Corporation undertook to pay the fees for all persons undergoing the operation, and the expenses of medical attendance.

Captured Treasure. In 1754, Newbury witnessed a novel procession. Two French merchantmen laden with dollars and gold and silver bars, having been captured and brought into Bristol by some English privateers, the treasure was placed in forty-seven wagons, and guarded by troops, halted in the Market Place, *en route* for London.

Accession of George III. In 1760, George III. came to the throne, a King who tried once more to establish personal government and to ignore the strongly-expressed wishes of his Parliament—an attempt which was, however, not found to be so easy as it had been in former centuries. He was proclaimed at the Market Cross at Newbury, 1st November, 1760, where six companies

---

* Underwood MSS. Hist. MSS. Com. 1885, p. 297.

of the Berkshire Militia, then recently embodied, were drawn up. The proclamation having been read, the soldiers fired three volleys, and all drank the King's health. The names of the following worthies of the town are appended to the proclamation:—Henry Cox (Mayor), W. le Marchant (Deputy Steward or Recorder), Thomas Penrose (Rector), Richard Budd, John Cox, George Calverly, Lypeatt Bodman, Lawrence Head, Thomas Goulding, Francis Page, Benjamin Merriman, John Kimber, William Bodman, Thomas Lovidge, George Jones, Samuel Toomer, and Edward Head.

Bread Riot at Newbury, 1766.

The costly wars in which England was engaged almost continuously throughout the eighteenth century had a most disastrous effect on the manufacturing resources of the country, and almost paralysed many branches of industry. Especially was this the case as regards the clothing trade, in which Newbury was at this time still considerably engaged, consequently there was a great scarcity of employment, and the common necessaries of life were raised to so high a price by those who were able to take advantage of the monopoly they enjoyed, that the poor were crushed down to a pitiable state of starvation and despair. It was, therefore, no wonder, although not to be excused, that when no one would stand up to be the poor man's friend, the bread-winners of that day at last rose in defence of their starving families, to vindicate the wrongs to which they felt they had been subjected. The millers and bakers of the town and neighbourhood were the especial offenders, as notwithstanding the price of wheat was not immoderately high, they kept up the price of bread much in excess of what was fair and legitimate. At last the long subdued feeling of discontent found forcible expression. On a certain market day in August, during the time the sacks of corn were being pitched for sale, the people broke out into wild riot. Upsetting the open stalls, they flung themselves upon the scattered provisions, corn, meat, butter, and eggs, wrecked a couple of houses, and so alarmed the bakers that they at once lowered the price of bread, and promised a further reduction. But the spirit of the mob was not easily to be managed. They proceeded to break into the mills, and throw the corn into the river; windows were broken, and damage to the extent of £1,000 was done. Several persons were injured in the fray, one of them fatally.

The military had to be summoned before this disturbance could be quelled. Happily, it was perceived that the rioters had much reason on their side, however unreasonable their mode of expressing their wrongs might be, and it is satisfactory to know that bread was afterwards sold to the poor at a cheap rate—9d. per gallon loaf—public subscriptions being raised for the purpose, while the millers agreed to grind their wheat free of charge. The Corporation made good the damage done to the farmers in the market, the ringleaders of the mob were tried and punished, and the town sank back to its usual peaceful condition.

Newbury Bridge. The old wooden bridge, which for centuries spanned the swift-flowing Kennet at Newbury, adorned with timber-framed houses over-hanging the river on either side like one continuous street, was taken down in 1769, and the first stone of the present structure was laid 28th July in that year. It was built by the Corporation at a cost somewhat exceeding £700. The builder was a Mr. James Clarke, an eminent man in his day, who also erected the Town Hall, the handsome block of buildings in the London Road, once the famous "King's Arms" hostelry, and most of the principal houses in Newbury of that date.

There is no more familiar landmark in the town than "The Bridge," which consists of a single elliptical arch with stone voussoirs and massive abutments, surmounted by a handsome open balustrade. It is altogether one of the most picturesque "bits" in the old town, and whether viewed from up stream or down, the sturdy old structure forms an exceptionally pretty picture, and as pleasantly embodied in modern verse :—

> The bridge is here—the silent river flows,
> And over both the stream of life still goes.
> Men pass and re-pass, toil and work—and die ;
> On *this* side toil—on *that* they sleeping lie.
> Here still they battle in defence of right ;
> Here still are loyal hearts and hands to fight,
> And men who, swift in danger's hour would spring
> To guard the same old bridge for "God and King."
>
> *May Rowland.*

Decline of the Clothing Trade. When the clothing interest was being rapidly extinguished in Newbury, the Weavers' Company, in order if possible to revive the manufacture, issued an advertisement setting forth that they had agreed to disannul their powers and right of settling the price which any person in the trade should give for making any kind of goods. Moreover they gave free liberty for strangers to come into the town and manufacture silks, muslins, cottons, linen, worsted, etc., without any interference from the Company of Weavers. This announcement concludes with the following paragraph :—

> "Newbury is a town well supplied with water and an extraordinary good market to supply its inhabitants with every accommodation that can make life comfortable, and it is well situated to carry on an extensive trade, having an easy conveyance to and from London by the River Kennet."

But it was too late, for the trade had been rapidly declining from the middle of the last century, and in course of years one improvement after another was introduced into the manufacture of woollen cloth. Then came the introduction of machinery, and with it the factory system, spinning-jennies, carding machines, and the like inventions, due to the spirit and industry of the clothiers in the large manufacturing districts of the north, which brought about an exodus of the distressed weavers of Newbury ; and the Weavers' Company became but a shadow of the once influential brotherhood which exercised such potent sway in the olden time.

Royalty in the Town. King George III. appears to have honoured Newbury several times with a visit during his long reign. The King and Queen with the young Princesses were here in 1784, and changed horses at the famous Pelican Inn at Speenhamland, *en route* to Tottenham Park, Marlborough. Also in 1789, when dense crowds lined the roadway to express their joy at the recovery of the King.

The following year, George, Prince of Wales, arrived in the town on his way to pay a visit to Lord Craven, at Benham Place, and the next day the Prince hunted with the Craven hounds. His Royal Highness was again at Newbury in 1797 and 1798.

Jubilee of George III. The town of Newbury most creditably bore its share in the demonstrations of loyalty evinced on the occasion of the national Jubilee to celebrate King George the Third entering the fiftieth year of his reign.

The ceremonies of the day being concluded, the company retired to the ball room at the Mansion House, which was honoured with the presence of the Margravine of Anspach and other nobility, and about 400 of the principal inhabitants of the town and neighbourhood. A local journal of the day thus summarises the proceedings :—

> "The town of Newbury in their corporate as well as private capacity, has ever manifested the most zealous respect for the person of the King and attachment to the Throne, but in its arrangements on this occasion has surpassed itself, and set an example worthy of the imitation of every part of the kingdom."

CHAPTER XI.

A Famous Coat—Loyal Celebrations—The Margravine of Anspach—The Canal—The Old Guildhall—The Queen of Portugal—Various Incidents—The Reform Bill—Public Rejoicings.

The Newbury Coat.—A Record of 1811. In connection with the ancient trade which made Newbury famous in former days, the remarkable achievement of converting wool from the sheep's back into cloth, and finally into a well-finished coat, between sunrise and sunset on a summer's day, has acquired a world-wide celebrity.

This remarkable performance in the sartorial art came about in this way. Mr. John Coxeter, a then well-known cloth manufacturer at Greenham Mills, remarked in the course of conversation one day in the year 1811, to Sir John Throckmorton, Bart., of Buckland, near Faringdon, "So great are the improvements in machinery which I have lately introduced into my mill, that I believe that in twenty-four hours I could take the coat off your back, reduce it to wool, and turn it back into a coat again." The vaunt thus spoken in jest made so great an impression on the Baronet that shortly afterwards he enquired of Mr. Coxeter if the feat was really possible. After a careful noting of the time required in the various processes, Mr. Coxeter replied in his opinion it could be done.

Not long after the above conversation, Sir John Throckmorton laid a wager of a thousand guineas that at eight o'clock in the evening of the 25th June, 1811, he would sit down to dinner in a well-woven, properly-made coat, the wool of which formed the fleeces of sheep's backs at five o'clock that same morning. Such an achievement appearing practically impossible to his listeners, the bet was eagerly accepted.

Sir John entrusted the accomplishment of the feat to Mr. Coxeter, and at five o'clock in the morning the worthy squire came to Greenham with his shepherd, bringing with him two fat Southdown sheep. Proceedings at once commenced, and no time was lost in getting the sheep shorn. The wool was washed, stubbed, roved, spun, and woven; the cloth was scoured, fulled, tented, raised, sheared, dyed, and dressed. The cloth was finished, as thus described, by four o'clock in the afternoon, eleven hours after the commencement of the sheep-shearing. The coat had now to be made. Mr. James White, of Newbury, superintended the tailoring, and cut the coat. Nine of his men with needles ready threaded, took the garment in hand at four o'clock, and completed the coat at twenty minutes past six. In the meantime the news of this extraordinary match against time had spread abroad, and an immense concourse of people assembled, waiting with intense excitement the achievement of the task. Taking his stand upon a platform, Sir John Throckmorton appeared wearing the coat in the presence of over five thousand people, and sat down to dinner with it on, together with forty gentlemen, at eight o'clock in the evening. The two sheep which had been despoiled of their wool were roasted whole, and cut up and distributed among the people, together with 120 gallons of strong beer, this latter being the gift of Mr. Coxeter. The garment is a large hunting coat of the then admired dark Wellington colour—a sort of damson tint. It had been completed in thirteen hours and ten minutes, the wager thus being won with an hour and three-quarters to spare.

A silver medal was presented to Mr. Coxeter by the Berkshire Agricultural Society for this wonderful achievement. This famous coat was exhibited at the great International Exhibition of 1851, where it attracted a great deal of attention. A few copies of the old coloured engravings from an oil-painting by Luke Clint, of Newbury, were eagerly bought up.

These are certainly days of speed, and though with the vastly superior machinery of to-day this remarkable performance could no doubt be easily eclipsed, it is interesting to notice that up to the present it has never been equalled in this country.

Peace Rejoicings. In commemoration of the Treaty of Peace, signed 3rd May, 1814, between Great Britain and France, nearly four thousand persons were entertained to a substantial dinner, the table being arranged in the three principal streets, and decorated with bunches of laurel. The toasts were announced by sound of trumpet, and accompanied by military bands. After dinner there were the usual festivities, and at night the town was grandly illuminated.

At Greenham, Mr. Coxeter, not content with his great achievement in connection with the famous coat, had a gigantic plum pudding made, which was cooked under the supervision of twelve ladies. This monster pudding measured 24ft. in length, and was conveyed to Greenham Mills on a large timber wagon, drawn by eight beautiful oxen, which were highly decorated with blue ribbons. The driver was similarly ornamented, and bore aloft an old family sword of state, presumably to give *éclat* to the occasion. Arrived at its destination, it was served up at a dinner given to 800 poor persons, at which Squire Croft presided.

The victory of Waterloo the following year (1815), was observed with general rejoicings. The Corporation, together with the Yeomanry and Volunteers, attended service at the Parish Church, and made a handsome contribution to the fund for the widows and orphans of the slain.

Coronation of George IV. The Coronation of George IV., 19th July, 1821, was but indifferently celebrated at Newbury. In the evening there was a dinner to celebrate the occasion, at which the Mayor presided. One of the members of the Yeomanry going out of his way to abuse the Queen, it was communicated to the crowd outside, who smashed many windows of the Hall, and one of the cavalry men had his skull fractured. Ultimately there was " a grand battle royal " between the members of the Yeomanry troop and the crowd, in which divers heads were broken and other injuries mutually inflicted. Anxious to prevent more mischief, the Mayor caused the Riot Act to be read, and by his firm and courageous conduct the disturbance was quelled, but it was some time before quiet was entirely restored.

The Margravine of Anspach. Of the many persons of note and importance who, though not actually resident here, were intimately connected with the public life of Newbury in the early part of the nineteenth century, few acquired a greater popularity than the Margravine of Anspach.

The Margravine was the youngest daughter of Augustus, 4th Earl of Berkeley, and when a little more than sixteen, married William, afterwards 6th Baron Craven, by whom she had seven children. On the death of Lord Craven, in 1791, she married the Margrave of Brandenburg, Anspach, and Bareith, nephew of Frederick II., King of Prussia, commonly called " The Great," and of Queen Caroline, consort of George II.. During her residence at Benham Place, which was built by her husband, Lord Craven, in

1775, the Margravine took a great deal of interest in public affairs in Newbury, and there was scarcely a function of any importance to which she did not give her countenance and support. At the time of the Napoleonic scare, the Margravine, who took an active part in promoting the volunteer associations which were then raised, presented a handsome silk standard to the local troop of Yeomanry, inscribed with her motto, "Salus Publica Salus Mea," and her many charitable and kind acts endeared her to all classes in the town.

In a very spirited public address upon leaving Benham in 1811, the Margravine says :—

> "I take this opportunity of assuring the people of Newbury and all the worthy Yeomanry of the County of Berks, that I only wish I had ten times as much landed property in the County as I have, to have ten times the means and opportunities of proving my attachment to it."

The Margravine died at Naples, 13th January, 1828, and was buried in the English cemetery in that city. The Margrave, who had pre-deceased her many years, was buried in Speen Church.

The Kennet and Avon Canal. With the improvements in communication by road, considerable impetus to trade was given, particularly in regard to the conveyance of coal by the construction of the Kennet and Avon Canal, which opened up direct communication by water between London and Bristol.

This canal which commences at Newbury, forms a continuation of the river Kennet navigation, connecting the Thames with the Severn, and was first projected in 1794, when an Act was obtained for its construction. It was completed in 1810, and water communication between London and Bristol was opened in the early part of the year 1811. The total cost of the Canal appears to have been £1,072,000, and was carried out by John Rennie, the celebrated engineer, who bestowed great pains not only on the survey, the designs for the viaducts and bridges, but also on the contruction of the works, which he superintended with rigid scrutiny.

In the year 1813, the gross receipts were £22,000, and the net, £11,800. In 1840, these figures had grown to £58,000 and £39,100 respectively. By 1848 the gross receipts had fallen to £33,200. But then the Great Western line was opened. Four years later they were down to £24,300, and then the proprietors in despair offered to sell their Canal to the Railway Company. So far it would seem the fight had been a fair one, but the battle was over, and the strongest had won. Such, at least, was apparently the opinion of Parliament, for the transfer was sanctioned, and in 1852 the Great Western bought the whole undertaking for £210,000, for a little less, that is, than one-fifth of its cost.

The interest of the Great Western was not, of course, to develop the canal for the purposes it was originally constructed to serve, and in 1888 the gross revenue had fallen to under £6,000, while the maintenance of the canal cost £9,500, besides £7,000 to £8,000 paid in the shape of interest to its former proprietors.

THE RIVER KENNET AT NEWBURY,

Previous to the construction of the Canal.

[From drawings by Mr. Joseph Toomer, who as a pupil of Sir Joshua Reynolds.]

The Old Guildhall. The old Guildhall, which formerly occupied a considerable part of the Market Place, was a very picturesque building, and interesting from its many historical associations. It was erected in the year 1611, and therefore in existence during the memorable period of the Civil War, when the bodies of Lord Falkland and other officers of note were laid out in one of the upper rooms before removal for burial. In 1684 a prison was built on the east side, and the west front was "beautified" at the latter part of the reign of George II. The upper floor, which was approached from the paved area below by a spacious flight of stairs on the north-west side, contained the ancient Council Chamber, which was also used for the County and Borough Courts of Quarter Sessions, and for other public purposes. The ground floor was principally occupied by butchers' shambles, and by dealers in poultry, butter, and other commodities.

THE OLD GUILDHALL.

At the south-west angle the Pillory and Whipping Post were fixed, and at the north end were the Parish Stocks.

In consequence of the old edifice having become dilapidated and considered an obstruction to the carriage-way to other parts of the Borough, the authorities under powers of the *Newbury and Speenhamland Improvement Act* of 1825, had the historic pile razed to the ground in 1828, and sold the rich and beautiful carved internal fittings and highly enriched external ornaments for a mere bagatelle.

Among the projects proposed by the above Act (1825), were a new Town Hall, a new Gaol and House of Correction, widening of the Mansion House corner, a new street from Bartholomew Street to Cheap Street through the "Catherine Wheel" yard, and various other improvements which are still in the dim and distant future.

The Queen of Portugal. It was now some years since Newbury had been honoured by a royal visit, and in the month of October, 1828, there was a considerable stir in the town when it became known that the Queen Donna Maria of Portugal, attended by the Marquis Barbacena, the Marchioness de Palmella, and a numerous suite had arrived at the Pelican Hotel. A great concourse of people assembled in the Broadway, and the Queen appeared several times at the front windows, and bowed in response to the crowd which had assembled to give her a hearty greeting. The royal party dined at the "Pelican," and afterwards proceeded to London.

Proclamation of William IV. William the Fourth does not appear to have paid any regal visit to Newbury. He was proclaimed, 5th July, 1830, with ceremonies usual on such occasions.

The Machine Riots. Soon after the accession of William IV. occurred the "great rebellion" among the farm labourers, who in order to obtain a rise in their then wretchedly low wages, and to compel the farmers to discontinue machinery for the purposes of agriculture, committed violent depredations by breaking in pieces the thrashing machines, and setting fire to barns, stacks of corn, and even to dwelling houses.

For the most part they were married men of previous good character, with families depending upon them for support, and many of the wives of the poor fellows begged as an act of mercy that they might be transported with their husbands. Three were sentenced to death at a Special Assize held at Reading, 1st January, 1831, and death recorded against about twenty-five more. Great sympathy was shown with the unfortunate men, and a petition signed by 950 persons was sent from Newbury for a commutation of the sentences. Only one man was executed, named Winterbourn, who bore his fate with great fortitude, although he knew his equally guilty fellows had been reprieved. Many were transported for long periods, and several ultimately became very successful colonists in the land of their banishment.

The Forerunner of the Motor. In the month of August, 1832, Messrs. Ogle and Summer's steam coach passed through Newbury on its way from Southampton to Oxford. It travelled over the hilly and rough roads between Winchester and Newbury at an average speed of twelve miles an hour, and ascending the steep hills at various parts of the route with the greatest ease. In 1835 a steam coach, invented by Mr. Hancock, of Marlborough, named the "Erin," arrived at Newbury. It performed the journey between London and Marlborough—75 miles—in 5 hours and 48 minutes.

The Reform Bill. Agitation at Newbury The subject of reform in Parliament was a considerable source of agitation in Newbury, and its inhabitants were greatly excited on the subject till its settlement—the measure being warmly and influentially supported in the town. Upon passing the Bill in the House of Commons there were great demonstrations with illuminations and other signs of popular rejoicing, which were repeated at each successful stage until the measure finally became law.

It being considered a favourable opportunity of obtaining political enfranchisement, a petition was sent from Newbury to both Houses of the Legislature soliciting that privilege, but the inhabitants were somewhat apathetic in the matter on it being explained to them that no person could vote both for the County and Borough upon the same qualification.

We may mention in passing that Sir Francis Burdett, the distinguished political reformer, who, for nearly the first half of the nineteenth century occupied such a prominent position in public life, was the owner of the Ramsbury Manor Estate, and well-known in Newbury and the neighbourhood. He died in London, and—it is a singular circumstance—only a short time after, Lady Burdett, who was the youngest daughter of Mr. Coutts, the banker, also died and both were buried at the same time. The funeral cortége, which consisted of the hearse drawn by six horses, four mourning coaches, and a carriage which had belonged to the deceased baronet, drawn by four horses, passed through Newbury, 30th January, 1844. Sir Francis and his lady were buried in the family vault immediately under the Communion table in Ramsbury Church.

William Cobbett, so well known also for his political labours on behalf of reform, was a frequent visitor to Newbury, where his friend and correspondent, William Budd, a local solicitor, and Clerk of the Peace for the County, resided. He frequently attended the market-ordinary at the "Pelican," and addressed his brother farmers on the great question of the day, where crowds gathered if only to catch a sight of the soldier politician, who, whatever his faults may have been, deserves to be remembered as one of the boldest and purest of English political writers. He died in 1835.

Loyal Celebrations. The rejoicings at Newbury on the occasion of the Coronation of Queen Victoria, 28th June, 1838, were of a particularly hearty character. About 3,500 persons dined at tables erected in the public streets, both old and young being liberally provided for. A report of the proceedings concludes with a prayer which has been so abundantly answered that insertion here may not be inappropriate :—

> "Long may Victoria reign in the hearts and affections of her faithful subjects ; may thousands to be born, after the hand which pens this sentence is chill with death, bless her ; may He from Whom all good things do come, bless, prosper, and protect her ; and may all her subjects when the hour of her departure shall come for changing an earthly into a heavenly crown, have reason to bless and cherish her memory."*

The marriage of the Queen with the Prince Consort was celebrated in Newbury with considerable spirit, and all classes combined in making it an occasion for a joyous meeting.

---

* The report mentions that among the visitors was a lady—Mrs. Hulbert, of Speen, 94 years of age—who remembered the Coronation of George III.,

CHAPTER XII.

THE OLD COACHING DAYS.

The town of Newbury in the old coaching days or rather that part of it called Speenhamland, occupied a unique position, standing almost mid-way on the great western road from London to Bath, which latter city was then in its glory and height of fashion. Speenhamland was the stopping place for all coaches, and scenes of great activity and animation were to be witnessed every hour of the night as well as day, and the old borough and hamlet were then in the full tide of their prosperity.

The Roads. Before the regular establishment of Mail Coaches, there were few roads in England that were more than mere tracks; sometimes the sandy soil was worn through by the traffic until these tracks were many yards below the surface of the surrounding country; in other places where the ground was harder and the so-called road ran parallel with a river, the bed of that river when not in flood was preferred as the easiest and most level track to travel in. The running footmen who attended the chariots of those rich enough to employ them, were by no means superfluous luxuries. Their services were frequently required to push the vehicle through sloughs of mud, and by supporting it first on this side and then on the other to prevent it being overturned by holes in the road, or ruts that in some instances measured four feet deep.

Of the execrable condition of the road between London and Bath before the era of turnpike trusts, we can form some idea from the local records, when on the occasion of a royal progress, men were employed to "digg up ye high waies against ye King passing by," and there was a general turn out of labourers and other workmen to mend the ways, and render the bridges at least temporarily secure. When the Judges went circuit in their coaches, Juries were often kept waiting until their lordships could be dug out of a hole or swamp by the aid of plough horses, and in the seventeenth century scarcely a Quarter Sessions passed without presentment being made to the Grand Jury against this district on account of the bad state of the roads.

---

78 years before. It was mentioned to the writer by the late Mr. John Tanner, of Speenhamland, that Mrs. Hulbert told him that she had often heard her mother say that she well recollected being held up when a child (in 1688) to see the Prince of Orange and his troops march down Speen Hill, and what impressed her most were the "black men" in the cavalcade. This seems to support the venerable lady's story, as Lord Macaulay graphically describes the negroes from the coast of Guinea, who attended on the English noblemen who had joined the Prince.

The old Bath road appears to have originally passed through Chilton and Ramsbury, and when the new road was opened it is reported that the driver of the Marlborough coach with a fine conservative spirit, obstinately refused to use the new and better route, and stuck to the old wagon track by way of Ramsbury. "He was an old man," he said, "his grandfather and father had driven the aforesaid way before him, and he would continue in the old track till death."

The Act for repairing and improving the turnpike road from Newbury to Marlborough was passed in 1744,* and with the improvement of the roads there was a corresponding improvement in locomotion.

The Flying Coach. In 1752, two years before the date of the Manchester Flying Coach, an enterprising Newbury firm—John Clark and Co.—started a new vehicle of this description which seems to have earned its designation by the fact that it proposed to travel at the rate of four or five miles an hour, and undertook to perform the whole journey from Newbury to London in twelve hours. Four passengers only were carried, and the fare was ten shillings each to or from London, and about as much more money as was required for the fare was expended in living on the road, not to speak of fees to guard and driver.

From London to Bath. At this time the Post Coach, starting from London on Monday, did not reach Bath till Wednesday, although the "New Bath Road," as we have seen, was made some years previously. *The* coach started from the Saracen's Head,† Friday Street, Cheapside, and the hour of departure was so early that travellers generally slept at the old inn the previous night. The proper outfit for a gentleman of the period with an "inside place" was an "ultramarine Joseph," the indispensable "Pocket Monitor of Tompions," and the probable as indispensable

* The date of the "New Bath Road" is still preserved on some of the mile-stones between Newbury and Marlborough, which were erected in 1746 at the moderate cost of £1 each. The tolls at this time from the three gates between the two towns amounted to £416 16s., or a little over £8 a week. Among the Commissioners of this Trust at the above date we find the names of Dr. Brickenden (of Inkpen), Rev. Alexander Thistlethwayte, Thomas Garrard (of Up Lambourn), Charles Garrard (Kingwood), Rev. Servington Savery (Marlborough), Edward Popham (Littlecote), Thomas Batson (Ramsbury), John Whitelocke (Chilton Lodge), William and Samuel Jones (Ramsbury), Toby Richmond (Crowood), Samuel Dixon (Wallingtons), Edward Lucas (Hungerford), Henry Craven (Chilton), Rev. Thomas Shirley (Welford.) The salary of the Surveyor for the Wilts portion of the road (William Bunce) was £15 a year, and the same was paid the Surveyor for the Berks portion (Mr. Samuel Rawlins.) The salary of Mr. George Garrard (Attorney), as Clerk to the Trust was £10 a year, and £5 as Treasurer, and the Toll Collectors—Thomas and Sarah Furnell, and Thomas and Jane Warnham—were paid £1 12s. a month for wages, or 8s. a week for each couple. In 1810 the tolls from Hoe Benham gate alone were let for £900 a year.

† The site of the Saracen's Head is now occupied by the warehouse of Messrs. Boyd & Co.

sword, or as it was then called "silver hilted rip of ice-brook temper." There was a social and not ungenerous spirit in those days. Parties who spent the night at the Saracen's Head previously to travelling together usually contrived to make themselves known to each other, and to sup together. Ladies were not at all "squeamish" in falling into this fashion, and generally in one respect, at least, to their profit, for it was the rule of the road that the majority in one sex should pay for the refreshments of the minority in the other, and as more men than women travelled in those days, the latter might journey far at little cost beyond that of locomotion.

This Bath coach breakfasted at

COLNBROOK,

famed in those remote times not for its "cooks," but for its exorbitant charges, and very short commons.

READING

was the appointed place for dinner, and there it seems to have been understood that the host should entertain his guests by waggery, just as the hostess and the maids do in the Inn scene in Erasmus. Between Reading and

THEALE

came the afternoon time, when songs were sung, stories were told, the bottle of pure Nantz passed round, and altogether many strange things were said, done, or suggested, that would never be thought of now. At Theale the travellers regaled themselves with cake and ale, for which the house (the "Crown") was famous, for no other reason than it kept such wares for sale. Thus fortified, and the coachman having hoped that the gentlefolk had not hurried themselves, progress was joltingly made to

NEWBURY,

the sleeping quarters for the night. But sleep was, of course, the *last* thing resorted to. Those who loved a carouse ordered punch, and caroused, drank, and smoked accordingly. Others, if it were summer time, paired off when such pleasant process was practicable, and walked and talked, and made or listened to gallant speeches, with matter-of-course love assurances that were taken for what they were worth, and were not meant to pass for greater value.

The second day's journey carried the travellers first to

MARLBOROUGH

to breakfast, which they had well earned by the bumping they had endured, and the curses they had ejaculated as they passed over the road of rocks, ridges, and ruts which took them into that town. After many perils met and avoided, the coach tottered uneasily on its way to *Aquæ Solis*, at scarcely a swifter rate than a couple to three miles an hour; "a Corporation trot to St. Paul's on Sundays" was popularly said to be a fool to it. This coach which arrived at

Bath

on the night of the second day, carried no heavy luggage, and ladies who wished to "make a figure" at Bath, generally were kept cloistered up in their lodgings till their baggage and finery arrived by the waggon.

These "flying coaches" were the precursors of the

New Mail Coaches.

What may be strictly called the coaching era was shorter than some people may suppose; indeed, it did not exceed sixty years. The first mail coach began to run in the year 1784, and coaching ceased to be the most important medium of travelling in England before the year 1844. The early specimens of the Stage Coach were very cumbrous conveyances, and weighed considerably over a ton. They were seldom washed or cleaned, and almost as rarely were they greased, consequently it was the exception when a day passed without a wheel taking fire. But the times are too late—or rather, perhaps, not quite late enough—to make it worth while to dwell upon the peculiarities and disabilities of the older Stage Coaches They have been described over and over again; so also have the developments in coaches during the first thirty years of the last century, and the immense improvement which took place in roads was relatively far greater than that in coaches.

The "Pelican." "The George and Pelican," usually shortened to the "Pelican," was one of the most noted and best conducted houses on the western road, and the subject of an epigram attributed to the Irish actor, Quin, written on one of the windows of this historic hostelry* :—

"The famous inn at Speenhamland
That stands below the hill,
May well be called the Pelican
From its enormous bill."

Possibly this may have been so in Quin's time, for we remember to have seen another *jeux d' esprit* of this period on a glass pane of the windows, which to the best of our recollection ran thus :—

"As often as ye bell ye handle
Ye'll have to pay for snuffing of ye candle."

Of course, when "all the world" went to Bath, and Speenhamland was the principal centre of traffic, the "Pelican" was crowded with notables, especially during the season, and participated in the movements of kings, statesmen, admirals,†

* The "Pelican" is mentioned as early as 1646, in the records of the Court Baron of the Manor of Newbury, and in 1658, when a regiment of horse was wanted by Cromwell to serve in Flanders, old soldiers willing to join were requested to apply to the Captain "at the sign of the 'Pelican' in Speenhamland."

† The immortal Nelson frequently stopped at the "Pelican" on his journeys to and from Bath, where his father for some time resided, and on one occasion asked old George Revell, the head ostler, whether he could get from Newbury to London "by water," as he was tired of riding along the dusty roads. Old George suggested "the barge," but the gallant admiral thought this would be even worse than the coach.

THE OLD "PELICAN" INN, SPEENHAMLAND. *From an old print.*

generals, and eminent divines, all of whom had occasion to relax and more or less familiarise at this famous posting-house. But the old yard then so full of stir and bustle—the once glorious yard where the post-boys, whip in hand, and always buttoning their waistcoats at the last moment, came running forth to mount and away—is now almost as silent as the halls of Balaclutha, and bears witness to the mighty revolution which a past generation has witnessed. The supreme dignity of this historic house may be said to have departed when the Duchess of Cambridge, accompanied by the late Duke and his sister, the Princess Mary, drove westward through its gates, after partaking of luncheon here on the 9th December, 1839, when on their way to the Duke of Beaufort's, at Badminton. After this time royalty only looked in for a moment now and then, like a visitor to a poor relation, and we can well remember the huge old place in its last stage as an inn, when everything everywhere expressed past coachfulness and obvious coachlessness, which in its silent way was eloquent of the change that had fallen on the road.

The "Pelican" proper is that part of the inn now used for livery stables, with residence adjoining, and belonging to the Shaw House Estate. The "George," where the guests were principally lodged, was re-built about the year 1730, and comprised the handsome block of buildings in the Broadway, occupied by Mr. Money, the architect, and the saddler's shop adjoining on the west, together with an extensive range of buildings in the rear, forming a quadrangular courtyard, which were taken down when Mr. Money purchased the property. It also included the premises occupied by Mr. Lipscombe and the "Pelican Coffee House."

The names of some of the proprietors of the "George and Pelican" have been handed down to us. From about 1730 to 1755 the host was Mr. John Cary or Carey, who is buried in the chancel of Speen church, under a black marble slab bearing his arms—*argent, on a bend sable, three roses, of the first.* He was succeeded by Mr. Samuel Hancock, who died in 1783. Mr. George Botham became proprietor in 1799, and on his death in 1827, his widow took over the management.*

The old Pelican garden, which was renowned for its fruit and vegetables, was in the Backway, and after the coaches were taken off the road, was occupied by Mr. George Linton for many years as nursery grounds. Here also the Bowling Green remains. It was first enclosed by Mr. George Phillips, of the "Bear," sometime previous to 1734. A law suit resulted between Phillips and one Thomas Cleaver, when the latter recovered the land.

---

* An interesting reminiscence of this famous hotel has been preserved in an oil painting, executed by the late Mr. John Osgood, a local artist, sometime in the thirties, of which, by the courtesy of H. J. A. Eyre, Esq., we are enabled to give an illustration on a reduced scale. The figures were all well-known characters at the time. Commencing with the first figure on the left, this represents Tom Wilmot, horsekeeper, who is returning from Edmund Seymour's saddler's shop with oil for the harness. No. 2 is "Natty Watts," one of the

The "Bear." The "Bear" was another notable old coaching-house at Speenhamland,† and occupied nearly the whole of the site of the premises between the "George and Pelican" and the "Chequers." It was to this house that the bodies of Lords Carnarvon, Sunderland, and Falkland were brought from the old Guildhall, whence they had been taken from the battlefield before being conveyed away for burial. The Cromwellian Sequestration Commissioners and "Triers" also sat at this inn. The Protector himself was here on more than one occasion, and Charles II., James II., William of Orange, and Prince George of Denmark are recorded as having been regaled at this house, which, like the "Pelican" retained its celebrity for many centuries. The "Bear" was also noted for its famous cock-pit, and some of the most renowned battles in the annals of this once popular sport were fought here at the time the inn was kept by a Mr. Thomas Phillips, who is described as "a mighty fox-hunter." He was buried at Speen in February, 1787, and at his own particular request, a fox's pad was placed in each of his hands when laid out in his coffin, and his funeral was attended by the huntsmen and whippers-in of the packs with which he had so often hunted. About the latter part of the 18th century, the "Bear" was shut up for some time, and never again opened as an inn, in consequence of a murder supposed to have been committed in some altercation between the mistress and her cook, when one or the other of them was thrown downstairs and killed.

The "Chequers." The "Chequers" was known along the road almost as well as the "Pelican." This symbol is a very ancient one, and was observed painted lozenge-wise, red, white, and yellow, on the house of Hercules, at the corner of the

---

old-fashioned four-horse coachmen. No. 3, John Franklyn, butcher, of Speenhamland. No. 4, a young Frenchman, a pupil of Mr. Osgood's. No. 5 is Jennings, the old waiter at the "Pelican." No man who travelled from London to Bath was ignorant of Jennings, and he and his mistress were as well known as any two on the road. No. 6, "Effie New," a horsekeeper of some repute. No. 7, Jack Ashton, stud groom at the "Pelican." No. 8, Mrs. Botham, the active, bustling landlady of the "George and Pelican." No. 9, Grant, coachman of the White Hart coach, who lived at Bath. No. 10, John Casson, a large coach proprietor, living at Speenhamland. No. 11, the Rev. Joseph Birchall, Curate of Newbury. No. 12, Dr. Henry Hemsted, of Speen Hill. No. 13, Griffiths, a coachman. No. 14, William Bulpit, a corn-chandler. No. 15, Mr. George Dibley, Attorney, of Newbury. In the foreground the White Hart Day Coach, belonging to Messrs. Pickford, of Bath, immortalised in the Pickwick Papers by the observation of Sam Weller:—"I'm blest if they ain't had the imperance to put my master's name on that e'er coach door." In the corner shop stands the figure of Mr. William Hall, sen., who then carried on the stationery business which is still in the family.

† In a work by John Taylor, commonly called "the water poet," printed by Henry Gosson, London, 1636, giving an account of the wine taverns in various parts of the kingdom, he thus refers to Newbury:—"Newbury is a rich town for the trade of clothing; it sprung out of the consumption of an old town which is neere it, called Spene or Spinhamlands. There are three Taverns, under John Grenaway, Thomas Howes, and Anthony Linch. Spinhamland hath two tavernes, under Richard Cox and James Garroway."

Strada Fullonica at Pompeii. It has been considered by writers on Inn Signs to be armorial, as the "Chequers" forms one of the quarterings of the Howards, Earls of Surrey, who had the grant of licensing public-houses, but its great antiquity consigns it to some other origin. It has also been suggested that the name is derived from the chequered board suspended over the money-changers offices in mediæval times. But it more probably owes its origin to the ancient game of *Chequers*, a board for which we formerly saw so frequently painted on the door-steads of old city taverns and village inns. The board is divided into sixteen squares, and is usually placed lozenge-wise as in the days of ancient Rome, *i.e.*, with a corner at the top and bottom. The game is mentioned in one of Dibdin's songs, as being played at by the seamen :—

"Dear Mary, adieu ! Can that love go to wreck,
When every plank bears your name on the deck ?
Yea, many true knots on the yards I have made,
While guileless at *Chequers* my messmates have played."

The old game of *Chequers* is better known in later times as Backgammon. Oliver Wendell Holmes refers to the game of *Chequers* or *Checkers* in describing a scene in a tavern of former days in New England "where games of *Chequers* were played on the back of the bellows with red and white kernels of corn, or with beans and coffee."

The "Angel." The "Angel" was also another coaching inn of some little importance in its day. Its site is partly represented by the modern "Star" inn, and the adjoining premises.

The "Bacon Arms." The sign of this well-known inn is commemorative of the family of this name, who once occupied a prominent position in connection with many local institutions, and whose principal seat was at Elcot, between Newbury and Hungerford. Mr. Anthony Bacon also rented for a time Benham Park and Donnington Castle House. He was joint master of the Craven Hunt, 1813–14, and for nearly 20 years the popular commander of the Donnington Castle and Newbury troop of the 1st Berks Cavalry, and was presented with a handsome piece of plate for his patriotic services. It may be of interest to note that Mr. Anthony Bacon, who was interested in ironworks in Wales, was the first person in England to introduce the system of heating conservatories by hot water, which had been strenuously advocated in 1828, but adopted by Mr. Bacon at Elcot in 1821. Mr. Bacon died at his seat, Aberavon, near Neath, in 1828, and was buried in the family vault in Shaw churchyard. His son, Charles Bacon, was Colonel of the Royal Berks Militia.

The "Cross Keys." Among the many famous coaching-inns at Speenhamland was the "Cross Keys," which has recently been pulled down and re-built. This was a very ancient hostelry, and its sign, the keys *in saltire*, represent the arms of the Papal See, emblematic of St. Peter, and they figure in the arms of several English Bishops. It is very probable that the "Keys" were adopted on account of the property being originally held under some religious house.

A COACH SUPPER AT THE CROSS KEYS INN, SPEENHAMLAND.

From a drawing by Geo Cruikshank, senr.

In reference to the "Cross Keys" we cannot refrain from introducing an interesting record in *Woodward's Eccentric Excursions*,* which serves to show the character and usages of such houses in the "palmy days" of the coaching era, and is accompanied by a very humourous sketch from the pencil of the elder Cruikshank, representing a coach supper at this well-known old tavern. This specimen of the lighter literary food provided for its readers runs as follows:—

"The 'Cross Keys' at Newbury is the usual place appointed for accommodating the coach passengers on the Bath and Bristol road with supper. On account of the constant succession, *a plentiful cold collation* is always in readiness, and it is truly humorous to observe with what *fervent adoration* the hungry disciples pay their devotions to the shrine of Epicurus; the most experienced lose no time in their oblations while the misinformed are *sauntering in the yard*, watching every *movement* of their *baggage* or holding a long discourse with the coachman till the guard arrives, displaying a face descriptive of the utmost impatience, with the gloomy observation that *all is in readiness for departure*! This direful call must be obeyed, and many a *supperless wight* re-enters the machine, grumbling at his own folly during the remainder of the journey. The moment of the summons is frequently productive of many *laughable effects* from the *consternation* and *hurry* thrown into the different countenances!"

* "Eccentric Excursions or Literary and Pictorial Sketches," by M. Woodward—Allen and Co., 1796.

The "Lamb and Flag." On the same side of the way was the "Lamb and Flag," which originally symbolised the Holy Lamb with nimbus and banner, and was the arms of the Templars. The old house, long since pulled down, was the reputed birth-place of the celebrated Dr. Twisse, his father carrying on the cloth trade at this place, then the staple manufacture of the town. It appears to have been a half-timbered building, with well-designed gables and barge boards, queer penthouse roofs springing from low-pitched first-floors, and surmounted with dormer windows.

The "King's Arms" and the "Castle." The handsome block of buildings on the north side of the London Road, now converted into private houses, was built by a Mr. William McLary, about the year 1755, and as the "King's Arms" was one of the most fashionable posting-houses on the western road, as was also the "Castle" on Speen hill, which was more than once patronised by royalty.

In the Borough itself there were several famous coaching inns besides those at Speenhamland, such as the "Globe" and the "White Hart."

The old "Globe." The old "Globe" was a house of very interesting historical associations, and one of the most attractive architectural relics of old Newbury. Its many pointed gables (eight in number), its barge-boards, its handsome pendants—on one of which was the date "1611"—its round-headed tiles, oriel windows, and massive stack of Jacobean chimneys in the centre, made the upper portion of the building extremely picturesque. The stack was of red brick, panelled, and consisted of fifteen separate flues. From one of the upper rooms a door opened into a blind flue, and this by a manhole permitted access to the roof. The staircases were wide and handsome, and the public room on the first floor measured 40 feet in length, 19 feet in width, and 10 feet in height, with panelled wainscot and stuccoed ceiling of rich design.

The house, previously to the dissolution of the monasteries, belonged to the Priory of Wherwell, in Hampshire, and dated back as a tavern at least as early as 1649, at which date it is referred to by Baskerville, the Berkshire antiquary as the inn where he dined and witnessed the procession of the various Guild Companies after they had attended service at the church, and which he describes as "a pleasant sight to behold." The "Globe" is frequently mentioned in the earliest Borough records, and appears to have been the house specially favoured by the corporate fathers for their convivial gatherings, and to have obtained a wide celebrity as a house of entertainment. In 1662 its proprietor was Richard Chadsey, and in 1679, Henry Chadsey, a family long connected with Newbury and the neighbourhood. In later times the names Pottinger, Willis, and King were familiar as landlords of the old hostelry. For at least 200 years the "Globe" had been associated with what is known as the "Tory party"—a term of varied significance at different periods, but what may be accepted as denoting the supporters of "Church and State." It was also much frequented by the Newbury quidnuncs, who collected there to discuss political and local affairs, and hold their whist parties in the evening. Among them were many celebrated players, who, during the seasons, visited Bath, Cheltenham, Harrogate, etc., where high play was the order of day, and gambling was less a diversion than a recognised branch of science, the pursuit of which was to bring profit sooner or later. The old house was last used as the head-quarters of the Conservative Committee at the General Election in 1868, when its windows were smashed by an excited mob. Soon after the property was sold, and the ancient building demolished, great regret being expressed on all sides at the unnecessary destruction of such a landmark in local history. Its site is now occupied by the premises of the Capital and Counties Bank, and the South Berks Club.

The "White Hart." From this house the first "Flying Coach" to London started in 1752, and it was here that the Southampton and Oxford Coaches had their local quarters. The portico of the old inn now occupies a similar position at the entrance to a house at West Mills to which the name of "The Chantry" has been attached.

The last journey made by the Southampton and Oxford coach was on the 4th May, 1846, when it discontinued running, owing to railway communication being opened up between these two places.

Some of the Whips of a Bye-gone Age. The men who "handled the ribbons" in the "good old days," we are told, "*could* drive and no mistake." Amateurs, it is true, drive four-in-hands now-a-days, but they don't do it like Jack Sprawson, Probert, "Nat" and John Watts, John Burnett and his son John, Brightwell, Stephen Knight, the brothers Stacey, Everett, Johnson, John Casson, Chandler, Adlam, Alfred Waller, "Jemmy" Marsh, of the "Cross Keys," Sam Hunt and his sons Josiah and George, or George Linton used to do it. But it is all over now. One after another the coachmen of the last generation have arrived at the last stage; we must all come to it sooner or later.

"All, all are gone the old familiar faces,"

and the dashing mail-coaches that once swept through the hamlet, under the care of the scarlet-coated guard and his armory of horse-pistols and blunderbusses, are now a thing of the past, and the place knoweth them no more.

The Golden Days. Speenhamland was not then as now—somewhat dull and silent—but resounded from morning till night with the crack of the whip, the rattle of the wheels, and the notes of the guard's horn. Forty-two coaches passed through Speenhamland every day, so that the inhabitants

THE BIRMINGHAM, OXFORD, AND NEWBURY STAGE WAGGON, 18TH CENTURY.

must have been continually in the state represented in the celebrated lines :—

"Go call a coach, and let a coach be called,
And let the man who calleth be the caller,
And in his calling, let him nothing call
But Coach ! Coach ! Coach ! O for a coach, ye gods."*

Their decline. Yet the gods did not continue to the hamlet the perpetual boon of these numerous coaches. Four-in-hands were destined to give place to steam ; the fatal day gradually approached in which the forty-two were to be represented by the lone "Star"—the last of its tribe ; and the construction of the Great Western Railway destroyed the glories of the old Pelican Inn,† which had accommodation for a whole army of travellers, and frequently as many as 300 horses were put up in its extensive range of stabling.

The Advent of the Locomotive. A staggering blow to the activity and prosperity of Newbury and Speenhamland was struck by the withdrawal of the coaches, and the great revolution produced by railways was remarkable. Of the change at Speenhamland we obtain a vivid picture from the pen of a noble lord, a soldier and *raconteur*,‡ who was familiar with the hamlet when in the hey-day of its prosperity, and re-visited it after an absence of thirty-five years, somewhere about 1850 :—

"At an early hour," he says, "I found myself at the Great Western station ready to take the first train to Newbury: after a sulphurous journey we reached that town, and I immediately proceeded to the "George and Pelican," where I first stopped on my way to my tutor's ; but, oh, how changed was the appearance of that once famous hostelrie ! A dark-coloured omnibus, a one-horse fly, two glass coaches, and a few pair of post-horses were all that could be seen upon that spot, where in times gone by three "fours" were sometimes wont to be changed in less than an hour, and where the best turned out mails and coaches in England were accustomed to stop. . . . . The plague seemed to have entered Speenhamland. . . . . The theatre is enveloped in a chancery suit, and is in a state of inward dilapidation. The Pelican of the wilderness, as it may literally be called, looked desolate and forlorn, and a portion of it is converted into a chymist's shop.§ The Sun and Moon, two of the best rooms in the house, which all the *elite* of the company were wont to occupy, are now eclipsed ; one is on the wane, while the other is devoted to senna, rhubarb, magnesia, aloes, cinnamon, and colocynth ; the only glasses that now "sparkle on the board" are for aperient draughts, the sole bottles are in the windows, containing blue, white, yellow, and red mixtures."

---

* *Chrononhotonthologos.*

† This celebrated Inn so much associated with our national and local life, finally closed its doors about the year 1843. Mrs. Botham, the highly respected hostess, was elected on the Duchess of Somerset's foundation for lay-widows at Froxfield, and died there in December, 1846, and is buried with her husband (George Botham), and others of the family in Speen churchyard, where so many old friends and neighbours rest in peace.

‡ Lord William Pitt Lennox, fourth son of Charles, fourth Duke of Richmond, who spent some years of his early life with the Rev. James Knollys, a tutor, at Donnington (now called Donnington Lodge), and afterwards joined the embassy at Paris as an attaché, and accompanied the Duke of Wellington to the field of Waterloo. These references to Newbury will be found in "Percy Hamilton, or the adventures of a Westminster Boy," 1851.

§ This shop, now a saddler's, was then occupied by Mr. Philip Childs, chemist.

While pausing to contemplate the transformation that time and the introduction of steam had brought about in the town, the returned traveller noticed at the door of the "Chequers" an old familiar face, that of George Revell (previously head ostler at the "Pelican,") when the following conversation ensued :—

"Great changes," said old George, "sad work this rail, see what it has done for our town!"

"*Done* for your town," replied the visitor.

"Nothing stirring now," added old George, "but now and then a pair wanted for a pic-nic at Highclere: ah! we shall never look upon old times again!"

But these gloomy forebodings have not been fulfilled, and the ancient borough requires no commiseration, for it has many compensations. In the place of the old spasmodic pleasures and excitement there is permanent content and business activity, and in many circumstances the moral difference between the present and the past is as significant as it is desirable, while the old hamlet has survived the troublous times through which it has passed far better than might have been anticipated.

The Old Theatre at Speenhamland.

It was during the Coaching Days, when so many passengers had to spend a night at the "Pelican," the "Castle," the "Chequers," or the "Cross Keys," that the theatre at Speenhamland was in the height of its glory as "a popular retreat of the regular drama."

For a considerable period the old house was under the enterprising management of Mr. Barnett, whose company also regularly visited Reading, Gosport, Guildford, Winchester, and Ryde.

Many of the theatrical celebrities of the day appeared on the boards here, including John Philip Kemble and Edmund Keen, two of the great tragic actors, Mrs. Kemble, widow of the actor Brereton, Mrs. Jordan, the beautiful Miss Brunton, whose charms captivated the Earl of Craven; Incledon and Braham, the celebrated vocalists; William Henry West Betty, *the young Roscius*; John Banister, of Drury Lane fame; Mrs. Powell, Mr. and Mrs. Middleton, Miss Foote, and many more distinguished comedians of the Georgian era.

The Theatre, which was built in 1802,* has long since fallen from its high estate, and little but the outer shell of the building still remains. It was used successively as workshops, an auction mart, stores, and lastly as a cow shed.

"The curtain falls, the Play is ended;
The Beggar packs beside the Beau;
The Monarch troops, and troops the Maid;
The thunder huddles with the Snow.
Where are the revellers, high and low?
The clashing swords, the lover's call?
The dancers, gleaming row on row?
Into the night go one and all."

* It appears from the Borough Records that previous to the erection of this theatre, an old building which stood on the site of the present Temperance Hall was used as a play-house.

THE OLD THEATRE, SPEENHAMLAND.

The last public entertainment which took place within its walls was on the day that the Prince of Wales (our present King), was married, when it was used to entertain as many old people of the hamlet as could be accommodated with a good dinner in honour of this memorable occasion.

The Newbury Race Meetings. It is not necessary to enter into the very accidence of local race-meetings, but it is quite evident that the sport was in considerable vogue here as far back as the reign of Charles II. From this time up to the period of the enclosure of common-lands, yearly races had been a feature of the life of almost every country town or big village, in which gentle and simple alike participated. Although the entries were not of a very high-class character, the country people enjoyed these friendly gatherings and local competitions, and naturally grumbled when the open spaces which had for generations served as playgrounds as well as racecourses should be taken from them.

Race meetings are mentioned in 1740 and subsequent years as being annually held on Wash Common, which, before the enclosure, extended over what is now part of the park belonging to Sandleford Priory. These sports were patronised by the officers attached to the cavalry regiments which from time to time were encamped on the common, and the inspection of these corps, which usually took place about the same time as the racing, was always a popular event for the townspeople, one of whom, writing in 1777, says that "when the 3rd Dragoons were inspected on the Wash this year, much curiousity was excited by the appearance of the drummers of the regiment, who were all black men." It was at this period, and much later, usual for "men of colour" to be attached to the regimental bands.

In the first decades of this century, races were annually held on Enborne Heath, and the meetings were patronised by the principal noblemen and gentlemen in the neighbourhood, who gave every encouragement to this national pastime, which brought many visitors into the town and greatly benefitted the trade of the place. The Corporation of Newbury gave annually a cup value £50, and the race week was the event of the year. In 1815 a gold cup was run for, value 100 guineas, and there were in addition a sweepstake of 20 guineas each, 5 subs.; a sweepstake of 15 guineas each, with 25 guineas added, 4 subs.; a sweepstake of 10 guineas each, 6 subs.; a sweepstake of 5 guineas each, with £25 added. 5 subs.: and a handicap plate, value £50. This represents about the average "events" competed for.

During the race week, "Ordinaries" were provided at the "Pelican," the "Globe," and the principal hotels in the town, a grand ball was given at the Mansion House, under the auspices of the Mayor and Corporation, and the Theatre was opened nightly with a special caste from the London stage.

On the enclosure of Enborne, Woodhay. and other adjacent commons over which the course extended, these annual fixtures that had so long been a feature in the life of the town and neighbourhood, were discontinued, and finally extinguished.

An endeavour is now (1904) being made to revive race meetings at Newbury, and the wide stretch of land abutting the Great Western Railway between Stroud Green and Bull's Lock (236 acres), which has formed the lower portion of the Greenham Lodge Estate (the property of Mr. Lloyd H. Baxendale), is now in course of preparation as a racecourse. The property has been acquired for £30,000 by the Newbury Racecourse Company, the directors of which are Mr. Baxendale, Mr. James Buchanan, Mr. John Porter, and Mr. Oscar W. Rayner, the Solicitor and Secretary being Mr. G. Gardner Leader, of Newbury; and for the convenience of visitors, a railway station will be provided adjacent to the course.

CHAPTER XIII.

THE MILITIA, YEOMANRY, AND VOLUNTEERS

The Militia. Previous to the establishment of standing armies, the defence of the several towns throughout the country was intrusted to the Trained Bands, or what was denominated the *posse comitatus*, who were called out by the Magistrates on any appearance of riot or disturbance. They were regularly summoned once a year to attend the Court Leet, and the Magistrates were authorised to fine such as did not appear at the time appointed. This gave rise to the custom of granting exemptions by which those who could not or did not wish to attend the general muster were excused on paying a small fine, usually a penny, but at the Newbury court the exempting fee was generally twopence. After the muster they were regularly trained to the use of the long-bow by shooting at the butts set up in each parish, which at Newbury were on the south side of the Enborne Road, near the site of the present Grammar School.

After the Restoration, the Militia was put under the management of the Lord Lieutenants and the Deputy Lieutenants by the statute of 14, Charles II., cap. 3, which contains some curious particulars as to the raising of the Militia force.

The first Act of modern date which consolidates the Militia Laws is that of 26, George III., cap. 107 (1786), which, after reciting that a respectable military force under the command of officers possessing landed property within Great Britain was essential to the constitution of the realm, continues the powers given to the Crown by several previous Acts from the time of Charles II., to appoint Lieutenants of counties, who were to raise and have the chief command of the Militia, and to appoint *twenty* Deputy Lieutenants within their respective counties if such number could be found qualified, and the Act fixes the number of private men to be raised in Berks at 560.*

Few persons are aware how completely the centralising power of Government in London has in modern days absorbed the cabalistic exclusiveness, or to use a modern term, the individuality of interest which characterised the various towns of England during the middle ages—a process unavoidable no doubt—while it has in great part removed that provincial exclusiveness which was so apparent down to a comparatively recent period.

The local functionaries of the Borough of Newbury were always ready to resent as an affront any intrusion not amenable to their territorial sway, and this feeling seems to have shown itself on the passing of the Supplementary Militia Act in 1796 for raising a certain number of men for the service of the Army and Navy. An order from the High Constable of the Hundred of Faircross was directed to the Churchwardens and Overseers of the parish of Newbury, setting forth that the Justices of the Peace in and for the said County at a General Sessions assembled under and by virtue of the said Act, had appointed six men to be raised from the said parish on or before the 19th day of December, then next ensuing. The authorities having failed to raise the six men in the time required, were called upon to pay the sum of £210 on account of the expense incurred by them in such default. This sum was raised by a rate of tenpence in the pound, made upon all the inhabitants of the borough and parish to reimburse the Churchwardens and Overseers for the costs incurred by them under the Act. It is, however possible that owing to the long war with France and the drain on the able-bodied men of the town for military service, the authorities could not succeed in raising their quota in the short time allowed. Further, the parish officials at this juncture frequently preferred paying sums of money for substitutes to supporting the wives and families of soldiers during their term of service. Allowances were, however, made to Militiamen's wives and families during their embodiment by the Magistrates to endeavour to render the service less distasteful.

The local Militia was established under the statute 48 Geo. III., cap. 3, which received the royal assent, 30th June, 1808, and the following year three regiments were raised in Berkshire. The Newbury Volunteers were the first corps in the county to offer

* The Berks Militia, which had been embodied since 1792, were quartered at this time at various seaport towns on the coast of Sussex and Kent from Eastbourne to Ramsgate. The regiment appears to have been admirably drilled, and equipped in scarlet coats with blue facings, white gaiters, hair powdered, and hats well cocked up, and the men were ordered "not to let down the cocks of their hats on any account, and also to keep the skirts of their coats constantly hooked up."

their services, and were enrolled in the 1st Regiment of local Militia, under Lieutenant-Colonel Page, of Goldwell. Their services were continued after the end of the then war until the year 1815, by the statute 55 Geo. III., cap. 76, which received the royal assent on the 14th June, four days before the battle of Waterloo.

The Yeomanry and Volunteers. In 1794 and the subsequent years, when the French, emboldened by their success on the Continent, contemplated the invasion of this country, and fitted out a fleet for the conveyance of the troops assembled for the purpose and called the "Army of England," the system of volunteer enrolments was again resorted to, and corps were speedily raised in all parts of the country.

At Newbury a provisional force of cavalry was raised in 1797, and the first drill, under its Captain (Richard Townsend), took place at Speen, 10th February of that year.*

An Infantry Corps was also raised at Newbury, under Captain Edward Sheppard.

On the 26th July, 1799, the whole of the Berkshire corps, both cavalry and infantry, were reviewed by King George the Third on Bulmarsh Heath, when the field strength of the Newbury troop of cavalry was 2 officers and 34 men, and the infantry numbered 5 officers and 104 men.

In the month of June, 1800, the Newbury troop of Yeomanry, under the command of Lieutenant Slocock in the absence of Captain Townsend, was called upon to suppress a body of rioters who were agitating for an advance in wages, and with being provided with food at a less price. A large body assembled at Highclere, and were pursued by the Newbury troop to Hurstbourn Tarrant, where a detachment charged and dispersed the malcontents before they had time to execute, or even arrange, any plan of serious mischief.

In 1803 another troop of Cavalry was raised at Newbury, another at Donnington, called the Donnington Castle troop, and in this year eight troops were added to those already in existence. The strength invariably exceeded the fixed establishment, and Berkshire could easily have put over 600 mounted men in the field.

The same year Volunteer Infantry corps were formed throughout the county—five companies being raised at Newbury—Matthew Montagu, Esq., of Sandleford Priory, being Lieutenant-Colonel-Commandant, and Speenhamland furnished a company, under the command of Sir Joseph Andrews, of Shaw House.

---

* The first troop of Berkshire Yeomanry was formed in 1794 at Abingdon, and the old colours now hanging in the Council Chamber, bear the date "April, 1794." The service of the Berkshire Yeomanry was not confined to the county, for it appears that in September, 1798, they were abruptly ordered to Bristol, where they were quartered under Major Stead, of Donnington Castle House.

On the 8th June, 1805, the Berks Yeomanry and Infantry corps were again inspected by the King on Bulmarsh Heath, when His Majesty was pleased to express "the particular gratification he felt in having witnessed the military perfection of his Berkshire Volunteers."*

The Infantry Corps existed until the foundation of the Local Militia in 1808, when most of them were disbanded, although many of the officers and men volunteered into that body, and continued to serve therein.

The First Berks Regiment of Cavalry, which comprised the Hungerford troop, the Donnington Castle troop, the Abingdon troop, the Vale of White Horse troop, and the Woodley troop, continued in force until the year 1827, when they were disbanded. But some of the troops were soon after revived, and were in existence in 1831, when they were called out to assist the civil power at the Bristol riots of that year, when the animosities between reformers and anti-reformers were more ferocious than those of the Hanoverian Whigs and the Jacobite Tories of the days of George I. Better times have succeeded, when reforms may be obtained by legal means, not by torch and pike, and among the best reformers are the peaceful philosophers who upset old false theories on a basis of new facts.

All these troops were ultimately disbanded with the exception of the Hungerford troop, which was about the year 1855, increased from one troop to a corps of three troops, and termed the Royal Berks Yeomanry Cavalry, and in 1895 the head-quarters were moved from Hungerford to Reading. The regiment is now divided into two squadrons, and with the Middlesex Hussars form part of the 1st Yeomanry Brigade, though in order of precedence in the Force they are numbered twenty-seven and twenty-six respectively.

The Volunteer Movement of 1859.

In 1859, when a wave of patriotic enthusiasm again rolled over England, the men of Newbury were quick to respond to the call of duty and conspicuous for the ready and loyal zeal they displayed in contributing a company to the county battalion. The first Commandant was the late Mr. H. R. Eyre, of Shaw House, who has been succeeded by Mr. G. C. Cherry, Mr. James Simonds, Mr. Henry Somerset, Mr. D. Denis de Vitré, and the present Captain, under whose leadership the corps has ever been maintained at a high standard of efficiency, while some famous shots have distinguished themselves and added prestige to the company.

---

* In the old days the uniform of the Berks Yeomanry consisted of a blue tunic with scarlet facings, buckskin breeches, and bearskin helmet with red tuft, somewhat similar to the then equipment of Oxford's Blues (Royal Horse Guards.) Previous to the adoption of the present khaki outfit, the uniform of the corps was very much like that of heavy dragoons—the tunic scarlet with blue facings, the helmet plume being white, and the lace silver.

Both Yeomanry and Volunteers nobly played their part in South Africa, and when in future days some historian more brilliant than the present shall tell of Newbury, he will emblazon this fact upon her annals, that when there arose a well-grounded alarm and distrust for England's safety, the men of Newbury, unbiassed and unbought, banded together for the common weal, and regardless of personal considerations esteemed that to which their country called them the post of honour, and set an example to their successors to do their duty wheresoever they find it, with the same patriotic and unselfish devotion.

CHAPTER XIV.

OPENING OF THE RAILWAY TO NEWBURY—CELEBRATION OF PEACE—THE MARRIAGE OF THE PRINCE AND PRINCESS OF WALES—THE PARISH STOCKS—MILITARY AT NEWBURY—THE FALKLAND MEMORIAL—RAILWAY DEVELOPMENT—QUEEN VICTORIA'S JUBILEE—THE NATIONAL RIFLE ASSOCIATION—FORMATION OF THE BERKS COUNTY COUNCIL—THE LAMBOURN VALLEY RAILWAY—THE SOUTH AFRICAN WAR—PRESENT ASPECT OF THE TOWN.

Opening of the Railway to Newbury. Notwithstanding the splendid position which Newbury should have occupied as a railway centre, it was without any adequate railway communication long after most other towns had enjoyed that advantage. As already remarked, the first misfortune to the town was when the main line of the Great Western, owing to the opposition of the landowners, was driven round by Didcot instead of following the natural route along the Kennet Valley. As early as 1845, a Manchester and Southampton line was planned, taking Newbury *en route*, but the scheme came to nothing. Meanwhile the Great Western constructed the Berks and Hants branch from Reading to Newbury and Hungerford, which was opened for traffic 21st December, 1847, and in later years has been carried on to Devizes.

Celebration of Peace. The town and neighbourhood of Newbury furnished a large supply of men for service in the field during the Crimean campaign, many of whom were distinguished for their bravery and soldier-like conduct before the enemy.

When peace was proclaimed in 1856, Newbury entered very spiritedly into the general rejoicings that took place throughout the country. There was a procession as usual of the civic and other authorities; many thousands of people were feasted at the public expense; amusements of all kinds were provided, and in the evening the town was brilliantly illuminated.

Through the representations of Mr. Alderman Edward William Gray, one of the old Russian guns, captured in the Crimea, was allotted to Newbury. For a considerable period it was allowed to remain as a derelict, but was ultimately mounted in its present position in the Broadway, Speenhamland.

The Marriage of the Prince and Princess of Wales. The wedding-day of the Prince of Wales and the Princess Alexandra, 10th March, 1863, was celebrated by the inhabitants of Newbury in a very loyal and hearty manner. A dinner for 3,000 people was provided, the chief throughfares were gaily decorated, triumphal arches were erected, and the town everywhere presented a very festive appearance.

The Parish Stocks. Possibly, Newbury was the last place in England where the Stocks were used as a form of punishment, namely in 1872. The Stocks, as is well-known, are a simple arrangement for exposing a culprit on a bench, confined by having his ankles laid fast in holes under a movable board.

Previous to the destruction of the old Guildhall in 1828, the Whipping Post and Pillory—one above the other—were placed close to the south side of the building, and the Stocks were at the opposite end. The latter were stowed away in the Town Hall cellars, where they had lain forgotten for fourteen years. But in 1872 these favourite instruments of punishment devised by the ingenuity of our forefathers, were once more brought into requisition, when one Mark Tuck, an incorrigible bacchanalian, was sentenced to four hours incarceration in the stocks for insobriety and creating a disturbance at the Parish Church. It being a pouring wet day, the stocks were not set up in the Market Place, but placed in the Shambles, while a constable was stationed close by to see that the prisoner was not molested by vengeful missiles or other indignities. Still the punishment was sufficiently severe, for Mark was surrounded the whole time by a crowd of jeering juveniles to whom the process was a novelty. Mark is reported to have borne up fairly well, fervently ejaculating every time the quarter-hour of the church clock chimed, "Thank God, another quarter gone," at the same time registering it in the accumulated dust of years that still lay thickly upon the stocks. At length the period of incarceration was at an end, and on being released and feeling his feet once more, the victim of this degrading punishment bounded into the Police-station, almost overturning an old woman in his haste to escape from the sarcastic onlookers.

Since Mark's involuntary appearance, this interesting relic of "the good old times" has reposed peacefully in seclusion, and only brought out at the Art and Industrial Exhibition of 1884, as a specimen of the punishments of a less civilised age.

Military at Newbury. In the autumn of 1872, a series of military movements were practised upon a large scale, and some 20,000 troops were encamped on Greenham Common on their way to take part in the manæuvres on Salisbury Plain. A vast number of people visited the camp, and Newbury held high festival on the occasion, and the whole neighbourhood was proportionately excited. The bands of the various regiments were conjoined and played in the camp, which aroused the greatest enthusiasm. The march of the troops through the town in the early morning was a sight long to be remembered. First came the Cavalry Brigade—the Life Guards and Royal Horse Guards leading the way. As this magnificent body of heavy cavalry marched through the old streets with their colours inscribed with names memorable in our English history, they were received with the enthusiastic acclamations of the inhabitants. On many a breast were the medals which commemorated engagements in which both officers and men had distinguished themselves in various campaigns, and the people of Newbury were anxious to show them by their cheers that they deserved well of their country.

Prince Arthur, now Duke of Connaught, was with the troops, and every window was filled with fair girls fluttering their handkerchiefs in honour of the young Prince, who smilingly acknowledged the ovation accorded him.

The Falkland Memorial. The 9th September, 1878, was an important day in the annals of Newbury, when one of the largest and most representative processions that had ever taken part in any public ceremonial, accompanied the Earl of Carnarvon (High Steward of the Borough), to Wash Common, where his lordship unveiled the memorial in honour of Lord Falkland and the Royalist officers and men who fell fighting for King Charles I., on the 20th of the same month, 1643, two hundred and thirty-five years before.

This interesting memorial consists entirely of Cornish granite, the base being formed of a series of rock-faced steps from the Lamorna quarries. Upon these rests a block of Penryn stone, weighing twelve tons, on which the four inscriptions are cut. The superstructure comprises an octagonal plinth with gablets on four sides, having sunk panels filled in with a cross on the front face, and coronets and ciphers of Lords Carnarvon, Sunderland, and Falkland carved on the other panels. The octagonal shaft which surmounts this is a monolith, 17 feet in height, the total height of the memorial being about 33 feet. About 40 tons of granite were used in the work.

Railway Development. The first sod of the Didcot, Newbury, and Southampton Railway was turned by the Countess of Carnarvon, 26th August, 1879, and was marked by general festivities. The formal opening of the Didcot to Newbury section took place on the 12th April, 1882, when the railway was declared open by Lady Loyd-Lindsay.

In the following July the Bill for the construction of an independent line to Southampton passed successfully through Parliament, after a protracted and costly struggle with the South Western Railway Company.

The opening ceremony of the section of the line from Newbury to Winchester was celebrated by a considerable demonstration at Newbury, 1st May, 1885.

Queen Victoria's Jubilee. The Jubilee of Queen Victoria's reign in 1887, was celebrated in Newbury in right royal fashion. There was a Thanksgiving Service at the Parish Church, and a handsome stained glass window was unveiled by the Mayor (Mr. Benjamin Smith.) There was also a United Service held in the Corn Exchange. On the 21st June the town was bright and gay with festive decorations. There was a monster procession; the school children and the poor were feasted, and in the evening there was a general illumination of the whole town, while the beacon fires blazed merrily on the neighbouring hills.

The National Rifle Association. In the year 1888 a spirited endeavour was made by the Newbury people and others in the neighbourhood, under the leadership of the late Lord Wantage, to induce the National Rifle Association to adopt Churn, two miles north of Compton station, as the site for the "New Wimbledon." A public meeting was held at Newbury, and a deputation waited on the then Secretary of State for War, but the railway facilities were insufficient to induce the Council of the Association to move so far afield.

Formation of the Berks County Council. The Berks County Council was constituted in 1889, in common with County Councils throughout England and Wales, under the Local Government Act of the preceeding year. The main principle of the Act is that it adopts to counties that form of municipal government which had previously pertained only to English Boroughs.

The first election of County Councillors for the Borough of Newbury took place in January, 1889, when the writer was returned unopposed for the East Ward. The other two Wards were contested, and resulted in the return of the late Dr. Ryott for the North Ward, and the late Mr. J. B. Stone for the West Ward. Mr. J. H. Mason, who contested the North Ward unsuccessfully, was subsequently made an Alderman of the Council.

Presentation to Mr. W. G. Mount, M.P. In January, 1893, a presentation was made to Mr. W. G. Mount, M.P. for the Newbury Division, of two handsome silver Monteith bowls and two candelabra, in recognition of the services he had rendered as Chairman of the County Quarter Sessions and of the County Council.

More Military Manœuvres. Further Military Manœuvres took place on the Berkshire Downs during the summer of 1893, and a large number of troops again encamped on Greenham Common, the frequent passage of the soldiers through the streets giving the old town once more a gay and military aspect.

The 66th, or 2nd battalion of the Royal Berkshire Regiment, took part in these manœuvres, and as it was the first time the county regiment had marched through Newbury, the officers and men were enthusiastically received, and an address presented to the corps by the Mayor (Mr. Alfred Jackson) on behalf of the townspeople, which was acknowledged in a spirited speech by Colonel Ponsonby, commanding the battalion.

Great Floods in Newbury. The year 1894 was chiefly memorable for the floods, which here, as in other places, turned some parts of the town into an inland lake, and rendered many of the houses uninhabitable.

The New Drainage System. The great work of carrying out an efficient system of drainage for the town was commencsd in 1895, under the direction of Mr. Anstie, C.E., after having occupied the attention of the Municipal Authorities for nearly a quarter of a century, and may be considered one of the most successful undertakings with which the governing body has been connected.

The Queen's Diamond Jubilee. The year 1897 will take its place as a memorable epoch in the history of Newbury in connection with the celebration of Queen Victoria's Diamond Jubilee, which was attended with much enthusiasm. The loyalty of the town has been well proved on many previous occasions, but gratifying as is the chronicle of the past, the old town in this instance imitated the example of the Queen, and absolutely beat the record. Never before has there been such a spontaneous expression of loyalty from all classes and creeds, and never did the burgesses more thoroughly rise to their responsibilities. The celebration was carried out by a representative committee of townsmen, "Queen's weather" favoured the whole of the proceedings, and everything passed off in the most successful manner.

A congratulatory address was presented to the Queen by the Corporate body. Bonfires were lighted on the neighbouring hills as in 1887, and fifty-three distinct fires were observed from the heights above Woodhay, and rockets were going up the full sweep of the horizon. Viewed from this spot, some 972 feet above sea level, the scene was very fine, and "as the sun set," says an observer, "beneath a gorgeous canopy of gold, purple, and red, it was just such a setting one could wish for such a day, whilst the sounds of drums and merriment proclaimed the fact that neighbours everywhere were in the height of enjoyment. As we listen, the old familiar strain of 'God save the Queen' floats upward to our eyrie spot, as note by note is struck on the bells of Newbury, proclaiming the close of another splendid Jubilee day, and our thoughts recurred to the Royal lady it was all about, and the millions spread over the wide world, who would be joining hand to hand, heart to heart, to wish her prolonged life and happiness."

The Lambourn Valley Railway. This undertaking was first commenced in 1876, in the shape of a tramway along the Lambourn Valley, but languished through a lack of financial support, and the tram lines never reached further than Donnington Square. Some years after a scheme was set on foot to run a railway between Newbury and Lambourn, which was started under the general approval of the landowners and public in the district. A good commencement was made with the line, but owing to the failure of the contractor to carry out his contract, the works remained in derelict condition for several years. Under the auspices of Colonel Archer-Houblon and other local gentlemen, the line was at length completed, and opened for traffic in 1898, and has proved of great convenience and advantage to the public generally, more particularly to Lambourn, which previously was entirely unconnected with any railway system.

Royalty at Newbury. H.R.H. the Princess Christian and her daughter the Princess Victoria, visited Newbury in 1898, when staying with Sir Francis and Lady Jeune, at Arlington Manor.

The South African War. The war in South Africa was the most absorbing event of the year 1900. The town and neighbourhood of Newbury patriotically as of yore, responded to the call of duty, and in all branches of Her Majesty's service, Berkshire men were to be found doing duty in most parts of the vast area over which the campaign extended.

The country passed through a patriotic phase during the early part of the year, induced by the call of volunteers for active service in South Africa, and their frequent departure amid scenes of much enthusiasm fairly aroused the old martial spirit which has ever been characteristic of the royal county.

A movement to recruit the Berks Yeomanry was attended with great success in various parts of the district, and nowhere did a larger number of young men respond to the call than at Newbury, The subsequent military training at Churn was of much practical advantage, and the Yeomanry, which had been threatened with disbandment, gave abundant proofs of vitality and usefulness. The volunteers also benefitted by the outburst of enthusiasm, and their ranks received many accessions. A company of Imperial Yeomen, under Colonel Ricardo, Captains Eyre and Bishop, was formed, and proceeded to the front. Later on a service company of Berks Volunteers embarked for the seat of war. The Newbury men were entertained in the Council Chamber, presented with useful gifts, and bidden God speed by the Mayor (Mr. Rankin) on behalf of the townspeople. A sum of £200 was subscribed to the Mayor's Reservist Fund, which, in co-operation with the Soldiers' and Sailors' Families' Association, provided for the wives and children of the men away on active service.

Present aspect of the Town. We have now traced the story of the life of Newbury during these many centuries—from its early unchronicled days, through the period of Roman and Anglo-Saxon occupation, of Norman Conquest, of sieges and battles during civil wars, of national and local dissensions, down to our own more prosaic time, when the welcoming back of soldiers who have fought far from home, the death of Queen Victoria, proclamation of our present King, the restoration of the Old Cloth Hall, and many gatherings of citizens and neighbours in friendly concourse are fresh in the recollection of our readers. We must not, however, close this section of the work without some slight sketch of the commercial, intellectual, and social aspect of the Newbury of to-day.

Situated as our Borough is, in the centre of a rich agricultural district, and surrounded by the many beautiful family residences which abound in this favourite neighbourhood, the local trade is considerable, and it is of the best kind—that between the resident tradesman and the consumer, whose interests are thus more materially blended, and more reciprocal than if there were a larger trade consisting of chance and passing customers.

Like many other country towns, through which coaches plied in its palmier days, Newbury has not made any striking advance in population, and the place has grown almost imperceptibly to its present increased dimensions in a leisurely and dignified manner, typical of old-world ideas of progress. In fact, it is questionable whether the changes it has undergone during several generations may be classified as growth, so gradually have they been brought about.

Unfortunately, up to the present it has had no chance of those rapid movements in prosperity which give occasional impulses to manufacturing towns and draw towards them a large population, yet on the other hand it is equally free from the reverses to which they are subject, and also from the noise, smoke, and discomfort which is so characteristic of the manufacturing towns of the north.

But notwithstanding the changing tendencies of the age, there are several businesses in Newbury which have attained a large measure of success, and have made the name of the old town known in almost every part of the civilized world. Prominent among these are the engineering works of Messrs. Plenty & Co., which, originally purely of a local character, have now acquired a world-wide reputation for the manufacture of marine engines and boilers.

Another prominent feature of the trade of the town is the Albert Moulding and Joinery Works, which possesses machinery of the most perfected description, whilst its productions are of such high repute that the business transactions extend to all parts of the globe, and among their patrons are some of the most distinguished architects of the day, both at home and abroad.

These two firms employ a sufficiently large number of hands to give the town a "manufacturing air" at certain times of the day, bespeaking, moreover, the extensive character of their trade.

There are two large corn mills in the town, and considerable quantities of malt are made here, which, as well as flour, is sent to London and all parts of the country.

Newbury can also claim to possess two of the oldest brewing establishments in England, both of which have been in existence for some centuries, which, with another firm, supply the town and neighbourhood. There are also several timber, corn, and coal merchants in a large way of business.

It is unnecessary to speak at any length of the many material improvements Newbury has witnessed during the past century, particularly as regards sanitation, and it is to this more than anything else we are indebted for the comparative freedom from those violent disorders which were once so fatal in England, and are still epidemic in some parts of the country.

An efficient water supply, gas works,* electric lighting, and a complete drainage system, all indicate that the place is now well abreast of the times, though, as a rule, improvements have only been introduced after rather long reflection on the part of the Municipal authorities. Unfortunately, this *laissez-faire* has resulted in the water supply and electric lighting passing into the hands of private companies, and thus sensibly affecting the future interests of the ratepayers.

A great change has been brought about in the growth of the residential district south of the town, but in many cases the intrinsic beauty of the neighbourhood has not been improved by the new structures which have been erected.

Of the social and intellectual state of Newbury, it is difficult to express an opinion. The general character of the town is quiet respectability, and a noticeable absence of that squalid misery which is to be found in the streets of places having a large and fluctuating population.

The Technical Institute, which is largely supported by grants from the County Council, comprises classes for instruction in art, shorthand, manual training, etc., and these are well attended by students of both sexes.

The town is to be congratulated on the transfer of the Museum —which had long been in a parlous state—to better quarters at the Old Cloth Hall, recently restored at a large expense by private enterprise, and presented to the municipality for this purpose, and promises to be a popular educational institution in a neighbourhood so abounding in memorials of the past.

---

* Newbury and Speenhamland were first lighted with gas on Thursday evening, 29th December, 1825.

It must also be a matter of especial gratification to those who have long been agitating for a Free Public Library that the object they have had in view is about to become a realised fact. Mr. Andrew Carnegie, whose name will ever be honourably associated with the good work of providing Free Libraries throughout the country having offered the sum of £2,000 on eondition that a site was found by the Corporation and that a rate of 1d. in the £ was levied for the maintenance of the Library. These terms have been accepted, and the new building will be erected on part of the site of the old Workhouse in Cheap Street.

Good intentions and public spirit are always deserving of respect, and the Newbury Art Society has certainly more than justified its existence by the annual exhibitions it undertakes of the performances of artists of reputation and aspiring amateurs. The quality of the work of the numerous exhibitors for whom the neighbourhood supplies an inexhaustible inspiration, is of average excellence, and invariably represents most careful and promising productions, besides drawing all those of artistic tastes into a pleasant and profitable association.

The Newbury District Field Club, established in 1870, with the two-fold object of promoting both the study of antiquities and natural history, has proved a source of great intellectual enjoyment, and the information collected and embodied in its published "Transactions" have been of much practical interest and value. At present it would seem that the area of operations undertaken by the Club is beginning to be archæologically exhausted, and when it is considered that thirty-four years have elapsed since the first of its annual gatherings, its stands to reason that there are few places in the district which have not been visited by the Club. A new generation of achæologists has grown up in the interval, and if the society is to continue it must begin again by retracing its steps, to which little objection can be taken, as with few exceptions fresh persons would be visiting new scenes, and there are many places which would reward a far more careful study than has yet been given them.

The revival of musical taste in Newbury during the last twenty years has given rise amongst other things to much interest in musical education.

Under the fostering influence of local patronage and the personal activity of Mr. J. Shepherd Liddle, Mus. Bac., Cantab., the Newbury Choral Society has made a favourable reputation, and the demand for sound musical training or in the supply of students worth educating, is shown by the continued and growing prosperity of the Newbury Orchestral Society.

The oldest educational institution in the town is the Grammar School, which is one of those numerous foundations dating from the reign of Edward VI. The school has, after many vicissitudes, entered upon a new career, and there is every reason to believe its upward progress is now established.

Elementary Schools in the Borough are numerous and efficient, and now that the local educational authority has taken over the work of the old school managers who gave such devoted service to the organisation, it is hoped the schools will be thoroughly worthy of the old traditions in the coming years, and give a good start in life for the young citizens of Newbury. A High School for girls has also been recently established, under the auspices of the Berks County Council and the Local Educational Authority.

In respect of buildings and establishments for charitable purposes there is not much to complain of in Newbury.

There is a large number of benevolent and religious societies in the town, foremost amongst which may be ranked the District Hospital; several social and political clubs and reading rooms, a volunteer fire brigade, angling, golf, football, and cricket clubs, a multitude of temperance organisations, friendly societies, and other institutions, a detailed notice of which the limitation of our space forbids.

CHAPTER XV.

THE MUNICIPAL HISTORY.

The Charters—Ceremonies—Municipal Corporation's Act—Borough Extension Act—The Maces—The Common Seal—The Town Hall—List of Mayors—High Stewards—Deputy Stewards or Recorders—Town Clerks.

The Charters. Newbury was created a Royal Borough by Queen Elizabeth "of famous memorie," in 1596, but the inhabitants appear to have exercised the rights and privileges of a community long prior to that reign, the town being described in the preamble to the Charter of Incorporation in which an earlier charter is referred to, as "an ancient and prosperous Borough which had enjoyed divers liberties, franchises, and privileges by the charters of many past sovereigns of the realm."

Under this charter, the government of the town is vested in a Mayor, High Steward, Deputy Steward or Recorder, six Aldermen, and twenty-four Capital Burgesses, assisted by a Town Clerk and other officers. The Common Council to consist of not less than sixteen of the members, being a majority of the whole number, namely, the Mayor for the time being, three Aldermen, and twelve Capital Burgesses.

The first Mayor under the Charter was Bartholomew Yate, the first High Steward, Sir John Wolley (the Queen's Latin Secretary)—an office subsequently held by Charles Howard, Earl of Nottingham, Lord High Admiral of the English Fleet which dispersed the Invincible Spanish Armada.

In 1627, King Charles I. granted to the Corporation and their successors the reversion (being then under lease) of the town and manor of Newbury.

On the restoration of Charles II., the statute passed for the corrections of the Corporations afforded ready means for an attack on the rights and privileges of Municipal bodies, and was also made a pretext for raising money and every species of usurpation. The old members of the Corporation were displaced, and no Municipal body had any chance of continuing its existence without compliance with the wishes of the King.

The town of Newbury was also thought to have justly called down judgment on itself, having been rendered obnoxious to the King by the side it took during the Civil War, and the occasion was therefore taken to call upon the Corporation to show by what authority they claimed to be a body corporate and to exercise the privileges specified in the Incorporation. The Corporation of Newbury, terrified by the arbitrary measures adopted, voluntarily surrendered the Charters it possessed on the promise of having new and possibly more favourable grants. The new Charter was granted in 1664–5 (16 Car. 11.)

The same arbitrary exercise of power was followed soon after the King's death by his successor James II., by taking the Corporations under his control, and in the grant of Charters in the place of those which had been surrendered, introduced, as his brother Charles II. had done in all those he had granted, the clauses which gave the whole power to the select bodies, and made them removable by the will of the Crown. The Corporation of Newbury again surrendered their Charters, and a new one was granted in the first year of the reign of James II. (1685), and is considered by the Corporation to be their governing charter, under which their title is "the Mayor, Aldermen, and the Burgesses of the Borough of Newbury." But its validity is extremely doubtful, and the fact that the Corporation immediately reverted to the usage of the Charter of Elizabeth upon the passing of the celebrated Proclamation of 17th October, 1688, annulling all the surrenders which had been made and reviving the ancient Charters, tends to confirm this opinion.

From this time the direct interference of the crown altogether ceased, the indirect interference became gradually lessened till in modern times it has become almost extinct, and no influence can be less exercised than that which belongs to the crown in regard to Corporation privileges.

Ceremonies. From many entries in the Corporation Journals we see that the members of the old Municipal body were very firm in their determination to observe all the minute ceremonials handed down to them by their forefathers, for the spirit of allowing each person freedom to act as he pleased in such matters was not then to be allowed in the ancient and royal Borongh.

In 1685 it was ordered that at Christmas, Easter, and Whitsuntide, the Aldermen and Burgesses of the Borough shall first meet in the Guildhall and then proceed to the Mayor's house, and from thence home again from Church and return to the Mayor's house. They were also required to meet again at the Mayor's house the next morning after every of the said three feast days, and then also accompany the Mayor to church from his home, "first taking part in the accustomed entertainment."

Apparel. The old Corporation very propeıly not only paid due regard to the maintenance of the customary state, but also to the apparel of its members

In 1687 (24th September), it was ordered "that every Burgess of the Corporation shall and will before Thursday next coming provide themselves Gownes with velvet Capes only and no Loopes, upon payne of everyone neglecting to forfeit £5 to the use of this company."

Again in 1741 it was ordered "that all Burgesses who had served the office of Mayor should on all public or Gown Days appear in a gown all of one sort and make, proper and suitable to the office of a Burgess, and the Town Clerk shall provide himself with an Attorney's gown to be worn likewise on the Gown Days."

The Mayor's Feast. The Mayors of Newbury in former days had an allowance made them of some forty or fifty pounds towards defraying the cost of the customary inaugural feast on election to the chief magistracy. In those times the Mayor's Feast was the civic event of the year, and was attended by the nobility and leading gentry of the town and neighbourhood. Fortunes were readily made in these palmy days of commercial prosperity, and as the cost of the banquets and other charges to keep up the civic state with becoming dignity was considerable, only those persons whose means would allow them to worthily sustain the traditions of the office were admitted to the "company" by the then self-elected authorities. The dinners appear to have been on the most costly scale, and on one occasion we read that the real turtle supplied weighed over two hundredweight.

The allowance to the Mayor was altogether discontinued with the advent of the Municipal Corporations Act, and the old reminder of the good old times of our Municipal forefathers is the sum of five pounds still paid to each Mayor on his entering office, and given by Richard Cowslade in 1715 "towards the Mayor's Feast."

The Mayor's Cake. It appears to have been a very old custom in Newbury to make a large cake for the Mayor's Feast, and so conspicuous was this costly item at the annual banquet, that in 1742 a special order was made by the Council concerning its discontinuance, and its approximate cost—£10—was to be disposed as "the Mayor, Aldermen, and Burgesses, or their successors shall see fit and expedient."

The Pewter Plates. Among the effects of the old Corporation dispersed a few years ago, some interest was manifested in a large collection of fine pewter plates stamped with the Borough Arms, which were bought in 1747 out of a fine of £20 paid by Mr. John Head, jun., for declining to serve the office of Mayor. These are now getting very scarce, and it is a matter of regret that they should have been sold by the Corporate authorities in the first place for the sake of a few shillings.

Desire for Parliamentary Representation. In 1699 the Corporation passed a resolution that £100 be offered to any persons who should procure the privilege of electing representatives in Parliament for the Borough, but with the cautious proviso that the money be not paid until the members be chosen and their election approved by Parliament.

At this momentous period the most strenuous efforts were made by the Whig party to return to Parliament as many members as they could who were favourable to the Act of Settlement, by which the accession of the Protestant House of Hanover to the throne of England might be effectually secured. Hence the anxiety of the Newbury authorities to acquire direct representation in Parliament, but as the Act of Settlement was passed in 1701 and their special object attained, the desire to obtain Parliamentary enfranchisement was not pursued with the like importunity.

The Municipal Corporations' Act. The Municipal Corporations Act of 1835 put an end to the old closed Corporations; all exclusive privileges of trading or of exercising any calling or handicraft by which a trade monopoly was maintained, abolished, and the election of the Council placed in the hands of the newly-enfranchised Burgesses.

Under this Act the members of the old Corporation, who by virtue of their office were Trustees of the Municipal Charities, ceased to Act, and other Trustees were appointed in their room.

In consequence of certain irregularities in connection with the administration of the different foundations, extending over many years, protracted and costly Chancery suits were instituted, which so impoverished the finances of the Corporation as to render them in their corporate capacity practically insolvent when the Municipal Reform Act became law in 1835.

An investigation of the charities followed, and the Government Commissioner considering it a case for mutual conciliation, endeavoured to persuade the new Trustees to effect some satisfactory arrangement in the matter. But the majority absolutely refused to administer to any of the assets of the old Corporation or concern themselves in any way with the arrangement of its debts. Accordingly further Chancery proceedings were commenced, and the town became overwhelmed with difficulties.

The whole of the Corporation property was sequestrated, even down to the furniture in the Mansion House, and the pictures, the maces, and other effects were sold by Auction by order of the High Court of Chancery made in a cause "The Attorney General v. Corporation of Newbury."

Several members of the old Corporation in the meantime had compromised with their creditors or took other means to escape payment of their share of the deficiencies, while the few surviving defendants had to pay the whole of the heavy costs for which they were in no way morally responsible.

The silver-gilt maces were bought in by a few spirited townspeople for £35 and £32 respectively, the new Council being apparently very indifferent as to the fate of these and other historic treasures. The two beautiful copies from Rubens' series of Allegories by Fioravante, presented to the town by the first Earl of Carnarvon and now hanging in the Town Hall and said to have cost 500 guineas each, were bought in for £33 5s. and £27 each. The handsome chandeliers were bought in for a little over £10, and the portrait of John Winchcombe, now in the Council Chamber, was secured for £5. Portraits of King William III., Queen Mary, and Queen Anne, probably presented by these royal personages themselves, were unfortunately allowed to be sacrificed for three guineas each. The old pewter plates were bought in—to be thrown away at a later date. A valuable set of old Worcester china with the borough arms was sold for a nominal sum. Two handsome china bowls, presented by Captain John Seeley in 1773, also bearing the arms of the borough, together with many other articles of great interest and value, were allowed to pass into the hands of strangers for a mere bagatelle. Such was the apathy and indifference that prevailed among the newly-constituted municipal authorities.

The maces and other property bought in by certain guarantors were loaned to the Corporation as occasion required, a charge being made for the same. A dividend was paid, but in after years the Corporation managed to resume the proprietorship of their civic belongings.

The Borough Extension Act.

By an Act (41 and 42 Vict. ch. 184) 1878, for extending the boundaries of the Borough, the municipal area was enlarged by the addition of certain portions of the parish of Speen (including Speenhamland), and Woodspeen, Church-Speen, and Greenham; the extended Borough being divided into two wards called respectively, the

"North Ward" and the "South Ward"—the former consisting of so much of the Borough as lies north of the Kennet and Avon Canal, and the latter that portion lying south of the same line of delimination.

By the same Act the municipal body is to consist of six Aldermen and eighteen Councillors—the North and South Ward having, respectively, three Aldermen and nine Councillors.

By an Order in Council, the town is now divided into three Wards, North, East and West, co-terminous with the County Council divisions.

Description of the Maces. The two silver-gilt maces, referred to previously, are known as the "Stuart Mace" and the "Kimber Mace," having been, respectively, acquired by the Borough during the mayoralty of Edward Stuart, 1707, and John Kimber, in 1758.

The Stuart Mace, which was made by Gilbert Sheath, of London, is thirty-nine inches in length, of the usual open-arched crown form, with orb and cross, the arches rising from a circlet of crosses patée, and fleur-de-lis, being richly foliated. Beneath the arches of the crown are the royal arms in relief, and round the bowl, which is divided into four compartments by demi-figures terminating in foliage, are the rose surrounded by a crown, with the initials A.R., the harp similarly crowned and initialed, the fleur-de-lis the same, and the thistle treated in a similar manner. The shaft is divided into three lengths by encircling bands, and, as well as the base, is chased. On the upper length of the shaft are engraved the arms, without shield, of the Borough of Newbury.

The Kimber Mace is also thirty-nine inches in length. The open arches of the crown, beneath which are the royal arms, rise from a circlet of fleurs-de-lis, foliage and balls, and the head or bowl which is "bulged" and decorated with foliage, etc., in relief, bears on a medallion the Borough Arms, the name and date. The shaft is divided into three lengths by massive knobs, which, as well as the base, are chased.

Recovery of the Charters. The Royal Charters of the town, after being alienated from the custody of the Corporation and their whereabouts unknown, were recovered by the agency of the present writer, in 1883, and formally handed over to the town, and are now in a case in the Council Chamber. They consist of the Charter of Incorporation by Queen Elizabeth, the Ordinances, Charter of Charles II., and the Charter of James II.

The Arms of the Borough. The official Arms of the Corporation of Newbury are: on a mount, a castle with three domed and embattled towers, on each a pennon; the centre tower having a gateway with semi-circular arch, and portcullis; the legend being, "Burgus de Newburie." This device appears on the Common Seal of the Corporation.

THE MACES OF THE CORPORATION OF NEWBURY.

STUART MACE. KIMBER MACE.

From "The Corporation Plate of the Cities and Towns of England" by the late LLEWELLYN JEWITT, F.S.A., and W. H. ST. JOHN HOPE, M.A. By kind permission of Messrs. Bemrose and Sons.

The Mayor's Chain. The Mayor on his election is now vested with a chain and badge of office, which was provided by public subscription during the mayoralty of Mr. Robert Johnston, in 1883.

This civic insignia, which is of 18 carat gold, the design being after the Italian Renaissance, is formed by large links, bearing shields, which have in part been since emblazoned with the arms of successive Mayors. The centre link bears the arms and motto of Mr. Johnston, enamelled in colour; other shields bear the arms of the then Earl of Carnarvon, High Steward of the Borough, and those of the Winchcombe family. The pendant bears the arms of the Borough of Newbury.

The Town Hall and Municipal Buildings. The Town Hall, also called the Mansion House, a plain, substantial building of red brick on piers and arches in a style more ponderous than beautiful, was erected between the years 1740–42, in which latter year there is an order in the Corporation Journal that "all accounts relating to building the new Town House should be audited and settled."

Formerly the basement of the building was fitted up with an extensive and costly cooking apparatus for the Mayor's Inauguration Dinner and other feasts, but as these functions have long since been discontinued, the space is now appropriated to other purposes.

The Municipal Buildings were opened by the late Earl of Carnarvon, in 1876, as part of a larger scheme by which it was proposed to remove the existing Town Hall and widen the roadway at this dangerous point, but vested interests again prevailed.

On the staircase are large-sized portraits of King George III. and Queen Charlotte, presented to the town in 1879 by Mrs. Louisa Goulding, of Wilminster, Henley-on-Thames, widow of the Rev. Edward Goulding, a former Vicar of Brimpton, and mother of Mrs. Hamilton, whose husband was for a time Vicar of Greenham. They were presented to Governor Burt on the occasion of his being sent out to govern the Leeward Islands. Mrs. Goulding's husband's grandfather bought the Maiden Erleigh estate, near Reading, of Governor Burt, and these portraits of King George and his Queen, then in the house, were purchased at the same time. They were supposed to be by Gainsborough, but there is far greater reason to consider them the work of Allan Ramsay, principal portrait painter to George III., and son of Allan Ramsay, the celebrated Scottish poet.

The Mayors of Newbury. The following Lists of Mayors, the High Stewards, the Recorders, and the Town Clerks of Newbury, since the Incorporation of the Borough, are as complete as can now be ascertained, the records as regards certain earlier periods being defective.

MAYORS OF THE BOROUGH.

From the date of Incorporation, May 28th, 1596, being the 38th year of the Reign of Queen Elizabeth.

ELECTED SEPTEMBER 21ST.

Date of Election.	
1596	Bartholomew Yate
1597	
1598	Gabriel Cox
1599	William Chamber
1600	
1601	John Chamberlayne
1602	Edward Holmes
1603	
1604	Bartholomew Yate
1605	Henry Coxe
1606	
1607	
1608	William Chamber
1609	
1610	Roger Weston
1611	Thomas Goddard
1612	
1613	Richard Waller
1614	Anthony Child
1615	Richard Waller
1616	
1617	John Hunt, Senr.
1618	
1619	Thomas Newman
1620	Thomas Goddard
1621	Thomas Houghton
1622	Richard Avery
1623	Richard Waller
1624	Hugh Hawkins
1625	Edward Longman
1626	William Howes
1627	Gabriel Cox
1628	Thomas Gyles
1629	John Houghton
1630	William Hunt
1631	Richard Avery
1632	Richard Waller
1633	Hugh Hawkins
1634	William Howes
1635	Gabriel Cox
1636	John Houghton
1637	John Cook
1638	Richard Waller
1639	Hugh Hawkins
1640	Timothy Averie
1641	William Pearse
1642	John Edmandes
1643	Gabriel Cox
1644	William Nash
1645	Philip Weston

Date of Election	
1646	Amos Averie
1647	John Burch
1648	John Cooke
1649	William Pearse
1650	John Edmandes
1651	Gabriel Cox
1652	Philip Weston
1653	John Burch
1654	Richard Claver
1655	Richard Fanner
1656	Robert Blunt
1657	John Gyles
1658	Shuff Pinfall
1659	William Waller
1660	John Seely
1661	Henry Linch Gabriel Cox
1662	John Edmandes
1663	George Cowslad
1664	John Mundy
1665	Thomas Cowslad
1666	John Rider
1697	Gabriel Cox
1668	John Gyles
1669	Thomas Cowslad
1670	Thomas Wilson
1671	John Rider
1672	George Cowslad
1673	Richard Pocock
1674	Levi Smith
1675	Joseph Garrard
1676	Abraham Stockwell
1677	Richard Reeves
1678	Thomas Paradise
1679	John Smith
1680	James Pearse
1681	Thomas Salter
1682	Thomas Wilson
1683	Joseph Pearse
1684	Church Simmons
1685	George Cooper
1686	Richard Cooper
1687	Francis Cox John Cook
1688	Nathaniel Collins John Burchell
1689	John Gyles
1690	John Hore
1691	Thomas Hughes
1692	Joseph Head, Senr.

Date of Election.	
1693	Bartholomew Hughes
	Levi Smith
1694	John Hedges
1695	Richard Gray
1696	Samuel Slocock
1697	John Burchell
1698	William Rider
1699	Adam Hill
1700	Abraham Stockwell
1701	John Rawlins
1702	Edward Weekes
1703	Thomas Seely
1704	Thomas Stockwell
1705	Nicholas Snow
1706	Edward Godwin
1707	Edward Stuart
1708	John Parsons
1709	Joseph Parsons
1710	Edward Smith
1711	John Gray
1712	Robert Nalder
1713	Joseph Head, Junr.
1714	Oliver Slocock
1715	Richard Berry
1716	John Beale
1717	William Townsend
1718	Edward Lovelock
1719	Francis Page
1720	Lawrence Head
1721	Benjamin Head
1722	William Cundell
1723	Richard Cartwright
1724	William Russell
1725	John Hinton
1726	Thomas Stockwell
1727	Edward Stuart
1728	John Beale
1729	William Townsend
1730	Edward Lovelock
1731	Robert Nalder
1732	Edward Smith
1733	Peter Ely
1734	John Bond
1735	Giles Townsend
1736	John Weeks
1737	Edward Walter
1738	John Head
1739	John Cox
1740	John Wellman
1741	Richard Walter
1742	George Calverley
1743	Linyeat Bodman
1744	Richard Budd
1745	Jonathan Knackstone
1746	Richard King
1747	Lawrence Head
1748	Richard Golding
1749	Charles Sutton
	Lawrence Head

Date of Election.	
1750	Joseph Bolton
1751	Thomas Golding
1752	John Townsend
1753	Samuel Slocock
1754	Francis Page
1755	Benjamin Merriman
1756	George Calverley
1757	John Cox
1758	John Kimber
1759	William Annetts
1760	Henry Cox
1761	William Bodman
1762	Edward Withers
1763	Richard Robinson
1764	Thomas Lovidge
1765	John Lynch
1766	George Jones
1767	Samuel Toomer
1768	Joseph Furnell
1769	Israel King
1770	Jo. Millett
1771	Osman Vincent
1772	John Townsend, Junr.
1773	Richard Baily
1774	Richard Townsend
1775	Samuel Slocock
1776	Richard Townsend
1777	Benjamin Barnard
1778	John Grantham
1779	Joseph Gray
1780	John Clark
1781	John Townsend, Senr.
1782	Thomas Lovidge
1783	Samuel Toomer
1784	John Grantham
1785	Joseph Gray
1786	Andrew Grove
1787	John Hasker
1788	John Webb
1789	William Budd
1790	Benjamin Hawkins
1791	Joseph Toomer
1792	James Bodman
1793	Richard Golding
1794	William Vincent
1795	Samuel Grigg
1796	Richard Atlee
1797	William Davis
1798	Andrew Grove
1799	John Hasker
1800	Benjamin Hawkins
1801	Joseph Toomer
1802	James Bodman
1803	William Vincent
1804	Samuel Grigg
1805	Richard Atlee
1806	William Davis
1807	Richard Compton
1808	William Green

Date of Election.	
1809	Alfred Slocock
1810	William Green
1811	Richard Compton
1812	Alfred Slocock
1813	Alfred Slocock
1814	Joseph Toomer
1815	Benjamin Barnard
1816	James Bodman
1817	Richard Compton
1818	Edmund Slocock
1819	John Hasker
1820	John Gater Marriner
1821	John Grigg
1822	Thomas Willmot
1823	Edward P. Haskins
1824	William Mills
1825	John Satchell
1826	James Hazell
1827	John Hasker
1828	John Grigg Edward P. Haskins
1829	William Mills
1830	John Satchell
1831	James Hazell
1832	James Bodman, Junr.
1833	John Alexander
1834	John Alexander
1835*	John Alexander
1836	Jere Bunny
1837	Jere Bunny
1838	George Payne
1839	Edward William Gray
1840	George Payne
1841	John Lewis
1842	George S. Higgons
1843	William Dredge
1844	Thomas Simmons
1845	Robert Martin
1846	George Adey
1847	Edward L. Farrow
1848	Theophilus V. Turner
1849	Theophilus V, Turner
1850	William Dredge
1851	William Dredge
1852	Joseph F. Hickman
1853	Joseph F. Hickman
1854	Thomas Deller
1855	John H. Mason
1856	Edward Wilson
1857	James P. Jackson
1858	Henry Keens
1859	Henry Flint
1860	Henry Flint
1861	John W. Randall.
1862	John W. Randall
1863	James H. Lucas
1864	Thomas Fidler
1865	Edward P. Plenty
1866	William H. Cave
1867	Wiliiam H. Cave
1868	Henry Dolton
1869	Robert A. Ryott
1870	Robert A. Ryott
1871	Samuel Flint
1872	Joseph F. Hickman
1873	Joseph F. Hickman
1874	William G. Adey
1875	William G. Adey
1876	James Absalom
1877	Charles S. Slocock

In 1877 the Borough was enlarged by the addition of Speenhamland, and portions of Speen and Greenham.

Date of Election.	
1878	Thomas E. Hawkins
1879	James B. Stone
1880	Charles Lucas
1881	Montagu H. C. Palmer
1882	Joseph Hopson
1883	Robert Johnston
1884	William Hall
1885	Richard Ravenor
1886	Benjamin Smith
1887	Henry J. Midwinter
1888	George M. Knight
1889	Robert Long
1890	Stephen Knight
1891	Alfred Jackson
1892	Alfred Jackson
1893	Joseph Elliott
1894	Harman S. Hanington
1895	Ernest Harris
1896	Robert Long
1897	Edward Gould
1898	William Edmonds
1899	John Rankin
1900	John Rankin
1901	John Rankin
1902	Joseph N. Day
1903	William E. Lewendon
1904	Frederic C. Hopson

* In 1835 the Municipal Corporations Act was passed, and the Mayor was elected from that year on November 9th,

HIGH STEWARDS.

Date of Election.	
1596	Sir John Wolley, the Queen's Latin Secretary.
1625 (prior to)	The Right Honourable Charles Howard, Earl of Nottingham, Lord High Admiral of England, and Commander of the fleet which destroyed the Invincible Armada.
1625	The Right Honourable William Fiennes, Lord Viscount Saye and Sele. A distinguished Parliamentary leader, at whose house at Broughton the secret discussions of resistance to the Court took place.
1685 (prior to)	Sir Anthony Craven, Knt.
1690	William, 1st Baron and Earl of Craven.
1697	William, 2nd Baron Craven.
1712	Henry St. John, Lord Viscount Bolingbroke. The celebrated Secretary of State to Queen Anne.
1715	Robert Packer, Esq., M.P., of Donnington Castle and Bucklebury.
1731	William, 3rd Baron Craven.
1739	Fulwar, 4th Baron Craven.
1764	William, 5th Baron Craven.
1769	William, 6th Baron Craven.
1792	William, 7th Baron Craven, created Earl of Craven, 13th June, 1801.
1825	Henry George, 2nd Earl of Carnarvon.
1833	William, 2nd Earl and 8th Baron Craven.
1869	George Grimston, 3rd Earl and 9th Baron Craven.
1884	Henry Howard Molyneux, 4th Earl of Carnarvon.
1890	George Edward Stanhope Molyneux, 5th Earl of Carnarvon.

DEPUTY STEWARDS OR RECORDERS.

The following are the names of the Deputy Stewards or Recorders, and the years of their appointment, so far as can be ascertained from the existing records :—

1640	Richard Tomlyns
1643	John Barksdale
1646	Thomas Flexney
1662	Richard Garrard
1675	Thomas Gunter
1687	Richard Knapp
1689	Joseph Cowslad
1710	Richard Cooper
1726	Richard Pottinger
1739	William le Marchant
1764	Robert Vansittart
1789	James Blackstone
1824	Charles Dundas, M.P.
1832	William Whateley
1842	Henry Selfe Selfe
1856	George M. Dowdeswell
1893	Arthur Hewitt Spokes
1894	Frederic M. C. Mackarness
1904	Francis Fitzgerald

TOWN CLERKS.

As the Corporation Journals do not commence earlier than 1676, we have no means of ascertaining the names of those who filled this office for some years after the Incorporation of the town in 1596.

1662	Gabriel Cox
1676	Richard Pocock
1676	Joseph Garrard
1687	Edward Godwin
1688	Joseph Garrard*
1695	Edward Godwin
1719	John Beale, sen.
1732	John Beale, jun.
1757	James Head
1779	Richard Townsend
1808	Thomas Townsend
1824	Robert Baker
1838	Mark Willis
1842	Robert Baker*
1849	Henry Bunny
1854	Robert Fuller Graham
1876	Henry Burke Godwin
1895	Francis Quekett Louch

* Re-appointed.

NEWBURY, FROM SPEEN HILL. [From an Old Print.

CHAPTER XVI.

THE MARKETS AND FAIRS OF NEWBURY—THE BOROUGH RECORDS—THE COURT LEET AND ITS PRESENTMENTS—THE COMMONABLE LANDS OF NEWBURY—"BEATING THE BOUNDS."

The Market. The Market of Newbury is older than the Fairs, and although there is no mention of it in Domesday, we have reason to believe from its central position that provisions and goods were collected here for sale from time immemorial. We can speak of its existence as early as 1205 with certainty, when the toll received from the market amounted to £8—a large sum in those days, and evidencing that it must have been established for some time previous to this date, in fact from the name Chepe Street or the Market Street we may safely carry the market back to Anglo-Saxon times.

We also find that the market day has for many centuries, at least, been on Thursday, as it is specifically referred to as being held on this day in a grant of the tolls to Sir Thomas Herbert in 1466.

Previous to the erection of the Corn Exchange, the grain was pitched in open market, and offered to the public in small as well as large quantities, thus defeating the artifices of monopolies, and holding out to the industrious, lowly hand, the chief nourisher of his existence at a fair market price. Another good custom was also observed here; that the farmer, let him sell much or little, had his money paid on the delivery of the article, thus verifying the old distich on Newbury market, that

"The farmer may take back
His money in his sack."

The corn market is still one of the largest in this part of the country, and the quality of the grain, as it comes from various soils within the distance of 20 miles in some directions, is adapted for every purpose that can be required.

The Market Cross. We must not leave the market without referring to the ancient Market Cross, which from time immemorial had stood at the south end of the Old Guildhall, and where successive sovereigns of the realm had been proclaimed up to the time of George III., and all public orders declared by the chief magistrate of the town.

The Cross was erected there to remind all good Christian buyers and sellers to keep in view the mutual demands of religion and justice. When this emblem of our holy religion disappeared is uncertain, but it was probably pulled down when the Old Guildhall was swept away, together with the whipping-post, pillory, and stocks in 1828.

The Corn Exchange. In 1862, the Corporation did credit to themselves and the town by the provision of a fine Corn Exchange, which is acknowledged to be one of the most suitable buildings for the purpose in the county.

The Cattle Market. A commodious new Cattle Market was provided in 1873, and the opening ceremony was an occasion of considerable festivity, being attended by the three county Members and leading agriculturists.

The Earl of Carnarvon, who was the principal guest, re-called the fact that his father, thirty-two years previously, had presided over the annual dinner of the Newbury Cattle and Agricultural Association. Political reasons had much to do with the extinction of the Society, which only existed about a dozen years. The cost of the new Cattle Market was about £5,000, and the accommodation thus afforded to agriculturists and dealers has been much appreciated.

The Fairs. The town of Newbury can boast of the continued existence of one of the oldest fairs in England, namely that formerly held on the day and manor of St. Bartholomew, Apostle and Martyr, but since the rectification of the calendar, on the 4th September. This fair was granted to the Hospital by King John by royal charter, dated at Cirencester the 7th July, 1215, and the profits are still divided between the seven brethren and seven sisters inhabiting King John's almshouses in the "City."

From St. Bartholomew's fair we have to pass on to the 5th year of the reign of King Edward IV., who, "in consideration of the good, gratuitous, and laudable Service" of his "trusty and beloved Servant, Thomas Herbert, the elder," granted to him and his heirs, male, one-third part of the tolls and profits of two fairs to be held on two of the Church's festivals—an interesting testimony to the principles and practices of our forefathers, that they tried as much as possible to associate religion with business.

The first of these fairs was to be held on the Eve of the Feast of Corpus Christi—a moveable feast kept on the Thursday after Trinity Sunday—and on the same feast and for two days thence next following; and the second on the Eve of the Nativity of St. John Baptist (whose festival is celebrated on 24th June), and on the day of the same feast, and for two days thence next following; the Crown reserving to itself two-thirds of the profits of these two newly-instituted fairs.

In the Charter of Incorporation of the Borough, 38 Elizabeth, 1596, four yearly fairs or marts are appointed to be held every year, namely, on the day of the Annunciation (25th March), on St. John Baptist's Day (24th June), on St. Bartholomew's Day (24th August), and on St. Simon and St. Jude's Day (28th October.)

These four fairs appear from the increase in the amount of tolls and profits to have obtained a wide celebrity, and the records show that dealers came from all parts of the country to purchase cattle, cheese, and other commodities.

About the year 1687, St. Simon and St. Jude's fair, which had been previously held in the town, was removed to Wash Common by order of the Mayor and Corporation as lords of the manor. Party feeling ran very high in those days, and the opponents of the Tories of that period made complaint to the Crown authorities that the removal of the fair to the Wash was detrimental to the interests of the town. Whereupon the Tory Mayor, Mr. Francis Cox, as a pretext, was summoned before King James II. and his Privy Council to show cause why the ancient fair had been removed. The Mayor duly attended, and the result was that the fair was ordered to be again held in the town, with a separate fair for sheep in West Fields, and the worthy chief magistrate, who had peremptorily refused to stoop to the odious service of supporting a King in his endeavour to subvert the best interests of the country, shortly after suffered the "glorious disgrace" of being expelled from the Corporation.

Some time previous to the year 1720, the chartered fair appointed to be held on the day of the Annunciation, was altered to Ascension Day or Holy Thursday—a moveable feast, the Thursday in Rogation week—that is the week following Rogation Sunday, or the fifth Sunday after Easter Day. The other moveable fair was then (1720) held on the first Monday in Lent, and there were three fixed fairs on 24th June, 24th August, and 30th November, respectively.

The Statute* or Michaelmas Hiring Fair was established some time prior to the year 1752, when, owing to the alteration in the calendar, an official announcement states that "the Market for Hiring Servants, which used to be held here on Thursday next after Michaelmas day, will this Year be held on Thursday, the 12th day of October next, and will for the future be continued to be holden on Thursday next after the Old Michaelmas Day." At the same time the fair (S.S. Simon and Jude's), held on 28th October, was ordered to be held for the future on the 8th November, and that on 24th June (St. John Baptist), on 5th July.

These fairs are still held, but with the exception of the Michaelmas hiring fair and St. Bartholomew's, have almost fallen into a state of desuetude.

The Borough Records. The principal municipal records which have been preserved consist of the Corporation Charters from Queen Elizabeth to James II., the Court Leet Journals, which are extant from 1640 with a slight gap here and there up to recent years; the Corporation Journals, which commence in 1676; and the Records of the Court of Quarter Sessions, which commence in the early part of the reign of Charles II.; finally the Chamberlain's Accounts, which commence in 1672.

* The "Statute Fair" we conclude was established by Statute or Ordinance of the Corporation as lords of the manor, and not by royal grant or licence.

The loss of the earlier journals and muniments of the Corporation can possibly be accounted for by the statement made by Gabriel Cox, Town Clerk, in a petition to Charles II. soon after the Restoration, wherein he states "shortlye after his appointment some factious spirits of the late tyrant's (Oliver Cromwell) faction there, put him out of his Town Clarke's Office, and put in a necessitous person in his roome they knew would better follow their turn," and adds that "combining together, gott into their custody the ancient register books and ancient deeds of the Corporation, which said books they have torne and defaced, and some deeds they have embezzled to the greate greefe and discontent of the petitioner."

The Court Leet. The duties of the Court Leet were very important ones, being a court of record and having jurisdiction of such crimes as are punishable by common law.

This court exercised a criminal jurisdiction, and took cognizance of all offences against the King's peace, as well as putting in force sanitary regulations and other bye-laws relating to various trades, and generally superintending the social conditions of the inhabitants; while the Court Baron, held with the Court Leet, dealt with matters affecting transfers of property and the rights of lands within the manor. The following are some examples of the presentments of the Court Leet.

In 1640 Mr. Dunch and William Howes are presented "for that they have done spoil to the Marsh Common by riding their horses there," and are amerced 12d. Richard Mayle, of Hungerford, and William Stroud, of Wantage, are presented "for exposing unwholesome beef and mutton to sale in the Market of Newbury," amerced 10s. each. Others are presented for exposing "trouts out of season," and each amerced 2s. 6d. John Cook, gent., and other occupiers of lands of John Gwillum, "shall skower the watercourse called Old Streame in Northcrofte, making it tenn foot wide, before St. Thomas' Day, or else every of them to forfeit 5li." Officers are duly elected—two Tithingmen for each of the principal streets, Bread and Butter Weighers, Ale Tasters, Flesh and Fish Tasters, Overseers for the Marsh and the ditch in Northbrook Street, Haywards for the fields, the Marsh, and Market Place. It is noteworthy to find that a few days after the first battle of Newbury, the Court met as usual and transacted its business in due course, the Record containing a list of presentments for non-attendance, with the usual fines imposed; three beer brewers are presented for "taking excessive gain in selling of beer and ale," and others for a similar offence with hay and oats. In 1644 an order is made that "considering the continual troubles of the times and daily businesses and services hourly happening, there shall be chosen six constables for the year following, out of which six the Mayor and Justices to have power to make choice of them to serve the year following.

Sabbatarianism. In 1646 we may trace the growing influence of the Presbyterian party by an order made that "Every father or master of a family that shall suffer his children or servants to play in the street or elsewhere in the parish on the Lord's day within this town, for every such fact, after they have information of such abuses, the father or master to forfeit 6d."

In 1696, there is an order that "the constables, bayliffs, and tythingmen doe walk every Sabbath Day, and make diligent search in all Alehouses after idle persons that they may be proceeded against according to Law, and if any neglect their duty herein, we amerce them 5s."

Strangers in the Town. 1647. Thomas Farneford is presented for entertaining Francis Paine as an inmate contrary to law; order that he remove him or for his neglect forfeit V li., and at a later date it is ordered that "every tithingman within this borough, once in every fifteenth day, make diligent search within his tithing what strangers are there, and give full account to Mr. Mayor under their hands in writing, and if any of them shall neglect to obey this order, shall forfeit 2s. 6d. to the use of the poor." The fear of such strangers becoming chargeable to the parish seems to have been the motive for these measures, as appears by the following enactment, that "no landlord or householder shall entertain any stranger or inmate in their houses to dwell, unless first security be given to the Churchwardens and Overseers of the poor, on pain of forfeiture of 20s. a month."

The Bellman. 1649. An order formerly made is recited that for the better preserving of the town from dangers of fire and many other great inconveniences that are likely to happen to the town, and for the apprehension of all pilfering rogues and suspicious persons, there should be a Bellman that should walk the streets from 9 o'clock in the evening till 5 in the morning, and from 9 of the clock in the morning till five in the evening, and shout a distinct and audible noise, to give notice as well of the present condition of the weather, as of the time and hour of the night, which Bellman is to have 5s. a week duly and truly paid him by the inhabitants, that is to say of every inhabitant paying a ½d. a week to the poor, to pay 1d. every three months; and everyone paying 1d. a week to the poor, 2d. for every three months, and so proportionately.

Muzzling Dogs. In 1653 we have the following early instance of the practice of muzzling dogs:—"We present Robert Gubbard and Edward Andrew for keepinge of bytinge dogges, contrary to the Statute about Muslinge, therefore we amerce them 2s. 6d. a piece."

Tumbrel or Cucking Stool. In 1660 we find the Court Leet Jury presenting that the Constables last year did not, according to order of the law, set up a Tumbrel or Cucking Stool, and are amerced 2s. 6d., and at the Quarter Sessions, 1672,

Margaret Adams, widow, appeared, and pleaded not guilty to her indictment for a common scold, and put herself upon the Jury, who being sworn, say she is guilty of the indictment against her, and that she is to be ducked in the ducking stool as the Mayor shall think the time fitting.

"Down in the deep the stool descends,
But here at first we miss our ends;
She mounts again, and rages more
Than ever vixen did before.
So throwing water on the fire
Will make it burn up still the higher;
If so, my friends, pray let her take
A second turn into the lake;
And rather than your patience loose,
Thrice, and again, repeat the dose.
No brawling wives, no furious wenches,
No fire so hot, but water quenches."

Bull Baiting. It is curious to find that Bull Baiting appears to have been encouraged by the authorities, not only as a pastime, but because it was supposed that the baiting made the bull-beef more tender and wholesome. At a Court Leet, 1661, Edward Caton and others are presented "for killing bulls without baiting of them according to custom"; they are fined 3s. 4d. apiece, and it is further ordered "that if any butcher shall henceforth kill any bull without baiting, he shall forfeit and pay for every bull so killed a similar fine."

Repair of Pavements. At a Court of Quarter Sessions, 8th October, 1677, an order is made that "every inhabitant shall, will, and sufficiently repair and pave their respective parts of the pavements in the three chief streets—Cheap Street, Northbrook Street, and Bartholomew Street—full six feet from the respective messuages towards the middle of the said streets, and the Surveyors to have power from time to time to make rates for raising money to defray charges for repairing the middle of the said streets." This order was confirmed by the Mayor and Corporation, and £20 was allotted from the Town Stock for the purchase of stones and other materials; and, further, order was made that 50s. be raised to be laid out by the Surveyor in "speedy making a brick bridge at Black Stream."

Religious Observances. In 1684 the following order was made at the County Quarter Sessions respecting religious observances, "that the Alehouses of Anne Hobson, widow, and Thomas Flaggott be suppressed, for that neither of them had received the Sacrament of the Lord's Supper according to the Liturgy of the Church of England within 12 months past."

At the following Court, the Constable presented several offenders, principally Quakers, "for not repairing to the Parish Church of Newbury to heare Divine Service and Sermon upon the two last Lord's Dayes, com'only called Sunday."

The Court Leet Jury is not now summoned in Newbury, and gradually all the uses and privileges of this ancient institution of our ancestors wore away as the Courts fell into desuetude. The inhabitants for many years past considering that they were not bound to attend on the Court Leet Jury, and the fines leviable for non-attendance being inadequate in amount and not worth distraining for, these venerable Courts, from disuse and neglect rather than decrepitude and inefficiency, have virtually ceased to exist.

The Commonable Lands of Newbury. From very early times, possibly from the Anglo-Saxon period of village communities, the parishioners and inhabitants of Newbury exercised the right of pasturage for cattle over certain open and common fields within the limits and boundaries of the borough and parish, known as East and West Fields, Northcroft, the Marsh, and Wash Common, together with other lands long since enclosed or appropriated.

With regard to the origin of these commonable lands, in feudal times nearly the whole of the land of England lay in an open and more or less unenclosed state. Each parish or township comprised different descriptions of lands, having been subjected during successive ages to specified modes of occupancy, under ancient and strict regulations, which time gradually converted into law.

These parochial arrangements, however, varied somewhat in different districts, but not widely. Under this ingenious mode of organisation, each parish or township was considered to be one *common* farm, though the tenantry were numerous. Round the township of Newbury, in which the tenants resided, lay a few small enclosures of *grass yards* for rearing calves and as baiting and nursery grounds for other farm stock. This was the common farmstead or *homestead*, which was placed as near the centre of the more cultivated lands of the parish as water and shelter would permit.

Round the homestead lay a suitable quantity of arable land, including the deepest and soundest of the lower grounds for raising corn and pulse, as well as to produce fodder and litter for cattle and horses in the winter season. In the lowest situation, as in the water-formed base of the Kennet valley, or in swampy dips shooting up among the arable lands, lay an extent of meadow-grounds or *ings*, to afford a supply of hay for cows and working stock in the winter and spring months.

On the outskirts of the arable lands, where the soil was suitable for the pasturage of cattle, or on the springy slopes of the hills less adapted for cultivation, or in the fenny *leases* (pasture-grounds) of the valleys, which were gravelly, water-formed lands and too dry to produce an annual supply of hay with sufficient certainty, one or more stinted pastures or *hams* were laid out for milking cows, working cattle, or other stock which required superior pasturage in summer.

The bleakest, worst soiled, and most distant lands of the township were left in their native wild state for *timber* and *fuel* and *common pasture* for the ordinary stock of the community, whether horses, rearing cattle, sheep, or swine, without any other stint or restriction than what the arable and meadow lands indirectly gave. Every joint tenant or occupier of the township having the nominal privilege of depasturing as many cattle, sheep or other live stock on these common fields in summer as the appropriated lands he occupied within the township or manor could properly maintain in winter.

Further, the appropriated lands of the township were laid out with equal good sense and fairness. That each occupier might have his proportionable share of lands of different qualities and lying in different situations, the arable lands more particularly were divided into numerous parcels of sizes according to the number and rank of the occupier.

East and West Fields. Taking these fields in the order named, we first come to East and West Fields. These common lands were divided into parcels, the property of freeholders, of from one, three, or five acres, divided from each other by strips of turf called *linchards* and *mere* banks, the course of the crops being, in general, first, wheat ; second, barley or oats with or without grass ; third, clover, peas, beans or fallow. From this course turnips were excluded, unless by agreement between the various occupiers, but potatoes and cabbages were largely grown.

Over these common field lands the resident householders in the parish and borough of Newbury enjoyed the right of depasturing cattle from the end of harvest till the 8th November, according to the quantity of land they held. They also had a right to any crops remaining in or upon the ground, and could cut any green crops and any stubble, and could dig up any roots. Neither the freeholder nor the person occupying the land had any power to prevent those having rights of common from exercising this privilege.

The sporting rights over the fields were vested in the Mayor, as Lord of the Manor, and it was customary at Christmas to apply to him for leave to shoot over these lands. As many as sixty guns might be seen out, and the townspeople thoroughly enjoyed this annual diversion.

Previous to the enclosure of the fields a certain landowner had taken in and fenced off a considerable portion of the land, which the townspeople naturally resented, and serious riots ensued ; fences were torn down, trees and shrubs destroyed, and other damage done, which was only stayed by a magistrate reading the Riot Act. Several of the townspeople were sent to gaol, and much bitterness evoked, and there were many later uproars connected with the proceedings.

Soon after the Enclosure Commission was established in 1845 to facilitate the enclosure and improvement of lands subject to any rights of common, the Corporation of Newbury made application for the dividing, allotting, and enclosing of these common fields, and a provisional order was made under seal of the Commissioners, 4th April, 1846. All the necessary provisions having been fulfilled, the award was made by Edward Grantham, of Croydon, surveyor and valuer, who allotted the proportionate shares of the common right lands to each proprietor, *pro rata*, according to the extent of his old rights.

The Enclosure Award was sealed by the Commissioners, 31st January, 1849, and thus these ancient common lands were lost for ever.

Northcroft. These fields, containing about thirty-two acres, are what are known as "Lammas Lands," that is commons on which the inhabitants have the right of pasturage, formerly commencing on Lammas Eve, the day before the festival of Lammas Day (the 1st August), till Lady Day, the 25th March. But for many years the ground has been opened on the 12th August, and closed for cattle on the 6th April. This alteration in opening and closing the fields was due to the change of style in 1752. The difference between the old and new style was eleven days. Thus the Eve or Morrow of Lammas Day, the 31st July, of *the old* corresponded with the 12th August of the *new* style, and the 25th March with the 6th April, as now adopted.

So far back as the year 1640 we find a Hayward of Northcroft was appointed by the Court Baron of the Mayor, Aldermen, and Burgesses of Newbury as Lords of the Manor, and strict regulations were made from time to time as to the day of *hayning** or closing, and *breaking* or opening the fields; and the records of the Court contain many stringent orders for the government of these and other common lands within the manor. In 1650 the Court Baron presented Henry Girle for putting twelve cows into Northcroft contrary to custom.

In earlier times men only kept as much stock as their land would maintain throughout the year, but it frequently happened that many of the inhabitants had considerable land in other places, and kept a large number of cattle, which so soon as Northcroft and the other common fields were opened, were turned in to eat up the feed—to the great prejudice of the townspeople. To remedy this wrong an Order was made by the Court Baron in 1663 :—

"That no inhabitant shall bring any cattle into Northcroft or the other open fields unless such as are usually kept in the parish, and no person to turn out above 4 hoggs† and 4 beasts, or 6 beasts and two hoggs at one time, upon pain or forfeiture of 2s. 6d. per each hogg or beast above the aforesaid number."

---

* The word "hayned" is an old English term, signifying to lay in ground for hay, by taking the cattle off, etc., and is used in that sense throughout the Records of the Court Baron.

† This does not refer to a pig. The term "hogg" as here used signifies a *lamb* after weaning, until it is shorn of its first fleece.

At the same Court it was ordered :—

"That no man, unless he be a householder and pay taxes and do other duties belonging to the Borough, shall have any privileges in the Marsh, Northcroft or any of the fields belonging to this borough, nor any other portion under any pretence whatever."

It was also ordered "that no Butcher should turn out 'fatt cattle' in any of the fields before the 25th March, excepting *Northcroft*, where they might be depastured five weeks after Shrovetide.

In 1675 it was ordered :—

"That no inhabitant shall put into our Commons at the Marsh and Northcroft at one time above 1 horse or 2 cows, except those who have land in Northcroft."

In 1680, the time for "breaking" or opening Northcroft is mentioned as Lammas Eve, "which is the last day of July," until 25th March.

At the Court Baron held in 1756, the following order was made by the Jury :—

"We direct the Hayward* of the parish to take sixpence for each horse or cow that shall be found in Northcroft or the Marsh that shall belong to persons not residing in the same."

And in 1771, the jury presented :—

"That according to the ancient custom of this manor no owner or occupier of Lands in Northcroft hath a right to hitch, inclose, or feed any of the land there from the usual time of its haining to the customary time of breaking, neither hath any person to lay and dry peat thereon. And that if any cattle be found in Northcroft contrary to the usual custom, the Hayward to impound the same."

The above are the most noteworthy entries in the Court Rolls which bear upon the rights of the inhabitants of Newbury in regard to Northcroft.

At a County Court held at Newbury in 1888, a case was heard in which the plaintiff, who had recently purchased a part of the Lammas Lands in Northcroft, sued the Corporation of Newbury for nominal damages and trespass for being prevented free access to his freehold land in Northcroft, and impounding his cattle, whereby he was prevented feeding his after-math ; his contention being that the Corporation had no right to exclude his cattle at any time, nor to exclude him access to the land. After hearing the evidence for the municipal authorities, the Judge gave a verdict for the Corporation, with costs on the higher scale.

The Marsh. There is a tradition that the Marsh was given to the town by two maiden ladies, but if so it must have been at a very early period, as it has been appurtenant to the town for pasturage of cattle for several centuries, and is open throughout the year ; every inhabitant householder having the right to turn out one horse or two cows.

* The word "Hayward" is in all probability derived from *hay*, a hedge or enclosure, and "ward" to take care of, i.e. a person who looks after the cattle and prevents them from breaking down the fences, etc., or the Warden of Common Lands.

In the fifteenth and sixteenth centuries the Marsh was largely used as a "Tenter Ground," or "Rack Marsh" for drying cloth by the Winchcombes and other clothiers whose factories abutted on this common-land.

At the time of the Civil War some rough outworks were thrown up in the Marsh, under the personal direction of Cromwell, and were only levelled a few years since.

The Marsh has been the scene of many merry-makings and rustic sports, and is usually chosen as a site for the travelling circuses which from time to time visit the town. It has recently been termed "Victoria Park," but it is to be hoped that the historic name of "The Marsh" will long retain its proper place.

Wash Common. The manorial rights of the Crown over the common-field lands, known as "The Wash," and containing 251a. 3r. 14p. were acquired by the Mayor and Corporation by a grant from Charles I. in the year 1627, who, by letters patent, in consideration of £50 and subject to a yearly payment of £25 4s. 2¼d., granted to them and their successors in fee the reversion of the said manor, etc. From this time these common rights remained open and unappropriated, subject to the rights of the inhabitants to common pasturage, until enclosed.

On the 24th January, 1855, a meeting of landowners and the inhabitants of Newbury was held at the Town Hall to receive consent to the enclosure of these common lands within the borough and parish of Newbury; a provisional order having been previously obtained from the Enclosure Commissioners by the Corporation as lords of the Manor. A long discussion took place as to who were entitled to rights of common, which rights were defined as belonging only to parties having land, and the extent of their right limited to so much cattle as the lands held by them within the borough would maintain winter and summer.

The meeting resulted in a motion by Mr. Edward Brice Bunny, seconded by Mr. T. V. Turner:—

> "That the enclosure of Wash Common is expedient in the interests of the town of Newbury."

This resolution was carried with three dissentients. Mr. Cornelius B. Davis acted as Surveyor and Valuer in the matter, and his Award was sealed by the Enclosure Commissioners, 25th February, 1858.

It is scarcely necessary to add that the householders of Newbury received no compensation when thus deprived of the valuable rights and privileges which had been enjoyed by the commonalty of the town for so many centuries, but their inheritance was bestowed on their more favoured neighbours, whose only claim was that they were already possessed, by purchase or otherwise, of land within the boundaries of the borough.

Beating the Bounds. The ancient custom of perambulating the boundaries of the parish of Newbury in Rogation week, in order to preserve in all classes a correct knowledge of and respect for the bounds of parochial property, was formerly strictly observed. Before the Reformation these perambulations were conducted with great ceremony. The Steward of the Manor with a large banner, priests in surplices and with crosses, and other persons with hand-bells, banners, and staves, followed by most of the parishioners, walked in procession round the parish, stopping at crosses, forming crosses on the ground, saying prayers supplicating the divine blessing on the fruits of the earth, and allowing "drinking and good cheer," which was remarkable, as the Rogation days were considered fasts. At the Reformation the ceremonies and practices deemed objectionable were abolished, and only "the useful and harmless part of the custom retained."

By the injunctions of Queen Elizabeth it was required that in order to retain the perambulation of the circuits of parishes, people should once in the year, at the time accustomed with the curate and the substantial men of the parish, walk about the parishes as they were accustomed, and at their return to the church make their common prayers. And the curate in these perambulations was at certain convenient places to admonish the people to give thanks to God as they beheld his benefits, and for the increase and abundance of the fruits upon the face of the earth. The 104th Psalm was appointed to be said on these occasions, and the minister was to inculcate such sentences as "Cursed is he which translateth the bounds and doles of his neighbour."

From the period when the Borough was incorporated—38th Elizabeth—it was customary—usually once in seven years—for the Court Leet Jury to continue the practice of processioning, or "beating the bounds," and the religious element was formerly strictly observed—the 104th Psalm being invariably sung at the "Burial Hill" on the Wash, and the perambulation ceremony was closed with the "Old Hundredth."

In later times the religious portion of the proceedings has been generally, if not invariably, omitted. The writer recollects more than one of these "processionings," and the fun occasioned by the boys being "bumped" against a brick wall, a tree, a post, or other object which happened to be near the parish boundary. This, it will scarcely be doubted, was an effective method of recording the boundaries in the memory of these "*battering rams*," and of those who witnessed this curious mode of registration. Refreshments were liberally provided for those engaged in the perambulation at certain points of the parish and borough boundaries, and the proceedings terminated with a dinner at one or other of the favoured hotels, generally the "Dolphin" or "Black Boys."

All the duties of the Court Leet have of late years been taken over by the Corporation, and when the boundaries were last perambulated there was little of the "pomp and circumstance" of this ancient ceremonial.

The boundaries of public property being now so accurately defined on the Ordnance Maps, there is no longer the same necessity for these parochial perambulations, which, although they have been revived in many places of late years, have, as a rule, fallen into desuetude.

The Mayor of the "City." The curious custom of annually electing a mock mayor of that portion of the borough called the "City," originated in a kind of convivial club, not only to eat and drink, but to take measures for preserving the public rights over the common fields, and to prevent encroachments. As the members were most of them poor persons, they agreed at every meeting to subscribe small sums in order to make up a purse for the defence of their collective rights. The chairman of the club was called the "Mayor," and from this beginning the mock usage became an annual event, and was continued until recent years.

CHAPTER XVII.

ECCLESIASTICAL AND RELIGIOUS HISTORY.

THE PARISH CHURCH OF NEWBURY.

The original church was founded in 1086, at the close of the reign of the imperious William the Norman, by a certain Ernulf de Hesding, who gave the advowson to the Abbey of Préaux, or in the Latin the *Abbatium de Pratellis*, in the diocese of Lisieux in Normandy. Monasticism was then near its zenith. In 1413, in consequence of hostile relations between England and France, shortly to culminate at Agincourt, the advowson passed to the Carthusian monastery of Witham in Somerset—the Abbey of Henry I., and of St. Hugh of Lincoln.* When the monasteries fell, the advowson of Newbury passed to the Crown, and is now vested in the See of Oxford.

The existing church of St. Nicholas is a large and imposing edifice of late Perpendicular date, of considerable beauty and dignity, was erected between the years 1509 and 1533, and owing to the munificence of past parishioners who bequeathed funds for its maintenance, has been fortunately preserved to us almost as intact as when it left the hands of its original builders.

* Witham was the first example of the singular Carthusian arrangement existing in England.

NEWBURY PARISH CHURCH.

INTERIOR OF NEWBURY PARISH CHURCH.

During the fifteenth and sixteenth centuries, the merchants and manufacturers of Newbury were so successful as to be able to realise large fortunes, and it is to the liberality of one of these worthies—John Winchcombe—who could exclaim in the words of another distinguished clothier:—

"I thank God and ever shall;
It was the sheep that paid for all"—

that we are mainly indebted for the noble edifice which is justly the pride and glory of the old town and the whole country-side.

The general effect of the interior of the church, which has sitting accommodation for 1,170 persons, is one of singular spaciousness and stateliness. It consists of a lofty nave and two side aisles, a south chapel of the same date as the rest of the church, and a north chapel, now used for vestries, and as the receptacle for the large and excellent organ. The windows down the two aisles are specially worthy of note, not only for the excellence of their glass, but also for the continuity of the subjects depicted in them. The north aisle is storied with our Lord's miracles, and the south with His parables. There is also a remarkably good window in the south chapel, and two poor ones, one at the east of the church, and the other at the west.

The roof of the nave is in the main old, but has been restored and decorated. The original bosses have been replaced, several of these bear the initials I.S., *i.e.* John Smalwode *alias* Winchcombe; and I.W. for John Winchcombe is also carved on one of the bosses in the north aisle. Above the corbels are figures of angels with open wings, each holding a shield, displaying the instruments and emblems of the Passion.

At the period of the Civil War, the church was occupied by the Parliamentary troops as a prison, a hospital, a guard room, and for various other purposes, and was, consequently, very much injured and defaced. Not only was the lead stripped from the nave and aisle roofs, but even the weathercock was pulled down from the tower, and the soldiers only desisted pulling up the lead on the tower itself by being paid its value by the authorities.* A clean sweep appears to have been made of all the old monuments, some of which, judging from the head of a recumbent effigy of heroic size found when the church was restored in 1865, came from its old Norman predecessors; while the ancient muniments and deeds which had lain for centuries in the parish chest were either destroyed or appropriated. The daily service was put down, and the prayer book replaced by the new order of worship, called the Directory.

After all the church had suffered at the hands of the soldiery, it must have presented a sad spectacle, and evidently was in a state

* The lead was, probably, appropriated for the purpose of making bullets, as recorded in many other instances.

of desolation for some years after the war.* That it was so, we have the corroboration of the Churchwardens' accounts, from which it appears that it was not until 1654 that steps were taken to clear out the accumulated "rubbish," to "level the tomb-stones in the church,"† and to again make it fit for divine service. A voluntary rate was then made, a house-to-house collection undertaken, and funds raised from many friends at a distance, the amount expended being little short of £1,000 according to our present currency.

There is an interesting brass, 1519, to John Winchcombe, the famous worthy, and Alice, his wife. On four small plates at the corners are emblems of the *Agnus Dei*, and a monogram of John Smalwode. Winchcombe being a clothier, the association of the figure of the Holy Lamb as the emblem of St. John Baptist, the patron saint of clothiers, is explained. Another brass which commemorates Hugh Shepley, rector, 1596, reads as follows :—

"Full eight and twenty yeeres he was your Pastor,
As hee was taught to feede by Christ his Maister ;
By preaching God's Word, Good Life, Good Example,
(Food for your Soules, fitt for God's house or temple)
Hee loved Peace, abandoned all strife,
Was kinde to Strangers, Neighbours, Children, Wife ;
A lambe-like man, born on an Easter Daye,
So liv'd so di'de, so liv's againe for aye ;
As one Spring brought him to this worlde of sinne,
Another Spring, the Heavens receiv'd him in."

Other brasses are inscribed to the memory of Francis Trenchard, 1635, and George Widley, M.A., "Minister of God's Word," 1641. The church also contains many interesting tablets, and other memorials.

The most marked feature in the church is the old Jacobean pulpit, presented to the parish in 1607 by Mrs. Margaret Cross, and from which many eminent dignataries of the establishment have

* It has been frequently asserted that the iconoclastic zeal of the Parliamentary soldiery has been much exaggerated, and that a great part of the destruction in our churches was not due to their fanatical views. But Lady Springett, whose husband was severely wounded at Newbury in the first fight where he commanded a regiment of foot for the Parliament, tells us in her autobiographical letters that he commanded his soldiers to break down and destroy every vestige of those objects that he regarded as Popish idols, whether crosses, statues, pictures or ornaments. It mattered not with what exquisite art the marble figure had been chiselled, or with what elaborate and successful skill the painting represented life, if it depicted or attempted to embody fanciful representations of the Saviour, the Apostles, or Saints, nothing could shield it from the fury of the Puritan soldier. "Be they ever so rich he destroyed them, and reserved not one for its comeliness or costly workmanship." Lady Springett further mentions that on one occasion her husband slashed several pictures from their frames in the house of a Parliament-man with whom he was associated in searching "Popish houses" in order to show his impartiality; the pictures which he deemed superstitious representing the Crucifixion and Resurrection. The posthumous daughter of Sir William Springett, married, in 1672, WILLIAM PENN, the eminent Quaker, and FOUNDER OF PENNSYLVANIA.

† Indicating that the vaults had been ransacked for the lead.

preached from time to time, and also John Wesley when he first visited Newbury.* Restorers have done all they can to spoil this invaluable relic by painting, robbing it of its sounding-board and door, besides putting it upon a stone pedestal, quite out of keeping with its arabesque oak wainscot sides and general character.

The font is modern, and has a lofty, elaborately carved pyramidal cover with figures of the Apostles under canopies, being suspended from a bracket of wrought iron-work. Around the head of the font, which is octagonal in shape, is the text:—

"*Jesus est nomen quod est super omne nomen.*"

Previous to the restoration of the church during the incumbency of the Rev. James Leslie Randall, the Commnnion Table was placed in the centre of the Chancel, a mere altar rail dividing it from the nave. This was one of the last instances of Puritan rule remaining in England, and is referred by Scudamore in his *Notitia Encharistica.*

In the vestry is an interesting portrait of Dr. Twisse, habited in ruff, bands, Geneva gown, and skull cap. He was Prolocutor of the Westminster Assembly of Divines, and, therefore, a man of note in his day. At his death in 1646, he was buried with Parliamentary honours in Westminster Abbey, but his bones at the Restoration were removed to a humbler resting-place in the churchyard of St. Margaret's, Westminster.

On the outer wall of the south side of the chancel is a noticeable monument, formerly inside the church, erected upon three columns. In the space between the first is the statue of a man in armour, kneeling, and between the other two are the figures of numerous sons and daughters. It commemorates Griffin or Griffith Curtis, of Greenham, M.P. for Ludgershall, 1562–3, ob. 1587, and is surmounted by a shield bearing the arms of Curtis—*Erm, or a chevron, gu., between three fleur-de-lis.* Crest—*An arm erect habited in mail, holding in the hand a sword.* The motto, "*Velle bene facere,*" has been obliterated.

In the churchyard under the tower on the south side, is a large mound beneath which are buried many of the soldiers who fell in the second battle of Newbury, 1644.

The Church Tower has contained bells for ringing purposes from the time of its completion in 1532, and the original massive old oak beams and part of the framework for the bells still remain in use. The ancient bells were re-cast by James Wells, of

* On the 3rd February, 1740, during the incumbency of the Rev. Joseph Acres, John Wesley, the founder of the great religious body of Methodists, preached in the Parish Church of Newbury, which is thus recorded in his Journal:—"1740, Feb. 1st. I set out, and on Sunday, 3, declared the Grace of God at Newbury from the words of the Prophet, 'I will heal their back-sliding, I will love them freely,' and though the Church was full of (chiefly) genteel, well-dressed people, they behaved as though they knew God was there." As is well known, Wesley was an ordained clergyman of the Church of England, having been admitted to Orders by Potter (Bishop of Oxford) in 1725. He was at Newbury on many other occasions in after years, but did not preach a second time in the Church.

Aldbourne, Wilts, in 1803, and the new peal of eight bells was rung for the first time on the election of Mr. William Vincent as Mayor of Newbury. The little bell or priest's bell, bears the name of "R. Cor," Aldbourne, predecessor of the Wellses, 1724.

The time-honoured Curfew bell (the tenor) has been rung at eight o'clock in the winter evenings, and nine o'clock in the summer from time immemorial—the winter curfew commencing on the Weaver's Feast Day, the Monday before St. Matthew's Day, and the summer bell at Easter.

The bell rung at three o'clock on Saturday afternoons is a survival of the "morrow-mass bell" to prepare for the early mass on the following Sunday morning.

A bell is also rung on Shrove Tuesday, a relic of the pre-Reformation custom of summoning the faithful to confess and be shriven previous to the forty days of fasting.

The Parish Registers. The parish registers of Newbury are complete from 1538, the year when registration was first instituted by Thomas, Lord Cromwell, Vicar-General to Henry VIII., and are as perfect as any to be found.

At the head of the Register of Baptisms is the following preliminary title:—"In the yeare of our Lord, 1538, and in the 30 yeare of the Raigne of o^r most noble Kynge Henry the Eyghth In Earth Supreme head undar Christ of the Churche of Ingland and Geven by hys most Gracious Instructions In thys yeare as follows."

This is somewhat varied at the commencement of the Register of Marriages, thus:—"In Ann^s dno 1538 And in xxx yeare of the Rayne of our most vartuous Kynge Henry the eyghthe In earth Supreme head undar o^r Savyor Jesus Christ of the Church."

It will be observed that not only is the King here introduced with his new title of Supreme head of the Church of England, but is also endowed with an apparent title of moral goodness, which seems very inappropriately applied to his character. Such a want of moral rectitude would not, however, effect these formal designations, and it may be explained that the word "vartuous" here signifies the possession of the sum of all the corporeal or mental excellencies of man rather than moral perfection.

Baptisms.

Among the worthies who received baptism at the Parish Church we find the following:—Thomas Lyripin, a well-known Fellow of Winchester College; John Harmar, D.D., Warden and Head Master of the same foundation, and Regius Professor of Greek in the University of Oxford; Thomas Hyde, Fellow of New College also Head Master of Wykeham's College; Roger Ockham, Chancellor of Sarum, who took an active part against the Protestants in Queen Mary's reign; William Blandye, Translator of Hieronimus Osorius; John Hassall, D.D., Prebendary of Lichfield and Dean of Norwich; Francis Barksdale, a well-known physician; William Bew, Major of Royalist Horse, then D.D., and Bishop of Llandaff; John

Chamberlain, owner of Donnington Castle, one of whose sponsors were John Jewell, Bishop of Sarum; Philip Jemmet, founder of Raymond's Almhouses; Edward Godwin, who became a celebrated Nonconformist divine; Robert Twisse (son of Dr. Twisse), first incumbent of the "New Church," Westminster (1627); Samuel Tomlyns, another noted Nonconformist minister; Penrose, the poet; Francis Baily, the renowned Astronomer; and many other natives of the town who became famous in their day and generation.

Marriages.

One of the most noticeable things in the first register book of matrimony is the frequent entries of the marriage of priests, following the Act of Uniformity (2 and 3 Edward VI.) by which these marriages were permitted. In 1541 occurs the marriage of Renold Golofer or Golafre, a family of very considerable note in this county and the adjoining county of Oxford. John Maunsell was married to Julian Barkeley, 1563. In 1570 Ralph Lucas is described as of *Spyne*, a close approximation to the Roman name of Spinæ (Speen.)

The most curious entry, perhaps, is that of the marriage of Hannah Snell, the famous "female soldier," in 1759. She served some time in a foot regiment during the Rebellion in Scotland, and afterwards joined the Marines. At the siege of Pondicherry she received no less than twelve severe wounds. On her recovery she was sent to England, and on her discharge obtained a pension for life, and also became an out-pensioner of Chelsea Hospital. In 1772, Hannah, becoming a third time a widow, married at Wickham Chapel one Richard Habgood. She died in 1792, and at her special request was buried amongst the old soldiers in the cemetery of the Royal Military Hospital, Chelsea.

Penrose, the poet, was married to Miss Mary Slocock in 1768. After the poet's death in 1779, his widow married the Rev. Thomas Best, Master of the Grammar School, who died in 1814. The Rev. Thomas Best, Curate of Shaw, and Richard Best, Surgeon of Newbury, were sons of the Rev. Thomas Best by his first wife. By his wife née Mary Slocock, Penrose left an only child, Thomas, who, as Dr. Penrose, is known as the owner of Shaw House.

Henry Hart Milman, afterwards Dean of St. Paul's, was married here, 11th May, 1824, to Mary Ann Cockell, daughter of Lieutenant-General Cockell, of Sandleford Lodge.

Burials.

One of the earliest burials, under the year 1538, is that of "Mr. Henry Brydges, Esq.," uncle to Sir John Brydges, created Lord Chandos of Sudeley in 1544. Master John Wayt, Parson of Newbury, and one of the Executors of Jack of Newbury, was buried in 1539. John Megott or Magott, a former prior of St. Bartholomew's, 1546. Joan Winchcombe, apparently the second wife and widow of Jack of Newbury, 1549. In 1557 John Smalwode *alias* Winchcombe, son of Jack of Newbury; in 1592, Philip Kistill, a famous clothier and benefactor to the town; in 1595, Christopher Bunney; in 1596, Hugh Shepley, Rector. Mr. Thomas Edmonds, "one of the Queen's Majesties Councell," 1603; Sir Smith Lewis, Knt., of Chamberhouse, the same year. On the 12th June, 1604, was buried *Newbury's first Mayor* (Bartholomew Yate.) Christopher Twisse, probably father to the Doctor, 1608. John à Windsor, an Astrologer, mentioned by Lilly, 1619; Roger Weston, a clothier of renown, 1620; Frances Twisse, wife of the Rector, 1624. In 1645, Lieutenant-Colonel Smith, a Royalist officer, shot by a Major Stuart in the Parliament's service. Stuart was surprised by a party of Royalists from Donnington Castle, as he was sitting by the side of his intended bride at a supper party at Greenham Manor, and shot dead on the spot. Both friend and foe were buried in the church.

The Rev. Benjamin Woodbridge, of Nonconformist fame, was buried in the church, 4th November, 1684. In 1713, Thomas Cowslade; and in 1718–19, Richard Cowslade, the great benefactor to the town. Rector Hinton, in 1720; in 1742 Thomas Cowslade; and in 1758, another Thomas Cowslade; in 1769, Thomas Penrose, Rector; in 1774, the Rev. John Geree, Fellow of Winchester College. Robert Keens, aged 108 years, in 1780, whose death is noticed in the *Gentleman's Magazine*; in 1793, John Kimber, founder of the Almshouses bearing his name; in 1801 is the pathetic record, "Harriett Emmet, aged 19, who died from Excessive grief, commonly called Broken Heart."

In 1838, the worthy Rector for 41 years (the Rev. James Roe), aged 80, was buried in the "Church Garden" at the east end of the Chancel. During the whole of this long period the registers were fairly transcribed in the beautiful handwriting of Mr. Roe, and who made most admirable indices of all the current volumes.

The burial ground attached to the parish church was closed against interment, except in certain vaults, by order of the Secretary of State, under the provisions of 16 and 17 Vict., chap. 134, and a cemetery was provided for the parish. The church portion of the ground was consecrated by Samuel Wilberforce, Bishop of Oxford, on Easter Tuesday, 2nd April, 1850.

The Dog-Rappers. There were formerly two ancient officers attached to Newbury Church, who were paid 4s. a year each, their duty being to walk up and down the church, each bearing a black wand, and show the inhabitants to their pews. They were in later years called Vergers, but the late Alderman Edward William Gray remembered when they were known as "Dog Rappers," so called from their being required to whip the dogs out of the church "for the quiet of divine service." The two wands now do duty as symbols of office borne by the Churchwardens. We have heard of the "Rapper" in another church going around the edifice during service, carrying a long staff, at one end of which was a fox's brush, and at the other a knob; with the former he gently tickled the faces of the female sleepers, while on the heads of their male compeers he bestowed with the knob a sensible rap.

LIST OF RECTORS.

The names of the following Rectors are derived from the Episcopal Registers of the Diocese of Salisbury from the time of Bishop *Simon de Gandavo*, in 1298, to the year 1836, when the whole County of Berks was detached from Salisbury and annexed to the Diocese of Oxford. The series is completed from the records of the latter See.

1213–26 (prior to) Gervase.
1327 Richard de Warmington (Warmington, co. Oxon.)
1349 Thomas Charles.
1394 (prior to) Thomas Newman, of Hadisco, co. Norfolk.
1394 John Maldon.
1401 Hugh Clifford, Chaplain.
1408 John Lynes.
1418 Robert Langrish, M.A., Fellow of New College and Prebendary of Sarum.
1454 John Stretton, LLD., Prebendary of Sarum.
1457 Thomas Water, B.A.
1460 John Ingylby, M.A.
1479 Christopher Twynho, Prebendary of Lincoln and Archdeacon of Bucks.
1488 John Esterfield, S.C.L., Fellow of New College.
1513 John Wayte, M.A.
1539 Edward Heydon, B.C.L., also Rector of Enbourn.
1551 Edmund Allen, B.D., Fellow of Corpus Christi College; Bishop-elect of Rochester.
1553 William Smyth.
1554 Henry Howman.
1559 William Forde, B.C.L., Fellow of New College. Deprived in 1560.
1560 Thomas Bromhead.
1562 Thomas Early.
1567 Hugh Shepley,
1592 Thomas Coldwell, M.A., also Rector of Shaw-cum-Donnington.
1618 Nathaniel Giles, D.D., Canon of Windsor.
1620 William Twisse, D.D., Fellow of New College, Prolocutor of the Assembly of Divines. He exchanged Newton-Longueville for Newbury with Dr. Giles.
1648 Benjamin Woodbridge, M.A. Dispossessed under Act of Uniformity.
John Hillersden, B.D., Fellow and Vice-President of Corpus Christi College. Dispossed of his preferments by the Cromwellian visitors in 1648, is mentioned in 1664 as "the late Incumbent."
Stephen Fowler, Fellow of St. John's College, Cambridge, is stated by Gough, the Antiquary, to have been Rector of Newbury.
1663 Joseph Sayer, B.D., Prebendary of Salisbury.
1675 John Hinton, M.A., Prebendary of Sarum, also Rector of Shaw-cum-Donnington.
1720 Joseph Acres, M.A.
1746 Thomas Penrose, M.A.
1769 Richard Davies, M.A., also Rector of Highclere.
1797 James Roe, M.A., also Perpetual Curate of Dorchester, Oxon.
1838 Hibbert Binney, D.C.L.
1857 James Leslie Randall, M.A., Fellow of New College, Rural Dean of the Deanery of Newbury, Archdeacon of Buckingham, Canon of Christ Church. Suffragan Bishop of Reading, 1889, when he received the degree of D.D. The great Church work done in Newbury during the time Canon Randall held the living, and in which he took such an active and decided part, was remarkable.
1878 Edward Imber Gardiner, M.A., Rural Dean.
1901 Lionel Robert Majendie, M.A.

ST. MARY'S CHURCH, SPEENHAMLAND.

There is not, probably, a parochial church throughout the country which can claim a higher antiquity than the mother church of Speen, so beautifully situated at the foot of the Roman station of Spinæ. We have the evidence of Ordericus Vitalis, the Norman-English chronicler, that a church existed at Speen previous to 1079, and there are some grounds for the belief that a Christian place of worship was erected on this spot by the British converts while the Romans governed here, to which we have already referred in our history of that parish.

Speenhamland was absolutely detached from the ancient parish of Speen, and formed into a separate ecclesiastical district in 1884. The Church of St. Mary was erected in the years 1829–31, from the designs of Mr. Savage, architect, at a cost of about £7,000, and consecrated 16th August, 1831.

The Rev. J. A. D. Meakin was appointed Perpetual Curate in 1834, and when Speenhamland was constituted a parish he became its first Vicar. Mr. Meakin was vicar for nearly forty years, and exercised a most beneficial interest in the parish. He died in 1873, and his successor was the Rev. Nicholas T. Garry, who resigned in 1875. He was followed by the Rev. J G. Gibbs, who resigned in 1889, when the present Vicar (the Rev. C. L. Jeayes), was appointed by the Bishop of Oxford, patron of the living.

The church contains sittings for about 800 persons, and has since been enlarged by the addition of a new chancel, designed by the late G. E. Street, R.A. The other part of the building has also been re-modelled.

THE CHURCH OF ST. JOHN THE EVANGELIST.

The ecclesiastical parish of St. John the Evangelist was founded in 1859 out of portions of Newbury and Greenham. The church was consecrated in 1860, was erected by Miss Hubbard in memory of her parents, from the designs of Mr. Butterfield, architect, and is of brick in the Decorated style. It consists of chancel, nave, north aisle, and a bell-turret with two bells. The church is entirely free and will seat 500 persons.

The first Vicar of the parish was the Rev. Thomas Hubbard, who had to resign through ill-health. He was succeeded by the Rev. H. T. Morgan, who resigned in 1884, and was followed by the Rev. T. Barlow Poole, whose career of usefulness was cut short by almost sudden death. The Rev. R. Dunn took up the work in 1888, and succeeded in making St. John's a model of activity and energy. Mr. Dunn resigned in 1900, when the Rev. R. Wickham Legg was appointed by the Bishop of Oxford, who is also patron of this parish.

CHAPTER XVIII.

NONCONFORMITY IN NEWBURY.

Benjamin Woodbridge — The Presbyterian Church — The Congregational or Independent Church — The Baptist Church—The Wesleyan Church—The Primitive Methodist Church — The Roman Catholic Chapel — The Quakers' Meeting House.

The earliest authentic information as to the position and numerical importance of the various congregations of dissentients from the Established Church in Newbury is from an official return made by order of Seth Ward, Bishop of Sarum, who, ostensibly, was determined to carry out, not only the provisions of the Act of Uniformity in all their rigour, but also the various penal Acts, passed just before and during his episcopate against various bodies of Noncomformists. Whilst, however, we are forced to admit the Bishop's iron rule as regarded a portion of what after all was his flock, we are assured that neither in the episcopal documents, nor in those of the city of Salisbury is there a syllable of evidence to support such a charge.

This report gives a list of conventicles of the different sects, their numbers, quality, and abettors in the various parishes within the County of Berks in the year 1669.* But before dealing with this return we must point out that Noncomformity in Berks as elsewhere, is of a much earlier date than the days of the Commonwealth, which is the period generally attributed to its origin.

There can be no doubt that not only in the Parliament of Elizabeth, but also among her chief advisers, there existed a strong bias on behalf of the Puritan party, and there were evident reasons for such a feeling. There was, first of all, particularly in Newbury, the remembrance of the Marian Martyrs, which caused a strong re-action in the minds of very many against all that favoured Romanism, with which these severities were identified. Then there was much to cause sympathy with foreign Protestants; this was especially kindled in Elizabeth's Court by the first news of the massacre of St. Bartholomew in 1572, the very year, as Keble remarks, "when the English Puritans began to be more open and combined in ther efforts, first in Parliament for legalizing the discipline, and afterwards in their several districts, for establishing it without law." Hence a strong wave of Puritanism swept over the whole country.

* Lambeth MS. 639, p. 237. There were in the county at this time 128 Churches and 37 Episcopal Chapels, making a total of 165.

Moreover, many of the Dutch refugees,

"They whom the rod of Alra bruised,"

who came to Newbury from the low countries, brought with their craft as cloth-workers, their dislike of episcopacy as they found it here; and, possibly, to these Dutchmen, Walloons, Flemings, and others from the Continent, we owe much of the Nonconformity which for several centuries has been so identified with the town. Still it must be confessed that not in a few cases dissent gained a more permanent footing from the work of those ministers who, ejected from their own benefices, settled in the place of their former ministrations or in some of the neighbouring villages.

Newbury at this period abounded with spiritual teachers, and notwithstanding the Act of Uniformity and consequent ejectment of the Independent and Presbyterian ministers, the Nonconformists, it is evident, considerably strengthened their position, and some of the most active amongst them got into trouble occasionally for creating disturbances with the governing authorities. The town was divided into two violent factions, and the various political and religious dissensions at this time engendered a vast amount of bitter party feeling. We have an instance of this recorded in 1664, when an endeavour was made to elect a party Churchwarden at a vestry meeting held in the Parish Church, which is thus described by a contemporary chronicler* :—"The Mayor and other authorities of the town being met in the church on Easter Tuesday for the purpose of chusing Churchwardens for the year ensuing, they were assaulted by a rude and confus'd multitude of all sorts of Phanatics, some crying one thing and some another, and though sundry times excluded by the Constables that were call'd to keep the peace, yet they still broke in with fresh clamours, crying out that it did not belong to the Mayor and Company, but the whole parish to make choice. In fine they came to this at last, that they did not matter who was chosen, so one *Pocock*,† render'd odious to the Rabble for his Loyalty to the King, were not one. But Sir Thomas Dolman coming immediately to Town upon notice of the disorder, with a Guard of Soldiers, seiz'd the chief sticklers, who were afterwards proceeded against according to their demerits." From a report of the proceedings taken against the chief rioters, rival orators addressed the meeting at the same time, and the language made use of appears to have been of a most profane character, ending in uproar, fighting, and consequent desecration of the sacred edifice. The result of this stormy meeting was the prosecution of the chief offenders at the Assizes held at Abingdon, at the instance of Lord Lovelace, the Lord Lieutenant of the county.

From the return to which we have alluded at the commencement of this chapter, it appears there were at that time (1669), three Presbyterian congregations in Newbury, one Anabaptists'

* Heath's Chronicle, 1676, p. 525.

† Richard Pocock, Attorney in the town, and Mayor, 1673.

meeting-house, and the Quakers' meeting. The Presbyterian meetings were at Mr. Bond's house, morning and evening on Sundays, where was the principal gathering, and lesser assemblies met at the house of Elizabeth Castle and Hester Gearing on week days. The Quakers met at Robert Wilson's house, and the Baptists' meeting was at Mr. Thomas Merriman's.

These meetings, we are told, "consist of such as have been engaged (as generally the whole towne was) in y[e] late warre ag[t] the King, And their abbettors are such as have been ejected upon y[e] Act for Regulating Corporacions." The ordinary attendance on Sundays at the several Presbyterian meetings was 600—a large number considering that the population of the town was then stated to be only 3,000. The numbers of the Quakers and Anabaptists are given as "very small." In answer to the question as to the "quality" of the congregations, it is stated that they are all ordinary persons, except the wife of Mr. Roger Knight, of Greenham Manor. The "chief abettors" are returned as Mr. Linch, Ditton, Collins, Bond, Cooke, Houghton, Sealy, junr.; Brice, Hunt, Foster, and others.

Benjamin Woodbridge.

Of the "Teachers" or ministers, Mr. Benjamin Woodbridge is the foremost, the others are given as Mr. Blackaler,* Mr. Thomas Blake, of Chute, Mr. Burgess, of Marborough,† Mr. Henry Dent, of Ramsbury,‡ and Mr. James of Staines.§ The career of Woodbridge was a very chequered and troubled one. He became a Commoner at Magdalen Hall, Oxford, in 1638, but on the breaking out of the Civil War he went with a party of his co-religionists to America, and took his degree of M.A. at Harvard University, where his name appears first on the list. He, subsequently, returned to England, and was admitted to the same degree at Oxford in 1648. Shortly after, he was appointed Rector of Newbury, and was ultimately ejected for refusing to comply with the Act of Uniformity.|| In 1665, he took Holy Orders, with the intention of conforming to the Church of England, but not

---

* MR. BLACKALER was assistant to the Rev. Benjamin Woodbridge. He was at Woodland, co. Devon, before he came to Newbury, and at the time of the revolution he took the pastoral care of a congregation at Shobrooke, near Crediton, and continued there until his death, 20th February, 1702.

† DANIEL BURGESS, of Magdalen College, Oxford. Incumbent of Collingbourn, Wilts. Ejected by the Bartholomew Act. Retired to Marlborough, and preached there till he was silenced by the Corporation Act. He died in June, 1679.

‡ HENRY DENT, M.A., of Wadham College, Oxford. Assistant or Curate to Mr. Wild, Vicar of Ramsbury. Refused to comply with the provisions of the Uniformity Act in 1662, and kept a school at Ramsbury. He died in March, 1695-6, aged 68.

§ JOHN JAMES, M.A., of St. Alban's Hall. Rector of East Ilsley. Ejected, 1662. Settled at Staines, and remained there nine years. He died in London, July, 1694.

|| The number of ministers in Berks who were ejected for Nonconformity was only 29, not more than the number of parochial clergy who were deprived of their livings on various grounds under the Commonwealth.

meeting with the preferment he expected, and being reproached for his change of principles, he returned to his former opinions, and preached in various Nonconformist places of worship in Newbury and elsewhere. Upon passing of the Five Mile Act, Woodbridge preached every Sunday at a chapel at Highclere where the attendance is returned as being "from 40 to 1,000 persons, of which only 18 are of the parish, the rest are strangers," from which we may infer that he attracted many of his old flock who were deprived of his services at Newbury. About this time, Woodbridge had a sharp and bitter controversy with a noted and fearless Quaker, named Oliver Sansom, of Boxford, from which it appears Woodbridge had stigmatised the members of the Society as "Infidels," and "but little, if any, more of Christians than the Turks."

After the Proclamation for Toleration, or Indulgence of Religion, was issued, in 1671, Woodbridge was permitted to preach openly in the Market Place at Newbury. Upon the discovery of what is known as the "Presbyterian Plot," in June, 1683, Woodbridge was at "hide and seek" for fear of imprisonment, and took sanctuary at the house of Sir Robert Pye, at Faringdon, and afterwards retired to Englefield,* where he died the following year, 1st November, 1684, and according to his own desire was buried in Newbury Church, the scene of his early labours.

In the interval between the date of the last return we have quoted and the next report of the state of the diocese as regards conventicles, it is evident Bishop Ward, who equally disliked the Quaker, the Protestant Nonconformist, and the Popish recusant, laboured hard to put in force the rigorous laws against Nonconformists, "not out of enmity to the dissenters' persons," says his biographer,* "but because he believed that if the growth of them were not timely repressed, it would either cause a necessity for a standing army to preserve the peace, or a general toleration, which would end in Popery, whither all things had an apparent tendency." It is, therefore, not surprising to find from "An account of Popish

---

* In his nuncupative Will, dated 20th October, 1684, Woodbridge is described as "late of Englefield," without any other description. The witnesses were Elizabeth Aleyn, Mary Aleyn, and Mariabella Charles. Dame Elizabeth Aleyn, wife of Sir Thomas Aleyn, Knight and Baronet, was buried at Englefield, 8th October, 1685. This lady appears to have been the wife of Sir Thomas Aleyn, Lord Mayor of London at the Restoration, and created a Baronet by Charles II., 14th June, 1660. He married Elizabeth Birch, daughter of a vintner of London, and died in 1690. The house occupied by Sir Thomas Aleyn, or Allen, is described by Rocque, in 1761, as the residence of Sir Henry Inglefield, and as being situated lower down in the village than the chief house, which belonged to the Marquis of Winchester. It was removed many years since. We may add that Elizabeth, daughter of Sir Thomas Aleyn, or Allen, married Sir Douce Fuller, of Chamberhouse, in the parish of Thatcham, who died in 1673.

* The biography of Bishop Seth Ward by Dr. Walter Pope, is printed by Cassan in his "History of the Bishops of Sarum," III, 31.

Recusants, Obstinate Separatists, and Conformists," taken in 1679, that the total number of declared Nonconformists in Newbury was returned at 40 only, out of a population of 3,000, and there was not, apparently, a Roman Catholic in the town. This diminution of the Nonconformists is observable throughout the country.

THE PRESBYTERIAN CHURCH.

But after the passing of the Toleration Act, 24th May, 1689, places of worship for the use of the Presbyterian and Independent Nonconformists sprang up all over the kingdom, of which the old Presbyterian meeting-house at Newbury is a very fair type. It is the oldest Nonconformist place of worship in the town, and although its time-worn walls of red brick, mellowed by the sun of many summers, are now for the most part enveloped in a coat of modern plaster, it still bears an air of antique respectability that bespeaks its former importance.

Previous to the erection of this chapel in 1697, the Presbyterian and Independent congregations used the same place of worship, which is referred to in an entry in the minutes of the Court of Quarter Sessions, 1696, as the dwelling-house of Mr. William Taylor in Bartholomew Street; and at the Sessions held in August the same year it is certified that the newly erected building on the east side of Northbrook Street, on a plot of ground late in the possession of William Lynch, is appointed for an assembly of persons for religious worship.

Mr. Taylor was a son of the Rev. William Taylor, Vicar of St. Stephen's, Coleman Street, and officiated at the chapel till his death in 1700. He was succeeded by James Peirce, one of the most distinguished and learned of the Nonconformist divines, and the pastoral office has since been filled by many men of literary ability and distinction.

Formerly the Presbyterian attendants at the chapel numbered some of the principal and most influential of the inhabitants, but the places of those who were removed by death or otherwise were not supplied by others, and those who now remain are comparatively few in number, and for the most part entertain Unitarian views.

The following is a complete list of ministers who have successively held the pastorate since Mr. Woodbridge :—

1686–1694	John Southwell
1696–1700	William Taylor
1700–1713	James Peirce
1713–1726	Joseph Standen
1727–1753	Daniel Mace
1753–1762	John Blackburn
1762–1804	David James
1804–1827	John Kitcat
1827–1828	Peter Thomas Davies
1829–1849	William Wilson
1849 (part)	Goodwyn Barnby
1849–1852	Cornwallis F. Smith
1852–1854	Robert Harris
1855–1856	Frederick Rowland Young
1857–1862	Richard Shelley
1863–1865	William Robinson
1865–1895	Charles Matthews
1896–1898	James McLuckie Connell
1899 (part)	Thomas Johnson Stewart
1899–	Ephriam Turland

THE CONGREGATIONAL OR INDEPENDENT CHURCH.

The Congregationalists of Newbury, more usually known in former years as Independents, are accustomed to date the origin of their church from the year of the Act of Uniformity, 1662. Strictly speaking, the actual formation of the Independent Church in this town did not take place until the year 1686, or even later; but the adherents of the Rev. Benjamin Woodbridge, already referred to, who with him separated from the Church of England in 1662, were, undoubtedly the progenitors of the Independent Church which has continuously existed down to the present day. After the death of Mr. Woodbridge in 1684, the Independent and Presbyterian bodies formed distinct congregations, although meeting in the same building and having a common fund, while holding separate communion services. The minister of the Independents was the Rev. Benjamin Merriman, who was ordained to the office in 1686, when only 24 years of age. He was a native of Newbury, and had studied at Oxford. It is stated that the joint services had for some time been held in a house at Stroud Green, and were, in 1687, transferred to a barn upon the site of the present Congregational Church, which was rented and adapted for the purpose. A few years afterwards differences arose between the two congregations, and in 1697 a rupture took place, the Presbyterians withdrawing and erecting what was known as the Upper Meeting House, near the river. The Independent Church in 1710 is stated to have consisted of 172 members, the number of "attendants" being much larger. The meeting-house, which during 21 years had been hired of a Dr. Cook, was found to be very inconvenient, chiefly through its liability to be under water through floods, and in 1716—the year after the accession of the House of Hanover, when religious liberty became more assured—the congregation made an effort to purchase the site and build a new place of worship. The old records, still extant, contain curious particulars of the steps taken for the erection of this building, including the contract for the bricks, the purchase of Christiania deals, conveyed by water from London, the measurements and plans of the building, the dealing with the workmen. and the collection of subscriptions, the amount raised being £458. Mr. Merriman died in 1734, after a ministry of nearly fifty years.* Early in the following century,

* Attached to the east wall of the present Congregational Church near the entrance, stands a memorial stone commemorative of the Rev. Benjamin Merriman, with the following inscription :—

Here lyeth the remains of the REV MR. BENJAMIN MERRIMAN,
Of this town, Born A D 1662.
He finished his studies in the University of Oxford A D. 1680;
Was ordained to the ministerial office among Protestant Dissentors,
In this Church, A D 1680;
Continued the beloved Pastor thereof until his death, October 22nd, 1734.
His bereaved church
Here bewails the loss of his eminent abilities,
Piety, and unwearied labours,

On the opposite side is a memorial to Mr. Sedgley, a succeeding minister of this congregation, steps were again taken with a view to building a new chapel, the old meeting-house, which had been in use for over a hundred years, showing signs of decay. Largely through the efforts of the Rev. William Dryland, a new and commodious place of worship was erected at a cost of over £3,000. It was opened in October, 1822, the preachers for the day being the Rev. John Cooke, of Maidenhead, and the Rev. William Jay, of Bath, two celebrated ministers of the denomination. The building was substantially the same as now existing, but in 1872 an apse was built at the west end to accommodate the organ, and other alterations were made, further improvements being also carried out at a later date. A spacious hall for the accommodation of the Sunday school, now known as the "Lecture Hall," was in 1857 built in proximity to the church.

The following is a list of the ministers who have successively held the pastorate of this church :—

1686–1734	Benjamin Merriman	1840–1860	Henry March
1734–1748	S. Phillips	1861–1864	Benjamin Beddow
1748–1754	W. Sedgley	1865–1866	Benjamin Waugh
1755–1771	Thomas Reader	1867–1884	Edward W. Shalders, B.A.
1771–1784	James Marchant	1885–1887	Edward Hamilton
1784–1823	John Winter	1889–1895	John Pate
1807–1838	William Dryland (co-pastor)	1896-	Edward H. Titchmarsh, M.A
1838–1839	Spedding Curwen		

THE BAPTIST CHURCH.

No precise date can be given for the founding of the first Baptist Church in Newbury, but it appears from a circular letter from the ministers of the Particular Baptist churches assembled here in 1826, that this church or society was in existence at least twenty years before the Act of Uniformity was passed in 1662. A traditionary statement exists to the effect that the first minister and the then members of the Baptists suffered much during the Civil Wars from the soldiery of King Charles's army when quartered in the town.

The earliest reliable information we have been able to obtain relating to this denomination, formerly called Anabaptists, and distinguished from other Nonconformist bodies by their opinions respecting the proper *subjects*, and the *mode* of baptism, is in an official return made in 1669 to Seth Ward, Bishop of Salisbury, of all Conventicles in his diocese, to which allusion has previously been made. From this interesting record we learn that at this time there was but one congregation of Anabaptists in Newbury, and they are returned as "very small." Their place of meeting is given at the house of Thomas Merriman, the *locale* of which is not recorded.

Though precise and definite statements may not be forthcoming, yet there can be little doubt that the first regular minister of the

Baptists, after they had so far developed as to form themselves into a separate society, was a Mr. James, who preached to a few followers in an upper room at the house of Mr. Jabez Hill, grocer, in Northbrook Street, which is still standing. This exceptionally interesting old structure, with its beautifully fashioned pilasters, dentil cornice, gables, and ornamented barge boards, denoting the abode of a citizen of some rank and consequence, is one of the most picturesque relics of "Old Newbury;" and as supporting the ancient tradition, it may be mentioned that until recently a hook was to be seen fixed to a beam in one of the rooms, from which the lantern is said to have been suspended when the members of this early Baptist congregation foregathered here for the exercise of their religious worship.*

The activity and exertions of Mr. James, who is said to have been the minister for upwards of sixty years, are recorded as having been very successful, and a worthy example to other churches—the difficulties which beset him proving rather a help than a hindrance in his work. And here we may remark that never, as it would appear to us, could there have been a more golden opportunity for the national Church than when at the Restoration she regained her old ascendency. But in the event we know how little she used the bright opportunity that was given her. The deplorable indifference

* This house bears on the pendants of the gables the date of "1669," the same year that the return of Conventicles was made to Bishop Seth Ward, and it must have been some time after this that the Baptist meetings were held here. It is now the property of Mr. George Wintle.

everywhere prevailed at this "glacial period" of the church, and the records of the diocese of Salisbury to which Newbury then belonged, are enough to show how low church feeling had fallen, and to this in a great measure we owe the rise of the numerous religious societies which were then rapidly spreading over the nation.

This state of things and the zeal and example of Mr. James must have contributed not a little to stimulate the progress of the Baptist denomination in Newbury, and about the year 1700 the members of the community had become too numerous for the upper room in Northbrook Street, and a new meeting-house in Northcroft Lane was built, which was licensed as a place used for religious worship at the Borough Quarter Sessions, October, 1702.

For some time after the death of Mr. James, who was buried near the pulpit in the then new meeting-house, there was no resident or stated preacher, and it was not until the year 1716 that a Mr. Jefferies came from Taunton to Newbury and took over the pastorate. He remained here five years, and at the time of his departure the members of the congregation numbered about 100, and the society was in a most flourishing condition, but the minister who succeeded, whose name is not recorded, is said to have been "rather wide" in his religious sentiments, and to have led many of the more influential members of the Baptist church from Trinitarianism through Arminianism to Unitarianism, and these are reputed on their change of sentiment to have joined the Presbyterians. It was at this time—about the year 1730—that many of the original English Presbyterian Churches became Unitarian, and it is far more probable that this was the denomination to which so many of the Newbury Baptist community seceded.

A Mr. Britton succeeded as pastor about this period, but remained only a short time, and was followed by a Mr. Taylor, who officiated as minister for a few years, removing to London, and afterwards embraced Presbyterianism. After a succession of ministers, of whom nothing especially deserving notice is recorded, in September, 1780, the Rev. James Bicheno was appointed to preside over the congregation, and from this period we may date the steady and onward progress of the Baptist community in Newbury. Mr. Bicheno had a very remarkable career. He was born at Over in Cambridgeshire, and when about fifteen or sixteen years of age went to London to seek employment. Here he fell into the hands of a notorious crimp named Crispe, the person alluded to in Goldsmith's "Vicar of Wakefield" as having decoyed the Vicar's son, and was shipped off to Virginia. On his arrival he was sold as a slave to a gentleman who was a member of the State Council, and in this situation he remained for upwards of two years, when having found means of informing his friends of his lot, they redeemed him. Returning to England, he qualified for the Baptist ministry, and after having been twelve months at Falmouth, came to Newbury. Mr. Bicheno, who was the author of several historical and other works, remained in the pastorate at Newbury until 1807, a period of twenty-seven years, when he retired. During part of this time he kept a school for boys at what is now known as "Greenham House," near the railway station. He died in 1831 at the house now attached to the Roman Catholic Mission Church in the London Road.

Mr. Bicheno was succeeded in 1807 by Mr. Perry, who remained as minister until his death in 1812. The following year Mr. Welsh entered on his duties as pastor, and remained until 1839, when he was succeeded by Mr. Pike, who held the ministry until 1844, when Mr. Trotman entered upon the duties. He resigned in 1845, when the Rev. James Drew—an earnest-minded man who left behind him not a few evidences of his care for those over whom he had been called upon to rule—was appointed. It was during his ministry—in 1859—that the new Baptist Church in Northbrook Street was built at a cost of some £3,000, and enabled the congregation to "come out of Egypt"—this being the name given to that part of the town where the old meeting-house stands, and take possession of their new and more commodious place of worship. Mr. Drew who worthily sustained the duties of Pastor for nineteen years, was succeeded by the Rev. T. M. Roberts, B.A., in 1864. and the name of each subsequent minister is recorded in the following list :—

1770–1780	Francis Lewis
1780–1807	James Bicheno
1807–1812	John Perry
1813–1839	J. Welsh
1839–1844	J. B. Pyke
1844–1845	D. Trotman
1845–1864	Joseph Drew
1864–1866	T. M. Roberts
1867–1873	John E. Cracknell
1873–1875	Frederick Robertson
1875–1884	George Howe
1884–1888	Elias George
1889–	George J. Knight

THE WESLEYAN CHURCH.

It was in the West of England and in many parts of the diocese of Salisbury that the trumpet of John Wesley was sounded at a time of spiritual deadness in the Church of England. Fixing his head-quarters at Kingswood, near Bristol, Wesley was wont to visit periodically many of the chief towns of the diocese, including Newbury. At the first, often repulsed by the authorities and ill-treated by the people, he persevered in what he believed in his heart to be the special mission committed to him by God. And for the long space of well nigh forty years he carried on his work, thousands at times listening to his open-air addresses, the worst weather, the worst roads being no hindrance to his faithfully performing all his engagements.*

* Charles Wesley, the poet, probably did as much as his elder brother John, the orator, for the permanence of Methodism. The magnetism of personal influence passes away, but the burning life of that wondrous psalomody, sung Sunday after Sunday by congregations full of faith, is imperishable.

The introduction of Wesleyan Methodism into Newbury was by means of lay agency, with occasional visits from Wesley and the "travelling preachers" as they were then commonly called, from Oxford. The Oxford Circuit at that time extended from Witney to Salisbury, and included the intermediate towns and villages.

Wesley's Journals contain frequent reference to his visits to Newbury, and on the first occasion he held his own service at the Parish Church. Shortly after that visit he writes:—"As I rode through Newbury my horse fell and threw me in deep mire; I was not hurt, but after cleaning myself a little, proceeded on my journey." On another occasion, 5th March, 1770, he says:—"I came to Newbury where I had been much importuned to preach, but where? the Dissenters would not permit me to preach in their meeting-houses; some were then desirous to hire the old play-house, but the good Mayor would not suffer it to be so profaned, so I made use of a workshop—a large commodious place—but it would by no means contain the congregation; all that could hear behaved well, and I was in hopes God would have a people in this place also."

In the year 1795, chiefly because of the long journeys the preachers had to take on horseback with their saddle-bags packed with religious books, a change was made—Newbury was separated from the Oxford Circuit and became the head of the Newbury Circuit, which comprised many of the neighbouring villages. In the same year two ministers were for the first time appointed by the Wesleyan Conference to be stationed at Newbury, who, as was then the custom, remained for one year only. This arrangement continued until 1819; since that date the changes have been less frequent, the ministers for the most part remaining three years.

The place first used as a Methodist Chapel was in Wharf Road, with an entrance from Cheap Street, No. 43. Part of the old building still remains as a chapel, and has been used as such by several denominations, while a portion of it has been converted into cottages. This old chapel having become too small to accommodate the increasing congregations, a new and substantial building was erected in 1804, accommodating 350 or 400 people, on a site which is now partly occupied by the Technical Institute, in Northbrook Street.

A more commodious building being required, the present chapel was erected in 1838, providing seating accommodation for some 650 persons. In 1898 a restoration scheme was carried out at a cost of £2,000.

Wesley Hall, adjoining the church, was erected in 1887, at a cost of more than £2,000, and is, happily, free from debt. It is a well-arranged and handsome structure, capable of accommodating several hundred persons. It is sometimes used for public meetings, but chiefly as Sunday Schools.

The Wesleyan Day School, established 50 years ago, stands high in public estimation.

THE PRIMITIVE METHODIST CHURCH.

The local records of Primitive Methodism date back no further than 1829, in the summer of which year two preachers were commissioned to visit the villages lying in the vale of the White Horse and the northern part of Berkshire. Their names were John Ride and Thomas Russell. For several months little or no success was apparent, indeed so dark was the prospect and determined the opposition, that it was almost thought the Mission must be abandoned. It is upon record that in this extremity the two men spent the afternoon of the 9th February, 1830, in prayer in a wood near Ashdown, and it is related that Russell eventually rose from his knees, and in an ecstacy exclaimed, "Yonder country's ours!" raising his hand and pointing in the direction of Newbury. From that time the tide turned, and in the revival which followed many villages were visited, but Newbury was not reached until some time later. It was in July of the year 1831 that a Miss Smith (who afterwards became Mrs. Russell) conducted a camp meeting at Little Hungerford, and a man from Newbury who was present was so impressed that he invited the preacher to come and hold services in his cottage at Shaw Hill. These services were afterwards transferred to another cottage at Stroud Green, after which Ebenezer Chapel in Back Lane, where John Wesley is stated to have preached on the occasion of one of his visits to Newbury, became the "local habitation" of the infant cause. A forward movement was made by the purchase, in 1837, of Union Chapel for £650. It was depreciatingly said that the whole of the members at this time could have been accommodated in its somewhat capacious pulpit, but the number of adherents so much increased that the gallery from the old Wesleyan Chapel was bought and erected in the newly-acquired sanctuary. It was in 1887 that this building, hidden away at the end of Union Court, was exchanged for a new site on the west side of Bartholomew Street, where a Gothic structure and school buildings had been erected at a cost of £5,000. By June 1895 the debt had been liquidated, impressive Thanksgiving Services being held on the occasion. In 1897 the church was renovated, new galleries introduced, an organ was erected, and the school buildings enlarged at a cost of £800. Appended is a list of the Superintendent Ministers of the Newbury Circuit:—

1832–37	John Ride
1837–39	George Price
1839–41	Henry Sharman
1841–50	Thomas Ford
1850–52	Samuel Wilshaw
1852–55	Henry Heys
1855–60	Samuel Turner
1860–63	Thomas Cummin
1863–66	George Obern
1866–67	George Price
1867–70	George Wallis
1870–73	Daniel Harding
1873–78	Edward Alford
1878–80	Levi Norris
1880–84	Daniel Harding
1884–87	Joseph Harding
1887–90	Charles Jupe
1890–93	John H. Green
1893–98	John T. Stead
1898–1905	John Neville

THE ROMAN CATHOLIC CHURCH.

The Roman Catholic Church (St. Joseph's) Speenhamland, was erected in 1864, and opened for worship on St. Anselm's Day, 21st April, the same year. There had previously been a mission here, and schools in connection with the Training College at Woolhampton.

PRIESTS IN CHARGE.

1852	V. Rev. Canon Dambrine	1898	Rev. Henry L. P. Kelly
1855	Rev. Robert St. Hodgson	1903	V. Rev. John Scannell, D.D.
1864	Rev. Ferdinand E. Riley		

THE QUAKERS' MEETING-HOUSE.

The Quakers or Society of Friends—a sect once numerous in Newbury, but now for some time extinct—had a small meeting-house near Bartholomew Street, which has long since been converted to other purposes.

Their burial ground, enclosed by a high brick wall on which part of the quaint coping bricks remain, is in an obscure position in front of some old cottages approached from Market Street by a narrow passage called "Mayor's Lane." Disused and uncared for, the place might readily be passed unnoticed did we not know it was the last resting place of the nameless and forgotten dead, many of whom were once amongst Newbury's foremost citizens, and, therefore, fraught with melancholy interest.

CHAPTER XIX.

THE ENDOWED CHARITIES.

There are few objects of benevolence more substantially valuable and important in the town of Newbury than the numerous charitable institutions which were in former days founded by liberal minded citizens, distinguished by their munificence and public spirit, in order to do good to their own age and to posterity, to their own country, and to their fellow men.

Honourable indeed were the motives which induced these worthies of the past, possessed with a sense of benefits received and gratitude due to the Author of their exceptional good fortune, to found and endow the large number of Almshouses which yet remain as permanent memorials of their charity and kindness. These were the men who, not ashamed of their humble origin, felt an honest pride that by dint of their own exertions they were enabled to assist that class from which they sprung, and smooth the path of their less fortunate brethren when it was toward evening and the day was far spent.

In this light our public charities have been a prolific source of good, and may be regarded as among the most beautiful and excellent emanations of that local patriotism which is one of the noblest ornaments of our land. Nevertheless, we are fain to admit that these institutions have at times been subject to most corrupt influences, and brought into the town many undeserving persons who have been a burden to the community.

The oldest and by far the most interesting of the many charities of Newbury is that of the

HOSPITAL OF ST. BARTHOLOMEW.

This hospital is said to have been founded by King John, and on the clock turret of the old almshouses belonging to this foundation, known from time out of mind as "King John's Court," is this inscription :—

Hospital of St. Bartholomew.
Founded by King John { 1200. 1215.
This building erected - 1698.

The Charter Rolls from the second to the fifth of King John are lost, and amongst them, probably, the foundation charter of this institution.

Gervase of Canterbury bears witness to the early existence of this hospital in his *Mappa Mundi*, compiled soon after the year 1200, for he includes in his list of Berkshire hospitals that of "Sancti Bartholomaei Neuberi." In 1215, King John granted to the already existing Hospital the right to hold a two days' fair for its support, as shown by the Close Rolls (17 John, m. 28), and this fair is still held yearly, being opened by the Town Clerk or his deputy with all the quaint formalities of former times; and the profits paid to the almspeople of King's John's Court. There is also collected at the time of the fair a penny from each licensed house in the town, the origin of which is not known. The earliest deeds extant refer to houses or lands in or near Newbury by various inhabitants of the place, dated respectively 1256–1261, 1302, and 1302–11, which singularly enough were purchased in London many years ago.

From various other documents we learn that the Master, Warden, Prior, or Rector as he is indifferently termed, was appointed by the commonalty of the town, and that in the year 1267 the Abbot and Convent of Préaux, in Normandy, patrons of the Parish Church, gave to the Hospital the right of free burial in the Cemetery of the said Hospital. One of the deeds dated in 1365 was executed "in the chapel of our house," and another, in 1477, is described as *sealed with the seal of the Hospital.**

---

* The Seal, which is of brass, is a circular one, 1 9-16 inch in diameter, bearing for device two conjoined crosses between four small stars, with the legend :—

*** DOMUS · ST. BARTHOLOMEI · IN NEWBURY.**

In 1545 the suppression of the Hospital was contemplated under the Act 37 Hen. VIII. c. 4, by which all Colleges, Chantries, and Hospitals were to be dissolved and granted to the Crown, an Act which became inoperative owing to Henry's death. Edward VI. passed a fresh Act of dissolution (1 Edw. VI. c. 14), but in this Hospitals were not included, and in the returns made under the second Act, St. Bartholomew's is not mentioned. It was, however, subsequently seized under the latter Act as a chantry, and leased by the Crown to one Thomas Burche, of Kensington, a yeoman of the King's chamber. The commonalty of the town resented such a high-handed action, and resisted the lessee's entry. Hence a lawsuit in the Court of Augmentations, in the records of which are contained many interesting facts about this establishment. The first witness is one of the almsmen of Donnington. He "sayth that of his owne knowledge he hath knowen this lxxxv yeres a howse of relygon in Newberye called the Pryore of St Bartylmewes;" that it was "an howse or pryore of chanons," and that they "wore whyte apparell after the order of chanons, that is to sey, an onder garment of whyte clothe, and over that a whyte rochett, and above the sam a vyolette gown sleveles.'" The chapel, part of which is still standing, is described as "a proper lyttell churche," and the chancel "seated with carolles," moveable stalls used by the brethren for daily private study and meditation. The Chapter House and the High Altar are also mentioned, and that on the sides of the chancel were two aisles "made between the bodye of the church, and the said chauncell with altars in them." According to Deloney, Jack of Newbury was married in this chapel to the widow of his wealthy master.*

The result of the case above mentioned does not appear, and a similar action was raised in Elizabeth's time, when the Queen's Attorney-General claimed the lands from the lessee, as being Chantry or Priory lands, and as such escheats to the Crown. From another deposition we gather that the Grammar School was engrafted on the Hospital Foundation in the reign of Edward VI.

Under the Statute of Charitable Uses, and by decree of the Commissioners, dated 1599, the property and management of the Hospital were handed over to the Corporation of Newbury, and this settlement remained in force till the passing of the Municipal Corporations' Act in 1835.

---

* The present chapel represents only a part of the ancient building which originally extended much further eastward, and on the south side. The chancel was cut off from the existing portion of the nave for the purpose of widening the roadway, which was carried out under the Newbury and Speenhamland Improvement Act of 6 Geo. IV., 1825. The old Winchester and Southampton road at this point was very narrow, and a portion of the ancient burial ground of St. Bartholomew's Hospital was also appointed for the roadway, when a great many human skeletons were removed and re-buried in the garden of the Litten.

In consequence of certain irregularities the Charity became involved in Chancery proceedings, and from 1836 to 1841 the Trustees endeavoured to get the case out of court, but without success. However, in 1846 this was accomplished, and new Grammar School buildings erected on the site of the ancient priory.

The Hospital and Grammar School Foundation are now administered under a scheme of 1883, and an Amending Scheme of 1899. New school buildings have been erected on another site at a cost of some £10,000, but the Almshouses have not been interfered with.

The Governing Body of the Grammar School Foundation consists of eleven Representative Governors, to be appointed—

Two by the Council of the Borough of Newbury;
Six by the Trustees of the Municipal Charities;
Two by the Berkshire County Council;
One by the Hebdomadal Council of the University of Oxford, and
Five Co-öptative Governors.

PRIORS OR MASTERS OF THE HOSPITAL.

	Henry, the Chaplain
1330	Richard Sersett
1340	John le Spene
1364	Thomas Eme
1365	Thomas Albon
1377	Stephen Clansfield
1389	Henry Halley
1447	John Bradstrawe
1451	William Mayhew, of Tackley, Oxfordshire
1459	Richard Aldeworth, of Sparkford, Somerset
1466	Thomas la Bale
1496	William Bray
1507	Edmund Worthington
1508	Robert Strete
1522	John Magott
1540	Roger Bromolde*

MASTERS OF THE GRAMMAR SCHOOL.

(prior to) 1559	William Ford, B.C.L.
(prior to) 1634	Rev. Thomas Parker
(prior to) 1662	John Woodbridge and Samuel Sprint
(prior to) 1686	Rev. Richard Simeon
(prior to) 1692	Rev. Benjamin Tassell, M.A.
1722	Rev. Philip Morgan
1764	Rev. Thomas Penrose, M.A. (Rector of Newbury)
1766	Rev. Thomas Best
1814-46	School discontinued
1849	Henry Newport, M.A.
1852	Rev. William Cole, M.A.
1867	Rev. Alfred Steane, B.A.
1876	Rev. J. Atkins, LL.B.
1902	E. Sharwood Smith, M.A.

THE CONSOLIDATED MUNICIPAL CHARITIES.

These Charities consist of that part which is applicable for purposes not educational of St. Bartholomew's Hospital and School Foundation, Kendrick's Morning Prayer Charity, St. Mary's Almshouse, and Raymond's Almshouse, in accordance with a

* Roger Bromolde, the last Prior of St. Bartholomew's, was a native of Newbury. He was born in 1506, became a Scholar and Fellow (1525-43) of Winchester College, B.D., and Canon of Lincoln.

Scheme sealed by Order of the Board of Charity Commissioners, 22nd June, 1900.*

The Trustees consist of fourteen persons, being the Rector for the time being of the Parish of Newbury, four Representative Trustees appointed by the Town Council of the Borough of Newbury, and nine Co-öptative Trustees.

St. Bartholomew's Almshouse Charity. There are twenty-four Almshouses attached to this endowment for an equal number of men and women.

Raymond's. Twenty-two Almshouses for an equal number of men and women, natives of the ancient parish of Newbury.

St. Mary's. Almshouses for six women, and out-pensions for women.

Kendrick's Morning Prayer Fund. The proceeds of this charity less expenses, are paid to the Rector of Newbury for the time being.

OTHER CHARITABLE FOUNDATIONS.

Church and Child's Almshouses.

The Church Almshouses comprise six for men and six for women. Child's Almshouses are for three men. These Charities and their respective endowments are now consolidated and administered subject to a scheme, dated 11th December, 1883, under the title of "Newbury Church and Almshouse Charities."

The Trustees are ten in number, of whom three are ex-officio Trustees, and seven non-official Trustees.

Cowslade's Charity.

Cowslade's gift to the Borough had an educational purpose. The donor by a deed dated 1715, provided for the education and clothing of ten poor boys, natives of Newbury, to be chosen by the Corporation. He also gave land for the yearly payment of £30 to the Organist of Newbury Church, and £5 towards the expenses of the Mayor's inaugural feast.

This Charity is now administered by the Rector of Newbury and three other Trustees.

Kimber's Almshouses.

These Almshouses stand near the Market Place, and were founded in 1795 by Alderman Kimber, and amply endowed, for six poor men and the like number of women, "natives of the town and not papists." Also for the education of a certain number of boys. Mr. Kimber directed that the officiating minister of Newbury should

---

* In 1857, a sectarian dispute arose in connection with the election of fresh Trustees, the number having become much reduced. Of the sixteen nominees whose names were submitted to the Charity Commissioners, ten were Nonconformists, and the Episcopal party in the town made application to the Court of Chancery for leave to strike out these names in favour of an equal number of Churchmen. Lord Hatherly, however, decided that the Charities were in all respects undenominational, and the request was refused.

preach a sermon the Sunday next after his decease, and on that day in every year, for which he shall receive one guinea yearly, "at which sermon should attend every person receiving the charity, unless prevented by illness, and in default thereof shall forfeit one week's pay."

The Trustees are six in number, the Rector being one ex-officio.

Coxedd and Pearce's Charity.

Thomas Pearce, a clothier, in 1671 endowed two Almshouses at West Mills for two decayed weavers, such as were free of the Weavers' Company, "of honest life and good manners."

Francis Coxedd, in 1690, gave two messuages at West Mills, "then in possession of his two poor almsmen," and also devised certain lands upon trust that the profits be applied first for the maintenance of the almsmen and repairs, and the surplus applied in the education of such poor children in the town as his Trustees should think fit. A scheme for the combined administration of these charities was ordered in 1883 by the Charity Commissioners. There are four almshouses for men in the Enbourn Road, and out-pensions are granted.

Hunt's Charity.

The donor of this Charity was one Thomas Hunt, who died in 1729. There are almshouses at West Mills for three poor widows, who receive a small sum of money weekly, clothing, and fuel.

Robinson and Crosse's Charity.

Benjamin Robinson, in 1754, built three almshouses for poor weavers in Northcroft Lane.

Crosse's Charity dispenses gifts of clothing to poor women.

Dangerfield's Charity.

Richard Dangerfield, by Will dated 20th January, 1826, bequeathed the sum of £400, the interest whereof to be divided yearly between the twelve almspeople in the Church Almshouses, and the interest of £300 between the almspeople in Coxedd and Pearce's Almshouses. He also made bequests to certain societies of Protestant dissenters in Newbury.

The Charity of John and Frances West.

The inhabitants of Newbury are entitled to a two-fifth part of the endowment of John and Frances West, applicable to children taken from the parish of Newbury, or from any parish or place contiguous thereto, on the foundation of Christ's Hospital. The proportion to be as near as may be of two boys to one girl, on the result of a competitive examination of boys and girls respectively, and being children of persons who have resided for two years in the borough of Newbury, or in default, in any parish or place contiguous thereto, some preference being given to West's Kin.

Pensions of £5 yearly are also enjoyed by a large number of persons in the town and neighbourhood.

Kendrick's Charity.

The founder, John Kendrick, who in his Will, dated 20th December, 1624, describes himself as a Citizen and Draper of the City of London, that is a member of the Drapers' Company, gave £4,000 to the Corporation of Newbury for the purchase of a house and garden "to set the poor on work," and with the residue of the same sum to make a common stock for the employment of the poor in the said house, according to the discretion of the said body corporate from time to time for ever. The Loan Charity consisted of £500 to be lent by the Corporation in sums of £50, to industrious clothiers for three years (or failing clothiers, to other tradesmen), free of interest. The third gift, £250, was to be laid out in land of the clear value of £10 a year "to maintain divine service to be said in the parish church by the parson or his curate every morning of the week at six of the clock for ever." This early hour has been altered to nine o'clock.

The bequest to set poor people to work, and the loan charities, are now incorporated with St. Bartholomew's Hospital and Grammar School Foundation, and now administered under that scheme; and the Morning Prayer fund is under the management of the Trustees of the Consolidated Charities.

CHAPTER XX.

POPULAR PASTIMES.

HUNTING.

As a hunting centre in a provincial district, the town of Newbury has, perhaps, few equals, the facilities afforded to sportsmen being very great, no fewer than five packs of foxhounds being within reach, of which three, namely, the Craven, South Berks, and Vine, have meets close at hand every week; while the Tedworth and Old Berkshire are frequently attainable in the best country of each.

The Craven Country.

The Craven is a very large country, comprising about twenty-five square miles, and it is surrounded on all sides by famous hunting grounds—as due west it is bounded by the Duke of Beaufort's country, north-west by the V.W.H., due north by the Old Berkshire, due south by the Vine and the Tedworth, and on the east side there is the South Berks.

It comprises almost every style of country, as there are some heavy woodlands, a vale with a good deal of water to cross, some sticky ploughs, and some of the most beautiful downs, whereon a holding scent is certain, and where hounds can race away from the best of horses. It is, in fact, a difficult country for hounds, requiring a lot of power and good noses, but as a somewhat rough and thoroughly sporting district, however, it can compare favourably with many others, and a very good class of hunter is required to admit a man riding straight to hounds across it.

SOME OF THE BEST MEETS.

The Vale proper runs from Hungerford to Kingsclere (between the Hampshire Hills and the Great Western Railway), the best meets in its somewhat limited area being Hampstead Mill, the "Olive Branch," Inkpen, Anvilles, Stype, East and West Woodhay, Crookham, Sydmonton Common, the "Harrow," Kingsclere; and a few more. Though not difficult it is trappy, and the fences out of the deep pastures require a clever horse and resolute rider to negotiate. Found in the Vale it frequently happens that foxes make for the hills that run from Ham Ashley to Sydmonton, and after a detour come back to the low country to die; so a nag must be able to gallop as well as jump on such occasions.

From each of the fixtures alluded to above many a good run has been had, also from the Coombe gorses and Three Legged Cross and Bull's Copse, on the brow of the hills, from which hounds often run into the Tedworth country.* Coombe Wood, a neutral covert, is usually full of stout greyhound foxes. On the east side a dip into the Vine country, near Fro Park and Sandford Wood, is generally attended with good sport, and though the coverts are somewhat thick and plentiful, the foxes are usually game and abundant.

Crookham Common with its chain of hangings is generally full of foxes, whilst the large woodlands round about Highclere, Penwood, etc., are usually sure finds. Perhaps the best bit of vale is that round Hampstead Mill, and runs from here to Red Hill; Enbourn and the Woodhays generally result. Inkpen, again, with coverts, round Inglewood, Wallingtons, and Titcombe always give a chance of a bit of jumping; while from the big woodlands of Stype many a good run has been chronicled across the Shalbourn vale into Bedwin Brails or across the river to Cakewood.

Immediately on the other side of Newbury a different district entirely prevails, the Benham coverts being the leading feature to

* One of the longest and straightest runs in the Craven Country was in Mr. Warde's time. The fox was found in a small covert called Waterman's, between Hampstead Park and Woodhay. Soon after he was found he was viewed by several persons, and was observed to have only half a brush. The hills at this time were covered with snow and were obscured by a thick fog. The scent, however, seemed to become better than ever, and leaving Coombe wood and village to the right, and over the open country towards Faccombe, the hounds went straight through Faccombe woods, running from north to south, by Netherton Bottom and up the opposite hill, still pointing southward. Crossing the Ibthorp water-meadows, he bore a little to the left under Pill Hill, but declined that, and running from scent to view was pulled down in the open near Tangley Clumps, and lo! when he was taken in hand he had the same half brush that had been observed at Waterman's two hours-and-a-half before.

the west of the town; the chief meets being Benham Park for Scots Wood, Hunt's Green, Elcot, the Kennels, Ash House, Kintbury for Hay Croft, Snelsmore Common, Winterbourne, etc. Round here we have few fences, large woods, and principally plough to ride over. Taking a wide cast towards the north we have a very similar country, if not so extensively wooded, Hermitage, Chieveley, Peasemore, Beedon, and Catmore Borders, the Ilsley Downs, Chaddleworth, Farnborough, and Woolley Park, present, with Lockinge brick kiln plenty of nice coverts, either wood or gorse, amongst the former Welford Wood.

The "Swan" at Shefford is the centre of a sporting plough district again, while a wide sweep to the east and north-east brings us to Ashdown Park—the extreme meet in this direction—and Lambourn, the great centre of coursing men in the past, when the far-famed Ashdown coursing meeting brought them together at a time when it had few equals in England. Baydon, Aldbourne, and Ramsbury Park, with Marridge Hill, brings us round to Mildenhall Borders, near Marlborough, and back to Chilton, Cakewood, and Hungerford Park—a worthy link to complete the chain, as it was from here Colonel Willes hunted the country for many years most successfully.

Masters of the Craven.

It is difficult to determine when the first regularly appointed pack of foxhounds was established in this neighbourhood, but the foundation of the Craven must have been laid by Fulwar, 4th Lord Craven, who hunted the country from the year 1739 up to the time of his death in 1764, and the Hunt was continued by the two next successors in the title. William, 6th Lord Craven, died in 1791, but the hounds apparently continued in the hands of the Craven family until taken over by Mr. Charles Dundas in 1804.

The following is a list of the Masters of the Pack :—

1739–1764	Fulwar, 4th Lord Craven
1764–1769	William, 5th Lord Craven
1769–1791	William, 6th Lord Craven
1804–1813	Charles Dundas, M.P.
1813–1814	Mr. Anthony Bacon and Colonel Stead
1814–1825	Mr. John Warde
1825–1828	Mr. Horlock
1828–1829	Mr. William Wyndham
1829–1833	Mr. Thomas Smith, "Hambledon Tom"
1833–1851	Mr. F. R. O. Villebois
1851–1856	Mr. Head Pottinger Best
1856–1857	The country was divided, Lord Portsmouth hunted the south side, Mr. George Montague the east, Mr. James Morrell the north, Major Willes and Capt. H. R. Seymour the west side
1857–1858	Mr. J. Cooke
1858–1862	Mr. Theobald Theobald
1862–1865	Mr. J. L. Coxe
1865–1871	Mr. G. S. Willes
1871–1872	Mr. J. L. Francklin
1872–1877	Mr. R. Harcourt Capper
1877–1879	Mr. G. S. Willes and Mr. W. H. Dunn
1879–1880	Mr. R. E. Wemyss
1880–1886	Sir R. F. Sutton, Bart.
1886–1892	Lt.-Col. G. C. Ricardo
1892–1895	Mr. E. R. Portal
1895–1900	Mr. W. H. Dunn
1900–1901	Mr. Lionel Barlow
1901–1904	Mr. W. H. Dunn. On Mr. Dunn's retirement in 1904, Mr. Pennefather accepted the Mastership, but resigned on account of ill-health
1905–	Mr. Peter Ormrod

FISH AND FISHING.

The right of Free Fishery in the river Kennet and all other waters within the borough boundaries has always been considered a valuable appanage to the manor, and in all the early charters and grants the " fisheries and waters appertaining thereto " are strictly reserved to the manorial lords.

In a Survey of the Manor of Newbury taken the 6th year of King James I. (1608), by virtue of a royal commission, the jurors report that

" The Lord the King hath the Free Fishery of the River Kenet and of all the water there."

It should here be observed that in legal parlance " Free Fishery " is an exclusive right of fishing in water running over the soil of other men's land, and as part of the corporate rights passed to the Mayor, Aldermen, and Burgesses of Newbury on the purchase of the manor from King Charles the First in 1627.* There are frequent references in the borough records relating to proceedings connected with breaches of the regulations concerning the Borough waters, and infringements of the rights of the burgesses. The Court Leet Journals also contain many presentments as regards illegal fishing, exposing fish for sale out of season, and other bye-laws, showing the jealous care with which the municipal body preserved their chartered rights and privileges in former days.

THE KENNET.

"The Kennet swift for silver eels renowned," rises near the village of East Kennet on the eastern side of Wiltshire, in the vicinity of Avebury, and after a sequestered course of about four miles, reaches Marlborough, it then enters the ancient village of Ramsbury, where trout are numerous, thence visits and refreshes Hungerford, where it begins to lose its character of trout stream proper, grayling and coarse fish now becoming numerous, and taking in that of a miniature Thames, proceeding thence to Newbury, where it becomes navigable, and continues its way to Reading.

After a course of some forty miles it joins the Thames between Caversham Bridge and Sonning—a function which is thus alluded to by Drayton in his quaint poem, the " Poly-Olbion " :—

" At Reading once arrived, clear *Kennet* overtakes
Her lord, the stately *Thames*, which that great flood again
With many signes of joy doth kindly entertain."

That this river has been famed for its trout from a very early period we have some evidence preserved in a MS.,† evidently of the time of Edward II. (1307–1327), which besides various tables relating

* The grant is thus expressed :—" All and singular the Waters, Water-courses, Fishponds, Fisheries, Fishings, of whatever kind, being part or parcel of the Town Manor, lands, tenements, and hereditaments and all other the premises appendant or incumbent thereto."

† Bodl. Lib. MS. Douce, No. 96.

to the ecclesiastical and civil divisions of the country, and other similar matters, contains a list of over 100 towns with the affix of what they were celebrated for, wherein Newbury is referred to as celebrated for its "Troyte" or Trout, which is so used in mediæval documents. The reputation of the Kennet trout also finds expression in Coxe's *Magna Britannia* (1720), where it is mentioned under Newbury that "among other things this Town is famous for its Trouts." Again, in Rocque's "Description of Berks," 1761, it is said "The Kennet abounds with fish, particularly trouts of surprising bigness."

But besides trout this river produces perch, tench, roach, chub, and dace. Barbel are supposed not to be found west of Newbury. Dr. Mavor, writing about the year 1805, mentions in his *Agricultural Report of Berks*, that Mr. Toomer, of Newbury, was famous for the very large size of the trout in his stews. Not many years previously he had three fish which weighed 15 lbs. each. Two of these were fattened by himself, the other was of that weight when taken out of the Kennet. At another time he had a trout which grew till it attained the weight of 17lbs., which was given to the then Lord Craven, who sent it as a present to King George III. Dr. Mavor also refers to having dined at Newbury with a party, who the day before had feasted on trout weighing 15½lbs., and which had been fed in a stew for about eighteen months. It measured 31 inches in length, 20¼ ins. in circumference, and the length of its jowl was 9⅛ inches. A trout of 1½ lbs. has in the course of a year grown in a stew to the weight of 8½ lbs. Instances have, indeed, been known of trout growing a pound per week.

At the Fisheries' Exhibition in 1883, trout from the Kennet at Newbury were shown, scaling 8¾ lbs. and 9¾ lbs., also four from the same river at Hampstead Marshall weighing, respectively, 20 lbs.* (taken by Lord Craven), two 10½ lbs., and one 8 lbs. Chub, 5 lbs. Perch, 2½ lbs. Barbel, 14 lbs. Dace, ¾ lb. Pike, 25 lbs., 27¼ lbs. (caught at Aldermaston), 16 lb. 20 lbs. (Speen Moors), 17¾ lbs., 19¼ lbs. (Kennet at Newbury).

Near Newbury the fishing is of much the same character as that obtained in the Thames. The trout only rise well to a fly in the May-fly and grannom seasons.

The greater part of the Kennet fishing is in private hands, but permission to fish is sometimes given. From Newbury to some distance below Aldermaston—a favourite spot—the Angling Association rent the whole of the Kennet and Avon Canal from the Great Western Railway, but some of the riparian owners question the power of the Company to let the fishing to the Association, and order anglers off.

A fair number of *Pike* are caught, but the fishing cannot be considered good. The pike, which has been poetically described as the "Wolf of Fish," affords much diversion to the angler. It is a

* This fish was not taken out of the river Kennet, but fattened in a stew.

great disturber of trout and other fish, owing to its size and strength. The best baits are gudgeons or dace. Pike are to be allured by a large bait, but one of moderate size is more certain to take them. The *Perch*, which is one of the most beautiful of our fresh-water fish and best eating, run unusually large, but owing to sewage pollution killing their spawn in former years, they are not numerous, although increasing. Some extraordinary catches of *Tench* have been made in the canal at Aldermaston, but this fish feeds in a fickle manner, and a success is not likely without elaborate ground-baiting. The fishing in the town of Newbury, where the river and the canal are incorporated, is principally for *roach*, *perch*, *chub*, and particularly *dace*, which like most other fish ran large when the sewage flowed into the river. There is good fly-fishing for large *trout* in private waters of the river Kennet during the May-fly and grannom fishing season, but at other times these Kennet fish in the neighbourhood of Newbury rise badly, the best fly water being above Hungerford. Fly-fishing for *dace* is often very good about half-a-mile below the town, near the "White House," also from Bull's Lock downward for a quarter-of-a-mile—a stretch of river and canal combined. *Chub* are very plentiful about the town, round the bridge at Bull's Lock, and generally below the various locks on the canal. Their favourite place is under trees and bushes. The *Roach* in the Kennet near the town are large and well-fed, but somewhat shy. *Bream* and *Carp* are also said to be in the river, but are rarely caught by anglers. A large extent of the canal is rarely visited by fishermen, though it is to be feared it is occasionally by poachers, and probably, well worth careful exploration. The best months for coarse fishing are September and October.

THE LAMBOURN.

The *Lambourn* is also a good fishing stream for trout. This river, which has its source amongst the chalk hills above the town of that name, runs on the left of the road between Lambourn and Newbury, and after passing through Bockhampton, Eastbury, East Garston, Great and Little Shefford, Weston, Welford, Easton, Westbrook, Boxford, Bagnor, Donnington, and Shaw, falls into the Kennet one mile below Newbury, at Ham Bridge.

This well-known trout stream is thus commemorated by the local poet Sylvester :—

"Little Lamb's Bourne
All summer long (while all thy sisters shrink)
Men of thy tears a million daily drink
Beside thy waste, which then in haste doth run
To wash the feet of Chaucer's Donnington :
But (while the rest are full unto the top)
All winter long then never show'st a drop,
Nor send'st a doit of needless subsidy
To cram the Kennet's wanton treasury
Before her stores be spent and springs be stayed :
Then, then alone, thou lend'st a liberal aid."

The Lambourn down to about East Garston is one of the intermittent streams, running low and sometimes altogther ceasing between Michaelmas and February (see Sylvester's lines above.) This intermittence has been explained by some writers on the principle of the supposition that in the hills from whence this small river issues there is a large cavity with a duct in the form of a syphon or crane, which begins to act as soon as the winter rains and snows filled the cavity, and ceases about the time of their return for want of a sufficient supply. But this variation is to be attributed to the water percolating the chalk and accumulating on clay gault, or other impervious strata below it. Thus the streams do not begin to run till the accumulated water has reached a certain height. In some exceptionally dry seasons the plane of saturation is reduced even below the level of the ordinary wells, and great dearth of water ensues. This river this winter (1903-4), has been higher than has been known for years, owing to the excessive rainfall, and has flooded many parts of the district through which it runs.

Trout are very numerous in the Lambourn, and are caught mostly between ½ lb. and 1½ lb.; a two pounder is an exceedingly large fish. The whole stream is now in private hands, the waters formerly rented by the Newbury Angling Association are now leased to the London Piscatorial Society. Much of this stream is eminently suited for fishing with the dry or floating-fly, but many fish are killed by wet fly-fishers, particularly about and after dusk in the hot months, very large "sedges," "governors," or "coachmen" being used.

Soon after the opening of the season there is usually a fair rise of *grannom* in the lower reaches, but a good sized artificial *March brown*,* ribbed with gold twist (a fly practically unknown to the fish) fished wet, often kills better than the *grannom*. This fly is infinitely more numerous in the Kennet than its tributaries. A small *red spinner* is a killing fly all through the season, and chalk stream flies generally will kill, though *duns* in their various forms are usually scarce. *Alders* are plentiful in June and July, and often will kill. A small *red palmer* with gold twist is a killing fly after May. The *Wickham fancy* is a favourite fly with local anglers.

About 5th June the rise of the May fly commences, which has a very brief terrestrial existence, lasting from a few days to three weeks. It sheds its eggs over the water, then dies—the eggs sink to the bottom and then hatch out in the course of a few weeks For how long the larvæ lasts under water is not known, probably two

* The *great red spinner* is the *image*, as it called, of the *March brown*—that is the March brown skin comes off, leaving the spinner. The *smaller red spinner* is the image of the *blue dun*, or *blue winged olive*. Duns are not numerous in the Lambourn as compared with other chalk streams such as the Test and the Itchen. Much interesting technical information on Fly-fishing in local streams will be found in "An Angler's Year," by Charles S. Patterson, M.B., M.R.C.S., F.Z.S., London; W. H. Russell & Co., 5a Paternoster Row.

years, and after various changes, one June morning they come paddling up to the surface; their back opens, and out steps a dull green May-fly. After a day or so this fly opens its back, and out steps a grey May-fly. Then comes the honeymoon, the shedding of eggs and oblivion. It is a popular error that the May-fly and the caddis worm are one and the same insect in different stages of development. The caddis are all connected with the sedge flies, which have flat wings along their backs when closed.

June is the best time to fish the Lambourn for trout. In July and August the fishing is principally in the evening, as above described. September is usually a good month unless the water is low. As regards the greater part of the water, *wading* is neither necessary or desirable.

Local anglers think they can distinguish Kennet from Lambourn trout, but they are identically the same species, only varying a little owing to local conditions and differences in feeding. There is also another point we may mention. Trout, as is well-known, change the colour of their backs as a rule, owing to the colour of the bottom over which they swim—an assimilation which may be regarded as protective colouration.

Of late years *grayling* have become common in the Lambourn near Newbury. These fish are also to be found in the Kennet. They rise badly and are difficult to catch with the fly here. Formerly the Lambourn and its tributaries, particularly at Donnington, was famous for its *crayfish*, which were caught in large quantities, in nets baited with animal matter, or dead fish. But some years ago an epidemic set in among the crayfish, which killed them fast, not only in England but on the Continent. This was the case in all the local streams, except the En, and the late Mr. Bunbury, of Marlston, who had a great partiality to the crayfish, which was considered a luxury "in season"—the season being the autumn of the year—had the river "Pang," which runs through the estate he then held, restocked, but, as he told the writer, they crawled out of the water one after another, and died on the banks. It was thought the water might have become polluted, but there were no grounds for supposing this to have been the case.

THE EN-BOURN.

This stream, which is called the "Aleburn" in boundaries mentioned in charters as early as the tenth century, rises near Inkpen, and soon becomes the boundary between this county and Hampshire, flowing through the Wash and Newtown, where for a considerable distance it forms the southern boundary of the parish and borough of Newbury. After leaving Sandleford it pursues an easterly direction till it has passed a place called Hyde End, it then takes a more northerly course, and dividing Berks, runs obliquely between Brimpton and Wasing, and falls into the Kennet near Aldermaston, after running about seventeen miles.

At Hyde End Mill (now disused), a Fishery has been established for producing trout by artificial means, and too much praise cannot be given to the intelligence and zeal which has been brought to bear in the art of Fish Culture at this Berkshire Trout Farm. This interesting enterprise appears so far to have been very successful, and when we recently visited the fishery there were some 40,000 trout eggs in the hatching boxes. When arrived at a sufficient stage of growth, the troutlets are transported in specially prepared cans to populate streams in far distant places. It must be a peculiar pleasure to those who make Fish-Culture a study and business to know that their well-directed efforts have done much to increase the stock of fresh-water fish in our English rivers, and that no sister art can compete with it in the extreme facility of its adoption, and the unqualified utility of its purpose. The trout raised at Brimpton are the Rainbow, the Brown, and the Loch Leven.

There are a fair number of trout in the En-bourn, but they are usually small, and seldom scale more than from 1½ to 2lbs. Pike from 8 to 10lbs. have been taken in the deep water at Abel Bridge and Shalford. Perch also are taken, and run from 2½lbs. upwards. Eels are getting somewhat scarce in this river. It is singular that while the Crayfish have disappeared from many local streams they have never been known to be absent from the En-bourn, and the same may be said of the river Loddon.

Such is a brief sketch of a method which, if universally adopted, would, in the opinion of many men of science, increase the stock of fish in the rivers of England a thousand-fold, and would of necessity tend to place within the reach of many, who, from its high price and scarcity are at present unable to obtain it, an article of food admitting of endless variety, and suitable to every palate.

CHAPTER XXI.

THE NEIGHBOURHOOD OF NEWBURY.

To give a list of the several places of interest within a comparatively short distance of Newbury would be to fill a volume instead of a few pages. On all sides the naturalist, the botanist, and the geologist will find treasure-troves in any of the surrounding hills and valleys, while the antiquarian traveller will discern much to interest him in all directions.

The following brief reference to a few of the principal places of attraction in the neighbourhood which can easily be reached by walk or drive from Newbury, may indicate, if but feebly, its surpassing interest to the traveller and tourist.

Shaw House. About a mile north-east from Newbury is Shaw House, which is by far the most stately Elizabethan mansion in the county, and in historic interest it yields to few in the South of England.

The house is built of red brick, with dressings of white stone; and its massive square-headed windows have mullions and cornices of the same materials.

Like many other houses erected during the reign of "Gloriana," its ground plan is a letter E, the porch projecting slightly less than the wings. It was completed in 1581, by Thomas Dolman, a member of an old Yorkshire family, who had settled in Newbury as a clothier, and having made a fortune, retired here to live as a country gentleman. The proceeding was distasteful to the townsmen, and they expressed their feelings in the lines :—

> Lord have mercy upon us, miserable sinners,
> Thomas Dolman has built a new house
> And has turned away all his spinners.

To which he retorted with the haughty couplet :—

> *Edentulus vescentium dentibus invidet*
> *Et oculos caprearum talpa contemnit.*
> (The toothless man envieth the teeth of those that eat,
> And the mole despises the eyes of the roes),

which may still be read over the portico; and above the lintel of the principal doorway is the appropriate motto in Greek :—

> Let no envious person enter here,

which is sad evidence that the eyes and teeth of his assailants were all too sharp for his repose.

It is said Dolman put up these verses as spells against those particular ill-wishers whose peculiar malice he dreaded.

The hall is lofty and well proportioned, and, like the rest of the rooms, panelled in oak, but the woodwork has unfortunately been painted over in a light colour. It is adorned with a bust of Charles I., and with a series of family portraits, including Chief Justice Eyre. The walls are hung with armour of the Civil War period, and of an earlier date, including a bridle and pair of gloves said to have been used by Cromwell, and in a corner is a heap of cannon balls and shells, the silent relics of the siege. In the windows are two large cavalry kettledrums, which may or may not be as old as the battle of Newbury.

We ascend up a handsome staircase of polished oak to the drawing-room, which occupies the south-east angle of the first floor. Here the panelling retains its original dark colour, and is of oak like that above described. In the wainscot of a bay window in this room there is let into the wall a brass plate perforated at a spot where a bullet may be seen. This is said to have been the work of a Roundhead soldier, who aimed at the King when he was dressing himself at the window, on the morning of the second battle of Newbury. The plate bears on it the following inscription :—

Tantis nequidquam ereptus periclis
Rex Carolus Primus
Hanc juxta fenestram
Instante obsidione
Scloppopetræ ictu tantum non
Trajectus fuit
Die Octob: XXVII., MDCXLIV.

On the opposite panel is an engraved portrait of the King "as he sate in the pretended High Court of Justice, Anno 1648, from the original at Oxford." In this room are portraits of one of the Parliamentary generals, by Vandyke; Emma, Lady Hamilton, by Romney; a lady, by Sir Joshua Reynolds; also several specimens of the pencil of Smith, "the English Canaletto." With other interesting relics in a cabinet is a snuff box which once belonged to Charles I., and which bears his portrait on the lid.

At the foot of the staircase are portraits of the leaders of the Royal and Parliamentary armies, a fac-simile of the death warrant of the King, and a "pass" signed by Fairfax.

Several generations of the Dolmans lie buried in Shaw Church, including the gallant defender of his house, who, at the Restoration, in 1660, was rewarded by a well-earned knighthood. There is a handsome monument in the church to the son of the hero of the fight, another Thomas Dolman, who was knighted by Queen Anne at Shaw House in 1703, on her return from Bath. The state bedstead on which the Queen slept is still preserved in the house, with tapestry hangings worked with scenes from Ovid's *Metamorphoses.*

The walls of Shaw House are such as would be well suited to stand a siege and an assault, being in many places six feet thick, as shown by the deep recesses in the windows. The roof, too, is a very forest of timber; and the foundations of the house and cellars look as if they had been constructed by their founder to last for all time. The cellars are very numerous and spacious, and mostly fitted with aumbries or cupboards. Some of them are dark, and are said to have been used as dungeons, but this may be dismissed as absurd, along with the local tradition which states that there was, and is, an underground communication to Donnington Castle, more than a mile distant.

The Rampart or Terrace. The question as to whether the terrace or rampart on the east side of the house existed previous to its being garrisoned for the King or was thrown up during the Civil War, has never been satisfactorily solved. But the view that it was raised for the defence of the mansion received some confirmation in an obituary notice of Sir Joseph Andrews, printed in the "Gentleman's Magazine" for January, 1801, in which it was said, "It was secured in the Civil War with a high bank or rampart of earth, still remaining, and served the King for a temporary retreat." This memoir was probably written by Henry James Pye, the poet laureate, of Faringdon, who was well versed in Civil War lore, and wrote some lines on the death of his friend Andrews. Never once were these defences penetrated, although assailed again and again. The house itself escaped injury, owing to the protection of the hillock on which now stands the water-tower, the surrounding trees and the ramparts. This elevated work has all the appearance of being of military construction, being sloped on both sides, that is larger at bottom than at the top of the parapet, and evidently the rampart was constructed to resist the enemy's great shot, and cover the house. There was formerly a very wide and deep ditch on the open side, and it followed, therefore, that as the earth of which the rampart is composed was taken from the outside of it, by so doing a fosse would be made at the same time. The present strip of garden on this side is of modern date. Sir Thomas Dolman was only 23 years old at the time of the battle, and it is traditionally reported that "King and Law" having been the password agreed on the night before the battle, Dolman announced it to the army by the command and in the presence of the King himself. In the heat of the fight next day young Dolman forgot the password, when the King himself lustily gave it to the youth, with directions to shout it to the soldiers, which caused such a volley of shot to be poured in upon the Parliament men as routed them from the garden, and turned the battle on this side in the King's favour. Hence the old stanzas:—

The charge-word lost, the young Squire, Tom Dolman, promptly shouted,
Our "*King and Law*," a hundred times Huzzah! Huzzah!
As the Royalists thus inspired, the Roundheads soon were routed,
From his father's stately house and avenues, and surrounding fields, at Shaw.

Then to the shrewd and zealous patriot galloping near his side,
His most sacred Majesty in great admiration loudly cried—
"Sir" Thomas Dolman henceforth let your *Armorial Motto* be,
The field-word which, thro' you, hath gained me Newberie.

The motto is still retained by the Dolman family.*

On the lawn in front of the house are four iron guns, said to have been left by the Parliamentarians as memorials, but there is nothing in the character of these guns to directly establish their connection with the Civil War.

The Woods of Shaw. Although lacking the bold and impressive features of some localities famous for exceptional picturesqueness, this side of the town possesses peculiar beauties to which full justice has never been done. There is in truth no more beautiful portion of rural England than that displayed in various parts of the umbrageous neighbourhood of Shaw, which, as its name implies, *shaw*—a wood or *shady* place, proves that the greater portion of this parish consisted only of woodland or wild moor. The Shaw woods were, in comparatively recent years, far more extensive than is indicated by the principal portion remaining, known as "High Woods," on the summit of a considerable eminence which commands an extended and diversified prospect. On the crest of the hill, at what was formerly the southern extremity of these woods, there was a deep and wide sunk ditch described in the evidence of Parliamentary officers taken in connection with the famous quarrel between the Earl of Manchester and Cromwell as the "High-Dyke." It was from this spot that Manchester's troops descended from the plateau in making their attack on Shaw House.

* The Shaw Estate was purchased of the representatives of the Dolman family by James Brydges, ninth Lord Chandos, and afterwards by creation the first Duke of Chandos. The Duke is said to have been the hero of the following story:—He was one day travelling from Bath, and slept at an Inn at Marlborough. In the morning, when he was about to leave, he was struck with compassion on seeing the ostler of the inn, named Jefferies, beat his wife in a most cruel manner. The Duke interfered, and touched by the sufferings of the beautiful girl, offered the husband a sum of money to part with her. This was gleefully accepted, and eventually the Duke placed her in his carriage and carried her away to Cannons, where he placed her under the care of the Vicar of Stanmore and his wife. The Duke at the time was a married man, but the Duchess died and so did the man who maltreated his wife, and then the Duke married the fair lady he had rescued. It was, however, his son Henry, the second Duke, to whom this dramatic story should be applied. The heroine's name was Anne Jefferies, and it transpired that she was a Newbury woman, the daughter of John Wells of this town. She was married to the Duke at Mr. Keith's proprietary chapel, Mayfair, on Christmas Day, 1744, he being then a widower, and the ostler Jefferies was dead. It has been stated that the incident of the ostler and his wife took place at the Pelican Inn, Speenhamland, but there does not appear to be the least foundation for transferring the scene of the occurrence from Marlborough. It may be added that the Duchess filled her new position to admiration, and died beloved and deeply lamented at Keynsham Abbey, Somerset, 12th August, 1759, and her remains were removed to Stanmore, and interred at Whitchurch (Stanmore Parva), on the following 30th August.

A fair visitant to this district, inspired by historical retrospection and incidental meditation, thus sweetly sings the charms of

THE WOODS OF SHAW.

Red of Autumn, slowly stealing over leaves that once were green,
Often have I watched thy beauty mingle with a golden sheen.
But I knew not thy perfection—miss'd thy glory till I saw
Fairest colours of October lightly touch the woods of Shaw.
Like a voice in farewell greeting, just as sweetly, and as sad,
So the trees are singing softly and the earth is crimson clad.
Smiling land of field and furrow! smiling land of vale and hill!
With no sound of harsh contention, though the great world rolleth still,
Rolleth still, but ah! so distant, that the creaking wheels of Time,
Only sound like echoes, beating to the cadence of a rhyme.
All the cares of life may vanish—gloom and sorrow have no lease
In the sunny land that lieth, here beneath the hand of peace.
Yet upon the hill-side standing, now my heart is filled with awe.
Why? oh why? ye cannot tell me; distant, tender woods of Shaw!
But I ask the heath-clad common, where the golden bracken falls,
And the silent river creeping down beside its willow walls.
"War!" the dying bracken whispers; "War!" the river murmurs low,
And the valley in its slumber, only utters "Long ago."
Long ago, some mighty conflict shook a nation,—shook a throne,
And the mighty oaks of England trembled as if tempest-blown.
Woods of Shaw! your Autumn leafage is not redder than the stain
That was once on yonder hill-side, 'mid the dying and the slain.
When the lurid smoke of combat from the death-field roll'd away.
Where the brave who fought and perish'd, lifeless on the greensward lay.
Lost amid the wild confusion, here perchance a soldier died,
Far away from friend and comrade!—broken weapons by his side.
Did a maiden bend in pity, did she shed a secret tear
O'er a fallen Roundhead trooper, or a silent Cavalier?
All unknowing, I may wander, over ground that once was blest
By the hallow'd dew of kindness, or a soldier's pray'r for rest.
Is it not that shouts of foemen mingle oft with sounds that weep,
And the drums that beat to battle, lull some warrior-souls to sleep?
Here the thunder of men's hatred smote the silence of a day,
But at mid-night, lo! one army in the moonlight stole away!
So a gentle deed may blossom by the rushing tide of strife,
And the sunshine chase each shadow from the battlefield of life.
Peace that follows in the war-wake, with her snowy crest unfurl'd,
Can subdue the sullen breakers in the ocean of the world.
Vision of the Past! release me from thy firm but slender hold,
Let some voices chide my singing,—I have left so much untold.
But the red of Autumn, burning, like that day that sinks to rest
Flinging ruddy light to eastward,—eastward from the glowing west,
Checks the effort of remembrance by the soothing pow'r it brings,
That my senses fain would slumber, 'neath the lullaby it sings.
Lest me roam the land, unheeded, with my idle thoughts my own,
Nature gives her best to pilgrims when they seek her all alone.
I would listen to the music that is whisper'd by the breeze,
And return the gentle friendship of the loyal-hearted trees.
I would watch the sunlight flicker; I would hear the wild rooks caw
As they wheel above the branches of the lovely woods of Shaw.

MAY ROWLAND.

Donnington Castle. One mile north of Newbury, high on a hill, and screened by venerable trees, rise the picturesque remains of the far-famed and romantic Donnington Castle. The castle, once occupied the whole of the crest of the hill, but is now limited to an ivy-mantled gateway (a fine specimen of early Perpendicular), with a tall tower on either side, and a piece of wall adjoining.

As the siege of the Castle and its successful defence against the Parliamentary forces, in 1644, is a matter of history already alluded to, we will pass on to

Donnington Castle House. Formerly the official residence of the Constables or Keepers of the Castle—an office once of some distinction.

The present house, which stands on the site of its ancient predecessor, was re-built after the siege of the castle and largely from its materials. It was occupied by successive generations of the Packers, owners of the castle and manor, and in later years by a Mr. Bagnall, whose daughter married Sir William Scott, afterwards Lord Stowell. The only surviving child of this union became the wife of the Prime Minister, Lord Sidmouth. Subsequently it was in the occupation of Dr. Byrne, Bishop of Meath, of Colonel Stead, Master of the "Craven," and Mr. Anthony Bacon resided here for some years. He was also a Master of the Craven Pack, as was Mr. Head Pottinger Best, and Colonel Ricardo later occupants of the house, and is now the residence of Mrs. Sperling, sister to the Squire of Aldermaston.

At the foot of the hill from which the old castle frowns down on Newbury stands

Donnington Priory, Built on the site of a small priory of Trinitarians. The Trinitarians (because their churches were all dedicated to the Trinity), or Maturins (because their first house was near St. Mathurine's Chapel in Paris), or Inghamites (because their first house in England was at Ingham, in Norfolk), had twelve houses in England, lived by an easy rule, and were mostly laymen. Donnington was founded by Sir Richard Adderbury, c. 1360, suppressed 1538, and valued in the *Valor* at £19 3s. 10d. revenue. There was a chapel attached to the priory, but this and the greater part of the house was destroyed during the investment of Donnington Castle, when all the buildings in the village were levelled with the ground to prevent cover for the besiegers.

Donnington Hospital On the opposite side was founded 1393 by Sir Richard Adderbury, and re-founded as Queen Elizabeth's Hospital by the Earl of Nottingham, to whom the patronage was granted, together with the honour of Donnington Castle, for his glorious victory over the Armada, to be held by tenure of presenting one red rose to the Queen every year on the Nativity of St. John the Baptist.

DONNINGTON CASTLE.

Donnington Grove. Just below the Castle, on a gentle rise above the river Lambourn, which here expands into a fine sheet of water, stands Donnington Grove, remarkable for the beauty of its situation—the grounds combining in the happiest manner all that can attract or charm in our local scenery. The house, in the Gothic of the period, was built by Mr. James Petit Andrews at the latter part of the 18th century. On his death, in 1797, the property passed to his half-brother, Sir Joseph Andrews, of Shaw House, who sold it to Mr. Brummell, Secretary to Lord North, and here he was visited by Fox, Sheridan, and other celebrities of the day. Mr. Brummell, High Sheriff of Berks in 1788, was father of Beau Brummell, who was an Eton boy when his father lived at the Grove, and it is interesting to know that his boyhood was spent at Donnington. Mr. Brummell's executors sold the Grove to John Bebb, Esq., an East Indian nabob, who frequently entertained the Duke of Gloucester. It is now the property of Mr. Marmaduke Head Best.

Returning to the town, about half a mile southward is

Sandleford Priory With its pleasant park and riverside woods—a parish containing thirty inhabitants, which stands on the site of a priory for Austin Canons, founded c. 1200 by Geoffrey Count of Perche, Earl Marshal of England, and Maud his wife. Its revenues were given to St. George's Chapel, Windsor, *temp.* Edward IV.

Its chief interest lies in its being a century ago the country house of Mrs. Montagu, the centre of literary society, and the reputed founder of the Blue-Stocking Club, and here Johnson, Stillingfleet, Burke, Goldsmith, Beattie, Garrick, Lyttleton, Gilbert West, Dr. Young, Hannah More, Reynolds, Mrs. Elizabeth Carter (our English Dacier), and Madame D'Arblay were among her visitors. Cowper commemorates a visit to Sandleford in the lines commencing .—

> **The birds put off their feathery hue**
> **To dress a room for Montagu.**

During her residence at Sandleford the house was rebuilt by Wyatt, and the old chapel of the priory was converted into a dining-room, and connected by an octagon drawing-room—a fact noticed by Mrs. Montagu in one of her letters.

Writing of Sandleford, Mrs. Montagu says :—" Why should I deprecate the monastic life? No one can be more retir'd than I am at present, and I inhabit a convent too, and live by rules, not indeed given by St. Francis, or St. Benedict, but by myself merely that I may have a reason for what I do. * * * My desk and I are placed under the shade of some noble elms. I prefer my sylvan palace to the Louvre, and indeed the work of a nobler architect, and the abode of worthier inhabitants.

The soul proud science never taught to stray
Far as the solar walk or milky way

may in these groves and meadows find enough to admire and delight in, and without the help of science investigate the great laws of the universe. On the terrace at Sandleford I have passed many happy hours in the conversation of the best of companions and the kindest of friends."

From the first recluse who shut himself up within the walls of the Priory to the witty, beautiful, and cultivated woman whose name has for a century-and-a-half been associated with modern Sandleford, how great a stride! Few monastic chapels have served such diverse purposes as that erected by the old crusader seven hundred years ago.

When Mrs. Montagu died in 1800 her nephew, Matthew Robinson, 4th Baron Rokeby, succeeded to the estate. Mrs. Montagu had adopted her nephew in 1776, after the loss of her one son, and only child. He was long resident with her, and continued to do so after his marriage with Miss Charlton, in 1785, till his aunt's death. On the death of Lord Rokeby, in 1834, his eldest son, Edward, 5th Baron Rokeby, succeeded to Sandleford, Denton Hall, Northumberland, and Montagu House, Portman Square. Lord Rokeby sold Sandleford to the late Mr. Chatteris in 1836. In 1875 Mr. Chatteris enfranchised the property by purchase of the Dean and Canons of Windsor.

Hampstead Park

the property of Lord Craven, and now occupied by Mr. James Bishop, is about $2\frac{1}{8}$ miles from Newbury by way of Enbourn, and forms a most delightful walk or drive. On the road the visitor will pass the Rectory, and National Schools belonging to the parish of Newbury. Immediately beyond the town, the valley in which it is situated opens out to a considerable width, presenting bold and fine elevations towards the north and south, and enclosing extensive lands on either side of the road.

After entering the park by the principal gates, and through an avenue of fine old limes, we arrive at the house, which originally was erected merely as a shooting lodge, but has been enlarged from time to time.

The manor of Hampstead was bestowed by Henry I. on one Gilbert, who took the name of Marshal, from his office in the Royal household. His grandson was John the Marshal, whose controversy with Becket about the manor of Pagham, in Sussex, gave occasion for the proceedings against the Archbishop. His son was William, created Earl of Pembroke, who became the Protector of the Kingdom on the death of King John. His five sons all became Earls of Pembroke, all died without issue, and the extinction of the male line was popularly looked on as a proof of the abiding anger of St. Thomas of Canterbury.

In the time of Queen Elizabeth the manor belonged to Sir Thomas Parry, the Treasurer of the Royal household, who built himself a stately mansion. In 1620, it was purchased by Sir William Craven,* the faithful lover of Elizabeth of Bohemia. It was to please her that he pulled down Parry's house, and replaced it by a magnificent pile that might remind his lady of the castle of Heidelberg. The architect, Sir Balthazar Gerbeir. died on a visit to Hampstead, 1667, and is buried in the church. In 1718 the great house was entirely destroyed by fire; its cellars can be traced just on the top of the hill above the church, Here on a breezy rise are eight pairs of splendid gate piers, some in brick, others in stone with scolloped niches, urns, and fruit and flower reliefs. A ninth pair, with the urns and trophied ornaments were taken away when Benham House was rebuilt, and re-erected at the western entrance lodge. Close to the house is a walled garden of eight acres, a grand-stand, and an abandoned race-course. The deer park at Hampstead with its interesting and ever-varying scenery, is very fine, with splendid timber, great slopes of bracken and ornamental water, and a double avenue leading up to the great house.

On the opposite side of the valley is

Benham Park, the seat of Sir R. V. Sutton, Bart., a minor. The manor of Benham-Valence, which derives its additional appellation from the family of Valence, Earls of Pembroke, after passing through various ownerships, was granted by Queen Elizabeth to "her faithful servant," John Baptist Castillion. His son, Sir Francis Castillion, sold the manor in 1630 to the trustees of Sir William Craven, from whom it passed through several stages of family descent to William, 6th Baron Craven, who built the present house in 1775, the old house of the Castillions having been burnt down the previous year. Lord Craven married, Elizabeth, youngest daughter of Augustus, 4th Earl of Berkeley, who married as her second husband the Margrave of Anspach. The manor of Benham-Valence was left by Lord Craven to his eldest son, who was created Viscount Uffington, co. Berks, and Earl of Craven, co. York, 13th June, 1801, from whom it was purchased by the Margrave, who died at Benham in 1806, and bequeathed the estate to the Margravine.

The house which has been much enlarged of late years, is an imposing building of the Ionic order, having an elegant portico in the south front, and stands at the head of a slight declivity. On the south is a fine sheet of water supplied by the Kennet, and on

*The magnanimity of this chivalrous nobleman throughout the whole of the severely-tried career of her he watched over, was as admirable as his heroism in the field and his magnificent generosity to his Sovereign. He gave the latter (Charles I.) £50,000, for which he was fined heavily besides by the Parliament; he headed the subscription list for the recovery of the Palatinate with £10,000, he gave his Palatine godson £1,500 worth of plate, and £200 a year; and he had to pay £20,000 for his own release in the Palatine cause.

the north side the grounds are well sheltered by woods, around which the great high-road makes a sweep to the western gate.

The following are a few of the principal attractions of the neighbourhood which can be reached by *rail* from Newbury :—

By the Newbury and Winchester Line.

East Woodhay. The first station from Newbury. Here was formerly a residence of the Bishops of Winchester, and three of the Rectors of the parish, Ken, Hooper, and Lowth became Bishops of London. *West Woodhay* House, contains the nucleus of a house built in 1635, by Inigo Jones, for the Darells. It has been much altered and enlarged by its present owner, but retains some of its old features, including good doorways over which are inscriptions: "Nisi Dominus ædificet frustra. "Exprome famelico animum tuum." "Perfla hortum meum." The situation is beautiful, and the house looks full on to the down, over a magnificent sweep of lawn, with some ornamental water. The old church, now pulled down, contained the tomb of Sir Benjamin Rudyerd, a poet, and an eminent politician of the Commonwealth. He died at West Woodhay, 31st May, 1658. On the summit of the range of hills is *Walbury*, a very fine ancient British hill-fort (783 by 550yds.), on the borders of the three counties of Berks, Hants and Wilts, occupies the highest elevation attained by the chalk in the South of England (972ft.), and commands a most extensive and beautiful view. Half-a-mile W. of the Camp is *Combe Gallows.* The existing gibbet is the third restoration of the original gallows on which were hanged (7th March, 1676), George Bromman and Dorothy Newman for the murder of two children of hers by a former husband. The bodies were hid in a pond at the spot.

Highclere is the station for *Highclere Castle and Park.* The Castle designed by Sir Charles Barry, in the style he adopted for the Houses of Parliament, is a magnificent edifice, containing a fine collection of pictures and objects of art. The Park, one of the finest in Hampshire, is 13 miles in circumference.

Burghclere is the most convenient station for *Beacon Hill*, and for *Kingsclere*, three or four miles distant *via* Sydmonton. The church is Norman, with central tower. On the south side of Cottington hill is the site of *Freemantle Park*, a favourite hunting-lodge of King John and the Plantagenet Kings. At the foot of the high land stretches the Roman road from Silchester to Old Sarum, known as the Portway. At Kingsclere is also the famous training establishment of Mr. John Porter, noted for its Derby winners.

By the Newbury and Didcot Line.

Hermitage. About half-a-mile from the village is the earthwork known as *Grimsbury Castle*, remarkable for its strength, entrance, beauty of situation, and skill employed in its construction. *Fence* or *Fetz* wood, on the outskirts of which the

Castle stands covers 700 acres, and is a noted game covert. *Marlston House*, the fine modern residence of Mr. G. W. Palmer, M.P., is in this neighbourhood.

Hampstead Norris. Two miles from here is *Yattendon*—a most charming old-world village. The church was built *c.* 1450, and is excellent Perpendicular throughout. There is a monument in the church to Sir John Norreys, of Netherland renown, with a long epitaph recounting his services.* Carte, the historian, is buried in this church. *Yattendon Court*, the seat of Mr. Waterhouse, R.A., occupies a commanding position on the hill above, and not far off is Frilsham House, the seat of Sir W. Cameron Gull, Bart.

On the road to Pangbourne is *Ashampstead Common*—a lovely tract of forest scenery.

Compton. Here, on the downs, are many evidences of ancient British and Roman occupation. South of the village is a remarkable Celtic encampment, known as *Perborough Castle*, from whence eastward a good view of "*Lowbury*," another ancient military station, rising about 620 ft., and supposed to be the chief position held by the Danes the night before King Alfred's great battle of *Ashdown*. This fortified post, with well-defined traces of a Roman camp, commands a view of a chain of no less than twelve military entrenchments.

Many race-horses are trained here at the establishment of Mr. W. G. Stevens, of Roden House.

Two miles away is *East Ilsley*, celebrated for its sheep fairs, which are the largest in this part of England. This is also a well-known racing centre, and among the horses trained on the neighbouring downs may be mentioned Lord Lyon, winner of the Derby and St. Leger; Achievement, Caractacus, winner of the Derby, etc., Gardevisure, Hawthornden, Elland, and many other horses famous in the annals of the turf. At Keat's Gore, near Ilsley, the celebrated *Eclipse* was foaled and trained.

On the highest point of the downs above East Ilsley is *Cwichelm's Hleaw*, the reputed burial place of Cwichelm, King of the West-Saxons.

About two miles from Compton is *Aldworth Church*, containing a remarkable series of altar-tombs and effigies of the De la Beche family.

---

* This epitaph suggests the impossible date, 1529, as the year of his birth, but he was born about 1547. The inscription also states that he died at his house at Yattendon, but this is also incorrect. He died in the arms of his brother Thomas at the latter's house in Mallow, co. Cork, 3rd July, 1597. His body was embalmed, and he is reputed to have been buried in Yattendon Church, but there is no entry in the parish register.

By the Line from Newbury to Reading.

Midgham, or Woolhampton, the second station from Newbury, is a most convenient centre from which a group of interesting villages on either side of the great Bath road may be explored. At Upper Woolhampton on the hill, $\frac{3}{4}$ mile distant, is the Roman Catholic College of St. Mary, founded 1838, but with considerable modern additions, and now conducted by the Benedictine Monks expelled from Douai. *Shalford*, near *Brimpton*, $1\frac{1}{2}$ miles south, the Templars had a Preceptory, written "Scaldeford" in the records, which at the dissolution of the order (1312), passed to the Hospitallers. The old house at Shalford is pleasantly situated on the Enbourn stream, and in the water-meadows is a raised yew alley, called the Nun's Walk. The date of 1582 is inserted in front of the house. At *Brimpton Manor*, also the property of the Hospitallers, there is a most interesting *Chapel*, though desecrated. The east window is good Decorated Perpendicular of 3 lights. On the south wall is a blocked piscina, and on the north a single very long lancet. There is an interesting north door, round-headed, with the scale diaper in the tympanum, and a raised Maltese cross in high relief. *Wasing*, 1 mile east of Brimpton. The church c. 1730, although there are earlier dates on the outside, and some traces of Early English work. There is some interesting Flemish glass in the windows, dated 1629–1669. There is a tablet in the east end to "Thomas Worrall, Rector of Wasing for 42 years, excepting the years y^t^ he was banisht for his loyalty." The church is most beautifully situated in the park of *Wasing Place*, the seat of Mr. W. G. Mount, for many years one of the representatives of the County in Parliament. *Bucklebury* is $3\frac{1}{2}$ miles north-west of Woolhampton. The manor belonged to Reading Abbey, and at the dissolution (1539), was bought by John Winchcombe, son of "Jack of Newbury." He built here a house as an approach to which the great avenue of oaks on Bucklebury Common is said to have been afterwards planted. In 1700, Frances Winchcombe, the heiress, married Henry St. John Viscount Bolingbroke, and where he was visited by Swift, Harley, Pope, Prior, Arbuthnot, Gay, and other members of the coterie of "all the talents." The church retains its ancient pews, and is interesting. On the tower is sculptured a crucifixion, a mutilated Maltese cross, and the rebus of the Winchcombes—a figure combing a *winch* or wheel. The inscription has never been satisfactorily deciphered, but seems to be "John Winchcomb," written (as on a carving at Newbury), without the vowels. The north window of the chancel has some heraldic glass from the old house, and a sundial dated 1649. Notice a wonderfully realistic fly painted at the side of the dial. The old house was pulled down in 1833, though some of its offices remain, and the deserted grounds, with fishponds and fine timber, are most picturesque. At *Bucklebury Cottage*, the residence of Mrs. Webley-Parry, is the original portrait of John Winchcombe, who purchased the manor, attributed to Holbein, and a most interesting collection of other portraits of the Winchcombes, the Packers, and the Hartleys, successively owners of the Donnington Castle and Bucklebury estates.

Aldermaston. The village is $1\frac{3}{4}$ miles from the station. This is one of the most picturesque villages in the neighbourhood, and the park, which is one of the wildest and most varied in this part of England, is 5 miles in extent and contains 1,000 acres. The present modern Elizabethan mansion, the seat of Mr. C. E. Keyser, F.S.A., was built in 1851, from designs of Philip Hardwick, but contains the fine old staircase from the Old Hall, with its balustrade of figures (engraved by Nash.) The church has been carefully restored by Mr. Keyser, and contains a very beautiful alabaster altar-tomb (1526), and some excellent modern mural paintings and stained glass.

THE ROMAN CITY OF SILCHESTER

is accessible by a most delightful walk of about 3 miles from Aldermaston station, or can be reached by road from Newbury by way of Crookham Common and Brimpton.

Padworth Church, 2 miles north east, has a small Norman apsidal church. The chancel arch has rich capitals, and the apse is vaulted. The late Norman north and south doorways are very good, and there is a Transition piscina.

About $1\frac{1}{2}$ miles from Padworth is *Ufton Court*, an historic mansion, finely situated on the brow of a hill, with a walled terrace at the edge, and is approached by a double avenue of oaks. It is of three stories, but from its great length preserves the repose of a two-storied house. It is built on the usual E plan, slightly modified, and there are no less than nineteen continuous gables. It is in the main Elizabethan, and was built by Elizabeth, widow of Sir John Mervyn, whose initials are seen in the hall. She purchased the property, then called Pole Manor, in 1568, married Richard Perkins, and died 1581. The Perkinses were recusants, and the house contains several hiding-holes for priests. One of the numerous Francis Perkins married, in 1715, Arabella Fermor, the reigning beauty of the day, and the heroine of Pope's "Rape of the Lock." There are seven fish ponds cut in the side of the hill, fed by a spring at the top, and discharging into the stream below. The barn to the left of the entrance to the eastern front possesses a fine open roof.

BY THE LINE FROM NEWBURY TO HUNGERFORD.

Kintbury. The church is a fine cruciform structure, and a low massive Early English tower, of which the door is Norman. It contains a monument to one of the Darells of Littlecote, who had an estate at West Woodhay and at *Balsdon* near Kintbury, the scene of a memorable sortie described in the "Battles of Newbury."

Two miles from here is *Avington.* The long low church here is Norman, and remarkably interesting. The font, which is rough Norman, has 13 figures in panels, of which many interpretations have been given ; they, probably, represent the twelve Apostles, with Judas, who carries the bag, and is being tempted by the fiend.

HUNGERFORD,

a town with many historic associations, but now possessing little of interest. Hungerford cherishes the memory of John of Gaunt, Duke of Lancaster, who gave the manor (previously royal) with all rights of common meadow-pasture and fishing to the inhabitants. Twelve of them, called Feoffees, with a Constable, hold a court at Hocktide as Lords of the Manor. In the modern Town Hall is preserved an ancient horn, reputed to have been given by John of Gaunt with the right of fishing. Another horn of brass, with the inscription "John a Gaun did give and grant the riall (royalty) of fishing to Hungerford toune from Eldren stub to Irish stil, excepting som several mil pond. Jehosophat Lucas was constabl,"* is used to summon the Hocktide meetings.

The *Bear Inn* was the head-quarters of Charles I. in November, 1644, and in the same inn, William, Prince of Orange, received James II.'s Commissioners, Lords Halifax, Nottingham, and Godolphin, in December, 1688.

The ancient church was ruthlessly pulled down and a new one built in the Gothic of 1814, since changed to that of 1880.

No one should visit Hungerford without, if possible, seeing *Littlecote*, the seat of the Pophams, 2 miles distant, in Wilts. It is a remarkable specimen of an almost unaltered mansion of the 16th century, built by the Darells, and sold by the last of that family, "Wild Darell," to Judge Popham, in the reign of Queen Elizabeth. Attached to the house is the wide-world story told in a note to Scott's "Rokeby."

---

* In an "Historical Sketch of the Town of Hungerford" by the present writer, published in 1894, a reference will be found to many manorial and borough records, including the Constables' and Churchwardens' Accounts. In the former, which commence in 1658, a very noticeable feature is the innumerable entries of relief given to poor destitute travellers, and payments for "carrying of cripples." The latter charges were somewhat difficult to interpret, and it was not for some little time after the above-named work was published that we obtained an explanation of these curious entries. It appears that in the year 1609, an Almshouse or Hospital in the city of Bath was founded and endowed by Thomas Bellott, Steward of the Household to Queen Elizabeth, for the reception of poor persons who might visit that city for the benefit of its waters. An Act had then been passed authorising Magistrates to license diseased and disabled persons to travel to Bath for the use of the hot springs, and *this licence compelled every parish through which they passed to assist them on their journey.* Hungerford being on the great high road from London to Bath, numbers of poor persons, crippled with rheumatism and kindred disorders, passed through the place on their way to the city of the *waters of the sun*, and obtained the necessary aid from the Constable, who was then as now, the chief magistrate of the town.

Returning to Newbury, the traveller may diverge to visit

LAMBOURN,

which is easily reached by a short branch railway. The chief features of Lambourn are, first—the fine cruciform church, in which evident portions of Saxon work has been found, having two chantry chapels of the Estburys, in one of which is the tomb of the founder, John Estbury, 1485, with a brass representing him in a surcoat, with his arms enamelled. His son founded the hospital near the church for ten poor men, and the almsmen—an interesting survival of pre-Reformation usage, attend divine service in this church every morning in the Estbury or Isbury chapel, kneeling around the founder's tomb. In the north transept of the church is the beautiful tomb of Sir Thomas Essex and his wife Margaret, 1558, with their effigies in alabaster. Reference to Lambourn would be incomplete without some allusion to its famous training quarters, and so widely known to people interested in the turf.

Ashdown Park. On the way to the White Horse Hill, Ashdown Park, the seat of the Earl of Craven, is passed, strangely situate in a desolate spot, high up among the bleak downs—an interesting specimen of its period, resembling a French chateau, its tall chimneys meeting in two massive quadrangular piles on either side, having a cupola in the centre, containing a lantern, which was formerly lighted as a beacon to guide travellers among these dreary hills. Tradition tells that Sir William Craven, who was Lord Mayor of London 1610-11, flying from the plague in the metropolis rode on and on, till on these lonely hills he espied a solitary farmhouse. There for the first time he felt he should be secure, and there he built himself "a lodge in the wilderness." It is said in consequence of this Ashdown was arranged with four avenues leading to the four quarters, and with windows on each side of the rooms, in order that if the plague came in on one side, it might go out of the other. The existing house, with which the original lodge is incorporated, was erected from designs of Webb, the nephew of Inigo Jones, the eminent architect, who inherited all his plans.

The Ridgeway. Ascending the steep hill leading to the White Horse the ancient road known as the Ridgeway, one of the four great Roman roads, and known by the name of the Icnield Street, is reached, which proceeds from the eastern coast near Great Yarmouth through several counties on to Land's End. Following the hill close to the Ridgeway we next came to the remarkable Cromlech known as

Wayland Smith's Cave, whose legend is familiar to every reader of Sir Walter Scott's romance of "Kenilworth." It is simply a denuded chambered long barrow of the Palæolithic or Old Stone Age, having a kistvaen of stones within it, to protect the place of interment, and represents a period of a thousand years or more before the Christian era. This sepulchral monument is of cruciform arrangement, having similar lateral chambers on each side, forming a Latin cross on the plan, corresponding to a rough outline of transepts, nave, and chancel. It was originally covered with earth, and surrounded by a circle of huge sarsen stones, many of which were broken up to repair the roads. It is mentioned as a boundary in an Anglo-Saxon charter of Eadred, A.D. 955, in which it is referred to as " Weland's Smithy." A pleasant drive along the Ridgeway will next bring the visitors to the celebrated

White Horse Hill. This spot is well-known for its panoramic view of the vale below ; but its celebrity is chiefly owing to the rude figure of a white horse formed on the north-west side of the hill, and being 374 feet in length, is visible from a distance of over 15 miles, when the afternoon sun is shining upon it. Its formation is ascribed to King Alfred as a memento of his celebrated victory over the Danes at Æscesdune, but may possibly be regarded more as a popular legend than an historical and well ascertained fact. The dimensions occupy about an acre of ground ; the white chalk between two and three feet deep and 10 broad. The head, neck, body, and tail, are composed of one line varying in width ; and one line or trench has also been made for each of the legs.

At the summit of the hill, which is 893ft. above the level of the sea is a large oval camp known as Uffington Castle, 700ft. in diameter from E. to W., and 500 from N. to S. The view from it is very fine, embracing objects in eight different counties.

Blowing Stone or King Alfred's Bugle. This singular natural production is composed of the substance here called Sarsen stone. It is pierced with holes on each side, of which seven are in front, three at the top, and several behind. The opening from which it is blown is at the top. The sound issues from the side, near the top of the stone, and can be heard in fine weather at Faringdon Clump, six miles distant. To quote a stanza or two from a poetical description of the antiquities round Lambourn, under the title of " A day on the Downs " :

" This stone, which utter'd many a blast,
In silence lay for ages past ;
By man unheard, by man unseen,
Tradition said it once had been,
And that for miles its loud alarms
Were heard when Alfred flew to arms ;
And this tradition had it still,
The stone was on the White Horse Hill.
From sire to son the Blow Stone tale
Thus circles round the White Horse Vale."

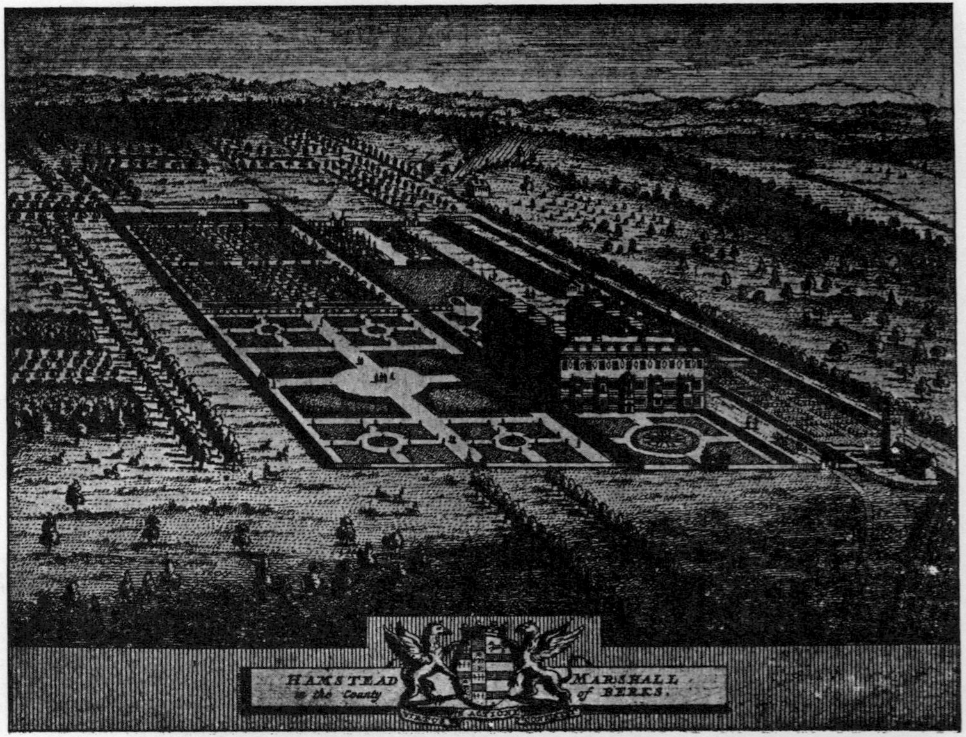
HAMSTEAD MARSHALL
in the County of BERKS.

THE GEOLOGY OF NEWBURY AND DISTRICT.

By E. P. Richards, F.G.S.

CONTENTS.

---

§ I.—INTRODUCTORY.

The floor of the Kennet valley at Newbury is about a mile wide, enclosed between wooded hills and plateaux; the river Kennet flows from west to east down the centre of the valley, and is joined about a mile below Newbury by the river Lambourn coming in from the north west

The town itself chiefly occupies the centre of the valley, but houses have crept up the southern side nearly to the plateau on which the Workhouse stands, and have extended northwards on to the slight hill that here separates the two valleys of the Kennet and Lambourn. In addition to the purely local geology, it has been found necessary in this paper to outline the general structure of Berkshire and to occasionally touch on continental geology, in order that the necessary contexts explaining the geology of Newbury may not be wanting.

The geological maps of the Newbury Division of Berkshire published by the Geological Survey will be found very useful, and with this help the paper can be followed with much greater ease.

The scale on which the above maps are drawn is one inch to a mile, and they are beautifully finished and remarkably cheap.

A list of some of the geological literature of Newbury and Berkshire is given in Appendix 1.

Geologists include all material forming the earth's crust under the term "rock"; and sand, clay, marl, chalk, gravel, limestone, shale, etc., are all "rock" to geologists.

The word "strata" is conveniently used when speaking of rocks that occur in great layers or sheets. (Latin, sterno, stratum, to spread out).

Professor T. Rupert Jones, F.R.S., F.G.S., has very kindly given the author his able assistance and has read the proofs of this little treatise.

I am also indebted to Doctor A. E. Slater, F.G.S., who read those portions relating to gravels, and sent me some useful notes.

§ II.—THE ANCIENT ROCK FLOOR UNDERLYING BERKSHIRE AND THE PROBABILITIES OF THERE BEING COAL UNDER NEWBURY.

[See plate I.]

All the rocks which form the present surface of southern and eastern England are found to rest upon a deeply buried worn uneven floor, composed of much more ancient strata.

These old rocks were once vast sheets of mud, sand, and clay, having been gradually laid down in their day in since long vanished seas. Some of this mud and sand was carried out into those seas by great rivers, and the remainder was worn away from those ancient shores by wave action; all this fine material in suspension settled down when it arrived in sufficiently tranquil water, and after ages of time had elapsed a great thickness of strata had accumulated (see fig 1, plate I).

Heat, pressure, chemical and mechanical action slowly converted the sand into sandstones and grits, and the layers of silt and mud into hard shales, fine clays or marls; and the abundant shells of sea creatures, the remains of crinoids, corals and other lime secreters also added enormously to the bulk of those ancient deposits by forming layers of limestone.

During the latter portion of that time, what are now coal seams came into being, and were interstratified between the layers of shale and sandstone; space will not permit an explanation of the origin

---

These maps can be obtained from the Ordnance Survey, Geological Department, Southampton. Map, No. 267 (Newbury 1898) New Series, price 3/-, hand coloured and Map No. 267 (Reading 1898) will be found very useful, price 3/-, hand coloured.

of coal to be given here, but it is well known that it resulted from tropical forests which grew on periodically subsiding sea flats.

The slow continuous cooling and consequent shrinking of the earth's interior, causes its covering of rocks to wrinkle up, rather like the skin does on an old apple when its interior dries and contracts; the wrinkles may be compared to mountain ranges on the earth's surface; and these great strata we have been describing were wrinkled, folded, and crushed, large areas being in this way forced up until they rose above sea-level and became continental dry land (see fig. 2).

This land was then subjected in its turn to the destructive action of rain and rivers, frost and heat, and to the ceaseless attack of the sea; thus it was carved slowly into hills and valleys, and its general surface gradually lowered; interminable wear and tear went on, until in places thousands of feet of those ancient layers of shale and grit containing the coal seams had been utterly worn away and dispersed to form new strata (see fig. 3).

Finally, changes in the directions of the forces which raised those old strata into dry land, caused them to gradually subside again below sea-level, and after thus being a land surface they became the ancient rock floor now deeply underlying the present surface of southern and eastern England (see fig 4).

To summarize here, four periods have been dealt with in the history of the strata now forming the ancient rock floor:—

(*a*) Their deposition as layers of sediment on the bottom of the seas of that time (see fig 1).

(*b*) Their hardening and change of character, accompanied by wrinkling folding, and crushing and their elevation above sea level into a land surface (see fig 2).

(*c*) The great denudation and wearing away of that land surface by rivers and the sea (see fig 3).

(*d*) The final slow subsidence below sea level (fig 4).

There have been at least two other important earth movements affecting the old rock floor since its first subsidence, but they will be described later on.

During the subsidence (period *d*, fig 4), when the old worn land surface formed a new sea bottom, the deposition of sediment at once recommenced. The continental land masses from which this new sediment was derived lay to the north and west of Great Britain; the submerged land surface was levelled up by the slow rain of sand and mud always filtering down upon it, and in due course the layers of sediment on the sea-bottom became practically horizontal; in much the same way a deep fall of snow converts the roughest ploughed field into a smooth surface.

During great ages the old rock floor became in this way buried under an entirely new set of strata (fig 4), which have since been partly elevated into land by further movements in sympathy with the old rock flood underlying them (fig 5). These new strata [as they are termed here for the purpose of this explanation] now form the familiar chalk hills around Newbury and the surface of S.E. England generally (fig 6); and it will be clear that in order to get to the coal seams in the ancient rock floor, it will be necessary to first pierce through all these younger strata which have been accumulated on the old submerged land surface.

By examining figs 1 to 6, it will be seen how portions of the once extensive coal seams have been preserved from denudation only in the "downfolds" of the old rocks, and therefore to be successful, any shaft or boring for coal in S.E. England must be made over one of these "down folds" or "troughs."

It is known that one of these ancient downfolds (belonging to period *b*) commences in Northern France, it runs beneath Belgium and crosses the sea to Kent, where its centre line continues, probably, to the north of the North Downs, under Newbury and North Wiltshire, thence towards the Forest of Dean Coalfield in Somerset, where it reappears at the surface.

This theory was first advanced by Godwin-Austen in 1858, and good coal has recently been found in Kent near Dover and Canterbury at a depth of about 1100 feet. In all probability we shall see this new coalfield gradually but surely explored and extended westward along the line indicated. Boring becomes year by year cheaper and more rapid, and we may expect to see experiments at no distant date being made along the line of this ancient downfold in search of coal. The great depth should be no hindrance, for there are numerous collieries over 3000 feet deep in Belgium, and not a few in England; our winding, ventilating, pumping, and coal getting plant are always being improved, and it is certain that in the future coal will be mined from much greater depths than at present.

It is impossible to accurately give the thickness of strata which may cover coal at Newbury, but it will certainly be much greater than at Dover, because greater denudation of the overlying rocks has taken place there than at Newbury. The section passed through beneath Newbury would probably be as follows:—

600	feet of Upper, Middle, and Lower Chalk.	Rocks deposited on the ancient rock floor since its subsidence and now forming the land surface of S.E. & Mid-England.
300	feet of Greensand and Gault.	
300	feet of Jurassic Strata.	
2000	feet of Red Sandstones and Marls.	
3200	feet.	

No geologist could definitely say that there is coal under Newbury, but the probability is great. Before spending money on such a speculation, it would of course be common sense to get a first class geologist whose special study was *stratigraphy*, to advise as to the exact locality for boring.

A recent boring has been sunk to a depth of 1302 feet at Lyme Regis in search of coal;* any geologist would have deprecated such

* Q. J. Geol. Soc. vol. 58, p. 279.

an attempt, for there is evidence indicating that the coal-bearing rocks have been quite worn away, and do not exist beneath Lyme Regis, in fact the town is probably situated over a worn upfold of the rock floor. It was anticipated that coal would be found at a depth of 600 feet, but the reader will be able to understand the fallacy of such a surmise; for Lyme Regis is situated on Lower Jurassic Strata, and had coal been there it could not have been reasonably expected at a depth of less than 2000 feet.

It is possible that the Kent Coalfield will be extended westward more by the actual following of coal seams already found there, than by speculative borings, unless the price of coal rises very much, which is quite unlikely.

The Permian sandstones and marls—the first layers deposited on the old rock floor—are believed to be missing under Newbury, and as the red Triassic marls and sandstones never appear at the surface in Berkshire, they will not concern us further.

The earthquake which occurred at Newbury on December 1st, 1904, is most likely due to a slight slipping along an old fault in the rocks of the deep-seated floor, and Prof. T. Rupert Jones thinks that a fault of this description extends up into the chalk along a line skirting the valley between Benham and Newbury. Tabulated observations of the quality of the shocks, taken immediately after the next earthquake, might at once determine if this is a focal line.

§ III.—BRIEF ACCOUNT OF THE HISTORY OF GEOLOGICAL EVENTS FROM THE SUBSIDENCE OF THE ANCIENT ROCK-FLOOR TO PRESENT TIME.

The old rock floor subsided very slowly and the seas which covered it were never very deep, because the sediment forming younger strata was deposited at a speed about equal to the rate of subsidence, and so the sea-bottom always kept fairly shallow; this slow depression continued with fair regularity until the following great masses of strata had been successively superimposed on one another:—

4th—The Cretaceous.
3rd—The Jurassic.
2nd—The Triassic.
1st—The Permian (wanting in Berks).

At the close of Cretaceous* time—that is after the formation of the Chalk—the subsidence of the rock floor ceased, the movement was reversed and the floor was again wrinkled a little along the ancient lines; the above three masses of strata were bent into ups and downs in sympathy, and slowly rose above sea level in many places (fig 5); those districts of elevation are now represented in S.E.

* Creta—chalk [Lat.]

England by the Chilterns and Cotswold Hills, and by the high ground of Kent, Surrey, Hampshire, Berks, and Wilts; from Kent to Wiltshire the Cretaceous strata were raised into a mountain range probably 3000 feet high, of which you now see but the weather-worn remnant when you look at Inkpen or Sidmonton or the low hills of Surrey and Kent; but between the Chilterns and this former mountain range lay a great downfold or trough, which became an arm of the sea, reaching probably as far as Devizes (see plate 2), extending eastward over London and the North of the Thames, covering Berkshire, Hertford, Essex and Suffolk, and bending N.E. as it became open sea.

In this gulf the Eocene strata were deposited on the top of the disturbed and submerged chalk, and these soft and young Eocene strata became dry land through a last great movement of the rock floor and its accumulated load of strata, which movement left the sites of Newbury and London high and dry. This movement took place in extremely recent geological time, but sufficient time has elapsed since then to allow the Thames and the Kennet to carve out their present valleys and remove hundreds of feet of Eocene strata (plate 3).

§ IV.—THE JURASSIC.

These are the oldest rocks that appear at the surface in Berkshire; they are well developed in the Jura Alps between France and Switzerland and take their name from that district.

As will be seen in plates 2 and 3, these strata are deeply buried in Berkshire by the overlying Cretaceous and Eocene rocks, except along the northern boundary, where they gradually come up to the surface; and, speaking generally, as you walk northwards from Berkshire you pass on to older and older rocks, until finally an ancient Palaeozoic rock-floor comes up and forms the general surface of the country in Derbyshire (see fig 6, plate 1).

It is hardly in the province of this paper to describe the Jurassic rocks, and they will only be treated of briefly; but it is necessary to mention them so that the geology of Newbury can be clearly understood.

The Jurassic beds of Berkshire are represented by the following strata in descending order (the lowest beds being the oldest):—

The Purbeck and Portland Beds The Kimmeridge Clay	Upper Jurassic.
Corallian Beds ... ... The Oxford Clay	Part of the middle Jurassic.

No Jurassic strata of greater age than the above are seen at the surface in Berkshire.

The Oxford Clay, cropping out in a band of country between Cricklade and Oxford, can be seen at Buscot on the south side of the Thames, where it is a shaly bluish-grey clay.

The Corallian limestone and sands, the former full of fossil corals, makes the land-surface in a second band of country between Coleshill and Oxford.

The Kimmeridge Clay forms a third zone between Swindon and Abingdon; it consists of dark blue and black clays and shales, containing plant remains, and numerous fossils of marine origin. It is named after the village of Kimmeridge near Swanage, where it is well exposed.

The Portland and Purbeck Beds are very irregular in thickness, and are represented in Berks only by a little group of limestones and sands about a dozen feet thick; they are exposed a short distance to the south of Shrivenham Station, about 5 miles from Swindon.

§ V.—THE CRETACEOUS.

This group of rocks is so named because its most important member is the chalk (creta, Lat.). In England the Cretaceous has been divided as follows:—In descending order, commencing with the chalk, which is the youngest and highest of the strata:—

	Character in Berks.
The Chalk	Upper.—Soft, evenly bedded and full of flints. Middle.—Rubbly and stratified, with only a few Flints and bands of chalk-marl. Lower.—White and grey marly chalk.
Upper Greensand	Dark Green glauconitic sands, calcareous sandstone and marl.
The Gault	Bluish Clay and Shale.
Lower Greensand	Loose brown and yellow quartz sand, with bands of ironstone.
The Wealden Clay The Hastings Clay	Both missing in Berkshire.

The Lower Greensand, the oldest and lowest member of the Cretaceous occurring in Berks, rests, as a rule, on the Kimmeridge Clay. At the close of the Jurassic period a slight earth-movement took place, which affected that area which is now Berkshire; but I have not previously mentioned it because only very important and extensive disturbances entered into the theory of Coal under Newbury.

This slight movement* which occurred at the close of the Jurassic and before the deposition of the Cretaceous, probably accounts for the local absence of the Purbeck and Portland Beds,

* The effects of which were too slight to be shewn on plate 1.

the Hastings Sand, and the Wealden series in Berks. The mingling of estuarine and marine strata in the Purbeck Beds is sound evidence of these local ups and downs; the Wealden and Hastings series were we know deposited at the mouth of a very vast river, which had a delta, that appears to have certainly extended from Kent to Hanover, and to have been about 100 miles wide The fossil remains of large land animals whose carcases floated out to sea are numerous in these rocks. The conclusion naturally inferred from the absence of these beds is that Berks was part of a temporary land surface for a short geological period during the deposition of the Wealden and Hastings Sands. This delta ultimately subsided and the movement extended to the site of Berkshire, and afterwards the Lower Greensand and the remainder of the Cretaceous rocks as above tabulated, were deposited on the deepened sea bottom.

The Lower Greensand is exposed in the N.W. part of the county between Faringdon and Balking, where the lowest layer is a gravel full of ancient rock debris and fossil sponges; it can also be seen on the right side of the road from Oxford to Sunningwell. The Lower Greensand varies in Berkshire from 25 to 50 feet in thickness and it is of very great importance as a source of water supply; the downward escape of rain-water that falls on the outcrop and soaks into the Greensand is prevented by the clayey strata of the underlying rocks, and the sand is often highly charged with good water; wells driven into the Greensand through the overlying Gault—which is also clayey and impervious—generally yield a good supply.

The Gault is a fairly regular stratum of dark blue or grey micaceous shaly clay, containing sulphide of iron and clay-ironstone concretions, and sometimes phosphatic nodules; it appears to have a thickness of about 200 feet in Berkshire, and is exposed in a continuous wide outcrop from near Swindon, via Wantage Road Station to the Thames at Wittenham.

The Upper Greensand, resting on the underlying Gault, owes its name to the green glauconitic sands of which the upper 25 feet of its thickness usually consist; glauconite is a mineral composed of silicate of iron and potassium, and gives a greenish or yellowish appearance to the rocks containing it.

The lower strata of the Upper Greensand are about 50ft. thick and are composed in Berks of a light coloured sandy limestone, full of an impure variety of flint (or silica) called chert. The Upper Greensand is valuable for water supply and is much more constant in its thickness than the Lower Greensand.

The Upper Greensand can be seen at Burghclere, where it forms a most instructive bit of country for Newbury folk. The section on plate 2 shews that the chalk overlying the Greensand has been squeezed into a sharp fold at these places* and the chalk forming the top of the upfold has been worn off, exposing the Greensand and now the worn edge of the chalk sheet surrounds the Greensand in an irregular oval. The cuttings on the railway to Winchester give an admirable exposure of the stratification of the Burghclere inlier. The village of Ham, eight miles to the east of Burghclere, is in the centre of a precisely similar "inlier." This long upfold of the Cretaceous, with the top more or less worn off, runs parallel to the downfold in the ancient rock floor that we believe to occur under the Kennet Valley, and this Cretaceous upfold is notably in sympathy with the geologically ancient line of upfold and upheaval running in the old rock floor from the Mendip Hills by way of Pewsey and Burghclere, under Kent, and thence to the Continent (see § 2).

The Chalk and its Relation to the Eocene Strata.

Most of the hills and valleys of the central and western areas of Berkshire are worn and carved in the chalk, but over that part of the country bounded to the north by a line passing through Reading, Hampstead Norris, Chieveley, Bedwyn, Highclere Kingsclere, and Basing, the chalk is covered more or less by the softer and younger Eocene Strata, and the hills and valleys are consequently worn out of these deposits; though the chalk is rarely buried anywhere to a greater depth than 400 feet in Berkshire.

The Eocene at the time of its deposition covered a much greater area than it does now, but through the action of rain and rivers, frost and heat, and possibly glaciation, it has been gradually washed away, the soft strata have offered little resistance, and the rivers in numerous places have cut quite through them into the underlying chalk; and so the bottom of a valley, although covered by river gravel, is often excavated in the chalk, and the hills forming the valley sides are found to be of Eocene strata. This amount of wear and tear has occurred at Newbury, and if you look at the section across the valley (plate 4) you will see that the Eocene strata have been cut through by the river Kennet, and quite removed in the centre of the town. The gravel covering the valley floor is the debris of this denuded Eocene and chalk; and it is there because it was harder and heavier than the fine silt and chalk and could not be carried out to sea by the rivers.

At Thatcham, where the chalk is more deeply buried, the bottom layers of the Eocene group are still intact and pass right across the valley, and the river gravel rests upon these instead of upon the chalk as it does at Newbury.

This gradual wearing away has left isolated patches of the Eocene beds resting on the tops of chalk hills (see plate 3), and

---

* This is purposely exaggerated a little in the sketch-notices.

such remnants are known as "outliers" because they "lie out," and are cut off on all sides from the now ragged edge of the once continuous sheet of Eocene strata, of which they formed an integral part; the description of these outliers comes under § 6.

Chalk is a marine deposit, chiefly composed of carbonate of calcium ($CaCO_3$); the mass of it frequently consists of the calcareous cases of foraminifera* but it also contains much silica, either in the form of flint nodules, or in the fossil remains of sea-urchins, sponges and sponge spicules, etc., which have been silicified since being deposited; the siliceous structures of minute radiolaria are also found in chalk. Calcareous fossils of numerous genera of shell fish also help to form chalk; remains of sharks and other fish are abundant, extinct crocodiles inhabited the rivers of Cretaceous times and gigantic reptiles inhabited the earth, which bore a sub-tropical vegetation.

The grey ooze—a few inches thick—that covers great tracts of the present Atlantic floor, is really a modern chalk, and is found to consist almost entirely of the shells of dead foraminifera. Most of them live at the surface of the water and their cases sink to the bottom when they die.

In Berkshire the northern boundary of the chalk follows a line drawn through Bishopstone, Ashbury, Woolstone, Childrey, Wantage, Hendred, Upton, Blewbury, and Cholsey. North of this boundary the chalk in England has been entirely removed by denudation (fig 6, plate 1), and the worn northern edge of the great layer now forms a long irregular ridge, commencing on the South Coast near Bridport, running up to Devizes, forming the Chiltern Hills, and finally ending on the Yorkshire coast at Flamborough Head. Whenever the reader goes north from Newbury or London he will find himself crossing this ridge, which is very noticeable.

The Lower Chalk is exposed round the edges of the Ham and Burghclere inliers, also at the bottom of the deep valleys in the downs N.W. of Aldbourne and near Wanborough. The Middle Chalk can also be examined at those places, for the Upper and Middle Chalk have been worn through and the Lower Chalk is thereby exposed.

The Lower Chalk is both grey and white, almost entirely without flints, and is at intervals interstratified with thick beds of "Chalk Marl." The base of the Lower Chalk in Berkshire usually consists of a chloritic Chalk Marl.

Marl is an intimate mixture of clay and lime, and it varies greatly in hardness and colour. It is soft and friable where it occurs in the prehistoric lake deposits of Newbury, but it forms

---

* Specks of living jelly, which inhabited tiny shell-cases, the latter pierced with minute holes through which the foraminifera obtained their nutriment (foraminifera—hole bearing. Lat.).

one of the hardest beds in the chalk. The clay it contains renders it more or less impermeable to water, and consequently rain falling on the chalk soaks in until it reaches the Chalk Marl, above which it accumulates or finds a vent where the marl crops out on the sides of the valleys, and this is the origin of many springs in N.W. Berkshire, where these conditions obtain. The Lower Chalk is usually about 220 feet thick.

The Middle Chalk in Berkshire is white and more or less stratified, it varies in hardness, and is often rubbly, it contains flint in the form of nodules and layers which occur here and there. The base is marked by a very hard chalk-limestone known as the Melbourn Rock*; and the top by a cream coloured limestone containing glauconite. The Middle Chalk is about 170 feet thick in Berkshire.

The Upper Chalk is easily recognised, for it is a well stratified soft white chalk, and the planes of bedding are defined by abundant white-coated flint nodules, of fantastic potato and kidney-like shapes.

Most of the chalk surface of Berkshire belongs to this upper division and it can be readily examined in any of the pits and quarries near Newbury where it is worked for lime or flints. It has an average thickness of about 300 feet, making the total thickness of the whole chalk about 700 feet. As I have already explained, the Chalk was squeezed up into land, and much denuded in many places before it was depressed and covered by the Eocene strata, and this of course means a great gap of unrecorded time in English rocks between the end of the Chalk epoch and the commencement of the Eocene period in England. The fossils of the two formations shew a great disparity, and hardly a single species of either fauna or flora that was abundant at the close of the Chalk period is found to have survived into the Eocene times of this country.

In Northern France, Belgium, and Denmark, however, the chalk was not raised into land, deposition went on steadily and a gradual change is recorded there by a long succession of passage beds from Cretaceous to Eocene times. The slow ordered march of life can there be clearly traced through an uninterrupted progression.

§ VI.—THE EOCENE STRATA.

(See plates 2 and 3.)

The Eocene (" Dawn of the recent " Gr.) is the lowest division of the great groups of rocks representing in this country the Tertiary or Cainozoic (" Recent life " Gr.) period; these names were given before the passage-beds between the Chalk and the Eocene had been discovered.

---

* From the village of Melbourn, near Royston.

The Eocene in England occupies two extensive areas which are spoken of respectively as the London and Hampshire "basins." They were once great downfolds of the chalk, depressed below and covered by the sea, and in these arms of the sea were deposited the clays, loams, sands and gravels, etc., which constitute the Eocene, and these strata have been classified in Berkshire as follows, in descending order:—

The Eocene of Berks.	The Bagshot Beds.	Upper Bagshot Sands.
		Middle Bagshot or Bracklesham Beds.
		Lower Bagshot Sand and Clay.
		The London Clay.
		*The Reading Beds.

The occurrence in the Reading Beds of fossilized leaves, the trunks of palms that have been similarly preserved in the London Clay, and numerous insect remains in the Isle of Wight Eocene, all go to prove that the materials of which the Eocene rocks are made were chiefly derived from the denudation of Cretaceous strata that formed the land around the Eocene basins.

The Reading Beds, so called because they are well developed and prominent around the town of that name, are the lowest of the Eocene Group and they rest directly upon the worn surface of the chalk. The base of the Reading beds is often well defined by about 8 feet of stiff dark grey or blue clay, with greenish sand intermingled. Upon this clay lies as a rule about 40 feet of unconsolidated sand, and this is followed by 40 feet of stiff plastic clays, variously coloured yellow, brown, or white.

The above is the average composition of these beds in Berkshire; at Reading they are about 90 feet thick, but thin out a little to the west. They can be seen resting on the chalk at Clay Hill near Newbury, the basal layer there contains fossil oysters (see plate 4).

The Reading beds form a more or less continuous band of country all round the Berkshire end of the "London Basin."

They can be seen forming the base of low hills to the west of Great Bedwyn, also at West Woodhay, to the south of Kintbury, at Hampstead Marshall, and around Enborne. The straight Roman road from Speen to Wickham is ruled along an undulating ridge composed of Reading Beds; the actual road surface is made upon a layer of Plateau gravel which here thinly caps the Reading beds. The London Clay and Bagshot Beds were of course quite washed away and removed before the Plateau gravel could have been deposited on Reading Beds, and this ridge is simply a remnant of the base of the Eocene strata.

A similar ridge commences at Donnington Castle and proceeds via Snelsmore to Chieveley; on this the Reading Beds are still

* Also known as the "Woolwich and Reading Beds."

covered by the base of the London Clay, the surface of which is coated with Plateau gravel, obscuring the thin layer of clay still intact. These two ridges are remnants of the once continuous sheet of Reading Beds that covered the chalk bottom of the London basin; and the valleys on either side have been worn through into the chalk, leaving these long outliers, which now form hills. Further east the Reading beds are not so denuded, and form large unbroken masses of strata.

The London Clay, the second deposit in ascending order of the English Eocene, is a very regular and persistent stratum throughout the London Basin, although it varies considerably in thickness; attaining 314 feet at Windsor, it gradually thins out to the west, its thickness at Ascot being 250 feet, at Burghfield 200 feet; 164 feet at Strathfield-Mortimer and 52 feet at Inkpen.

The land surface—whose shores were being eroded by the Eocene Sea and whose great rivers assisted the action of the waves in spreading this wide deposit of clay—lay to the north and west and south of what is now Berkshire. The deposition of fine easily-floated silt and mud took place more readily some way out at sea, where the currents of the rivers and tides were diminished and the water was quiescent, hence the thickening of the London Clay and other Eocene strata generally, as they are traced eastwards.

This division of the Eocene appears to be very devoid of fossils in Berkshire, but in the Isle of Sheppey it has yielded abundant fossil remains of the extinct palms, eucalypti, magnolias, oaks and other trees that grew in beauty and waved on the land round the Eocene Seas; also of extinct reptiles, tapirs, and birds, and of a rich marine fauna. The climate, as indicated by the fossils, was very warm or tropical.

The Bagshot Beds were laid down fairly evenly over the London Clay, and take their name from the district around Bagshot where they are much in evidence.

The Lower Bagshot Beds are some 100 feet in thickness, and consist of yellow, white or brown sands, interstratified with thin layers of white and chocolate-coloured clays, and a few seams of pebbles. These strata may be examined around the edges of the commons of Greenham, Newtown, the Wash and Cold Ash, where they form plateau and are capped by the Plateau gravel. The latter obscures the Bagshot beds even at the edges of the commons in many places, as at the Workhouse, between Greenham Lodge the Wash Common, where the gravel has slipped down.

The Middle Bagshot Beds, also known as the Bracklesham Beds (Sussex Coast) are only found in Berkshire near Sunningdale, where they are about 50 feet thick, the upper half being composed of sands and the lower half of clays. The Upper Bagshot Beds may be found on the eastern boundary of the county at Bagshot and Finchampstead where they are buff-coloured sands of an uninteresting character.

It will be seen in plates 2 and 3 that the Upper and Middle Bagshots have been worn away in western and central Berkshire, leaving only portions of the Lower Bagshots remaining on the high ground in the vicinity of Newbury.

§ VII.—PLEISTOCENE, PREHISTORIC, AND RECENT.

Under this section are included the quite superficial deposits in the neighbourhood of Newbury that have been formed since the Tertiary Rocks of Berkshire began to emerge from the sea. The surface gravels, sands, clays, and loams which you see resting indiscriminately on the Chalk and Eocene, are simply debris and wreckage resulting from the gradual denudation and destruction of those rocks, and they have been sorted and arranged into their respective layers and terraces almost entirely by the erosion of rivers, except in the case of the Plateau gravel, which probably owes its origin to the action of the retreating Eocene Sea.

It will, I think, be already clear to readers, that the present hills and valleys of Berkshire are of post-Eocene age; although the contours of the high chalk country began to be formed before Eocene times, and much of this high ground has probably been subjected to continual denudation since the end of Cretaceous times.

The peat and fresh water marl are the result of small lakes and marshes that existed in prehistoric times.

The following table gives in descending order, a list of these superficial strata:—

Historical.	The Black Gravel of Newbury.
Pleistocene and *Prehistoric.	The Neolithic Lake series. The Palæolithic River gravels
Pleistocene, but without evidence of man.	The Donnington gravel and loam. †Clay-with-Flints, overlying chalk. The Plateau gravel.

The term Pleistocene (pleistos, most, kainos. recent. Gr.) is now taken generally to include all Post-Tertiary deposits up to the end of Prehistoric times. Originally this word was only applied to the period between the end of Tertiary time and the beginning

*Prehistoric times are divided in England into three great divisions : (1) Palæolithic, the ancient stone age, represented by a long-headed race in England, who made very rough and rude tools and weapons of stone and flint. (2) Neolithic, the newer stone age ; these people were round-headed, and fashioned tools and weapons very beautifully out of bone, flint, and other stones. (3) The Bronze age, when man first acquired the use of metal.

†I have placed the Clay-with-Flints here provisionally, but its age is not very certain and it may be older.

of Prehistoric times, but increased knowledge and evidence now shew conclusively that man has certainly existed in some parts of the world from the end of Tertiary times.

The Plateau Gravel (see plate 3) is found in the eastern and southern areas of the county, where it appears to have once formed a thin but very regular and continuous sheet. It forms the surface of many of the plateaux that separate the valleys. The levels of these little table-lands range from 350 feet to over 500 feet above sea level; the rise being gradual from east to west. As an example, the level of Greenham Common may be taken to be about 380 feet, and at Chisbury near Little Bedwyn—a distance of about 15 miles further west—the Plateau gravel occurs on the top of a hill 580 feet above sea level.

This gravel is found usually resting on a rather smooth planed-down surface of Eocene strata. It was spread out apparently before the present river system of Berks existed; for it occurs in outliers in much the same way as do remnants of the Eocene strata, and it is perfectly clear that this partial destruction of the once continuous gravel sheet has been done by the present river system since the gravel was formed. I consider the evidence afforded by this gravel goes far to prove that the first denudation of the Eocene was chiefly effected by wave-action; these soft strata emerged so slowly that the sea destroyed them before they could form a land surface; a more rapid rise following, would then raise the planed-down strata into dry land, and this land would be covered with a layer of gravel resulting from that partial destruction.

The present local river system would then come into operation and carve the valleys, leaving the remains of the wide gravel sheet on the plateaux between them.

The gravel itself is composed almost entirely of much oxydised flints, about 60 per cent being sub-angular and 40 per cent well rounded and rolled, and the matrix is of sand and clay. There is an almost entire absence of Greensand and northern debris, and the gravel appears to be wholly due to the destruction of Eocene strata; it rarely exceeds 20 feet and averages about 8 feet in thickness.

This gravel contains no fossils and is so pervious to both air and water that shells, bones, or vegetable remains would soon be entirely decayed and removed.

It decomposes into a barren soil which is often peaty and is usually covered with heather, ling, and gorse; it can be seen to perfection on Greenham or Snelsmore Commons; it also forms the surface more or less between Inkpen, Great Common and Heath End. It can be examined at Wash Common, Newtown Common, Crookham Common, Headley Common, Wickham Heath, Stockcross Village and Snelsmore East Common. The Church at Cold

Fig. i.—*Section near Donnington Square.*

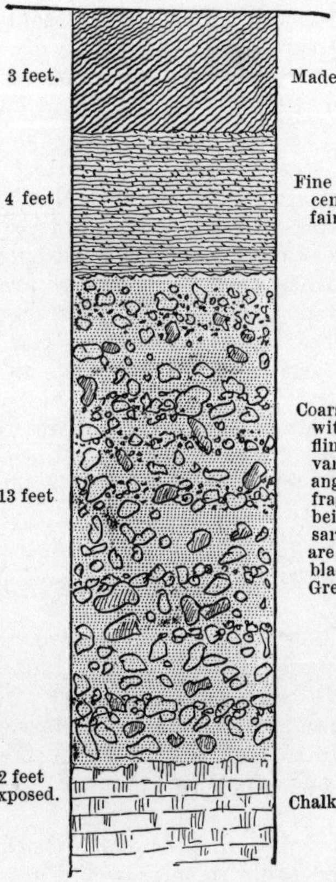

Ash is built upon plateau gravel. It will be seen from the foregoing, how the charming commons of Berkshire depend on the occurrence of this very interesting gravel.

The Clay-with-Flint, is spread over the surface of the chalk in a ragged and patchy zone about 5 miles wide, extending more or less east and west over the Downs lying north and N.W. of Newbury. In the centre of this band lie the villages of Compton, Beedon, Leckhampstead, East and West Shefford, and Ramsbury. The Church at Chieveley is built upon the Clay-with-flint.

The clay is a stiff reddish-brown deposit containing large unworn flints, it rests directly on the chalk and has been found to pass under Boulder Clay, and it may therefore be of pre-glacial age. It has not been fully examined, and Newbury geologists might very well study it closely and try to determine its true age. This clay is probably due to atmospheric decomposition of the chalk. Dr. Salter says it has been forming from the time the chalk was first exposed up to the present day. It is not shown on the maps accompanying this memoir.

The Donnington Gravel and Loam (fig i). This is another enigmatical deposit; it lies usually on an eroded surface of chalk-with-flints, and occupies a small area, the centre of which appears to be Donnington Square. It was exposed in the adjoining cutting on the railway from Newbury to Lambourn where it rests on eroded London Clay. [Fig ii & plate 4.]

Fig. ii.—*Section in the Lambourne Railway-cutting.*

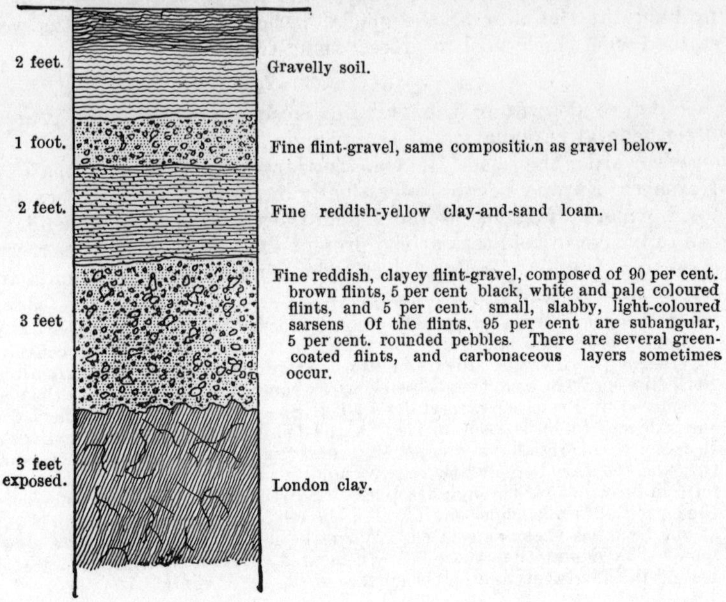

It consists of a lower mass of coarse roughly bedded sandy flint gravel, of a rusty reddish colour, varying from a few inches up to 13 feet in thickness. The upper portion is a red or cinnamon-coloured loam or brickearth, 50 per cent of it being tenacious clay and 50 per cent fine flint sand, intimately mixed together, and thin carbonaceous layers occur sparingly.

The base of the gravel contains sub-angular sarsens* of all sizes, up to 3 feet long. Both sub-angular and well worn flints are intermingled; about 85 per cent of the flints are brown, the remainder are of various colours; some of the latter are quite bleached, and have, I believe, been derived from the Plateau gravel.

Occurring as it does at the ancient confluence of the Kennet and Lambourn, and in view of its composition, I think it is a river gravel largely composed of local Plateau gravel, with an addition of Eocene debris of later formation than the Plateau gravel. The loam lies conformably on the gravel and averages about 4 feet in thickness. I have obtained no bones myself from this gravel, but remains of Elephas primigenius (mammoth) were found when making the adjacent railway cutting, and they came from either the gravel or loam (fig ii).

In Donnington Square I found—in 1894—a bone in the loam which Mr. E. T. Newton, F.R.S., has referred to either bison or bos primigenius (a gigantic extinct ox).

These bones are important evidence of the age of the Donnington gravel and loam, for they indicate a sub-arctic climate, probably at the close of the glacial period. The mammoths were clothed with thick wool to protect them from cold.

Before describing the gravels, freshwater-marl, and peat, a little general explanation of their origin is necessary.

Towards the close of the Tertiary period, the climate of Northern Europe began to gradually become colder, for we find fossil genera of shells in the Upper Tertiaries whose descendants can only live in cold seas at the present day; and in the Pleistocene clays and gravels, fossils of arctic shells and animals abound, and

* "Sarsens" are irregularly shaped blocks, boulders, or pebbles of an extremely hard fine sandstone, the grains of which are powerfully cemented together with silica, or silica and iron. Sarsens are found in nearly all the Berkshire gravels, and they also occur as boulders on the surface; they are considered by Professor Rupert Jones, F.R.S.,—who is a great authority on the subject—to have been formed in the loose sandy strata of the Bagshot Beds by a concretionary process, due to percolating water, which cemented the sand together here and there; resembling on a large scale, the lumps that form in brown sugar through dampness. Sarsens have also been referred to the action of humic acids that affected the felspar with which the sands may at one time have been associated. When the soft Bagshot Beds were slowly removed by denudation, these heavy cemented blocks and boulders were left behind in the gravels and on the surface of the bared chalk.

we know that the northern part of the Northern Hemisphere was covered with a great cap of snow and ice, which may have crept south as far as the Thames Valley in England, and seems to have covered most of Ireland. The ice sheet extended to the Pyrenees in Europe and far southward in North America. The tropical and sub-tropical flora and fauna of Tertiary times either died out or gradually retreated south, and were replaced by northern arctic types. It is not within the scope of this paper to discuss the causes and proofs of these phenomena, but the evidence we have is clear, abundant, and absolutely conclusive as to their occurrence.

During the "ice age" England south of the Thames Valley was very similar to the present habitable part of Greenland which lies between the coast and the edge of the permanent polar ice sheet. Newbury appears to have been just out of reach of the ice, for actual evidence of glaciation seems to be entirely absent in the neighbourhood. When these arctic conditions began to be replaced by a more temperate climate, the ice slowly retreated and the rivers were doubtless of much greater volume than they are now, and during the glacial summer there would be extensive floods. To these causes we may attribute many of the wide sheets of coarse heavy gravel that are spread over the valley floors in the South of England, and in particular in the Kennet Valley at Newbury. The bones of animals belonging to arctic species have been found in these gravels and are of course valuable evidence of the climate existing at that time. The peat and freshwater-marl mark the sites of ancient marshes and lakes, and always occur on the top of the gravels; their fauna at Newbury is that of a "coldly temperature" climate, and they record the gradual change of climate between the glacial period and modern times.

The Upper Palaeolithic River-Gravel. — On each side of the Kennet Valley at Newbury, there are fine broad terraces of river gravel that were deposited by the river Kennet in Pleistocene times when its bed was about 260 feet above sea level. Since that time the river has cut its way about 25 feet lower and has wandered more or less from side to side of the valley, gradually leaving the flat terraces high and dry. The action of rivers is complex and cannot be fully described here, but I may remind the reader that a river always cuts away at the concave sides of its curves, and carries the material removed down stream; it re-deposits some of this material on the convex sides of its curves, from which it is always receding, quickly or slowly according to the rate at which it eats away the concave side opposite.

In course of time, such river curves travel diagonally across a valley-floor until they reach the side of the valley, leaving behind them a smooth meadow which has a slight inclination towards the river, because the river bed is also being worn deeper. The subsoil of such meadows is river gravel and sand. On arriving at the valley-side, or the edge of a terrace of older and higher gravel, the river continues to eat its way in, until a high steep bank is formed; a mass of this bank ultimately falls off, as a rule, and reverses the conditions, causing the river to recede from the bank at a point opposite the fallen mass (or accumulation of fallen debris); in this way a curve is commenced that gradually travels diagonally away from the high bank to the other side of the valley.

If these few facts are considered when looking at the Newbury gravels, it will be easier to follow their history.

A most comprehensive view of the Upper River-Gravels can be obtained from the Great Western Railway Bridge in Gas-House Road.

The highest river gravel left on the sides of any valley is the oldest; younger gravels being left at lower levels as the river cuts its way deeper down.

I have already pointed out that the river Kennet was of much greater volume in Pleistocene times, and it was then able to carve away, deposit, and re-deposit gravels on an extensive scale.

On the south side of the river, at Newbury, the edge of the Upper River-Gravel lies parallel to, and just north of the Great Western Railway; Eastfields, St. John's Church and the "Black Boys" Hotel are all built on the Upper River-Gravel.

On the north side of the Kennet the Upper River-Gravel is not so clearly defined, because of the confluence of the Vale of Lambourn; but a terrace of this gravel commences near the Jubilee Clock, it skirts the valley-side past the Waterworks and continues more or less regularly towards Kintbury. A similar terrace may be discerned on the south side above and below Newbury. This Upper River-Gravel is usually about 12 feet thick at the edges of the terraces, and is composed of all kinds of flints, with a few well rounded flint pebbles and subangular sarsens intermingled. (see fig 9). Irregular lenticular beds of soft yellow or green sands are occasionally intercalcated with the Upper River-Gravel. The gravel contains roughly made rude palaeolithic flint implements, and these constitute the most ancient record we have of man in the neighbourhood of Newbury. Flint implements, turned up by the plough, can be found on the surface of fields that lie on the Upper River-Gravel. I found bones of the following animals in this gravel.

Ovis. (sheep) species undeterminable.
Bos tauras. (an ox).
Sus scrofa. (wild boar).
Equus caballus. (a nearly extinct horse).
Rangifer tarandus. (reindeer).
Bos primigenius. (gigantic extinct ox).

In making excavations in the Upper River-Gravel for the Great Western Railway goods station, remains of the mammoth were found. The reindeer and mammoth are of Pleistocene age, and their presence indicates an extremely cold climate, and points to the vast antiquity of man, for climates change very slowly indeed when measured by the lives of men and animals. A section in Enborne Road of the Upper River-Gravel shews it resting upon an eroded surface of hard dark green sand; this section is near the base of the Reading Beds at Newbury and the chalk is not far below the bottom of the section.

Fig. iii.—*Section at the Pumping-station of the Drainage-works.*

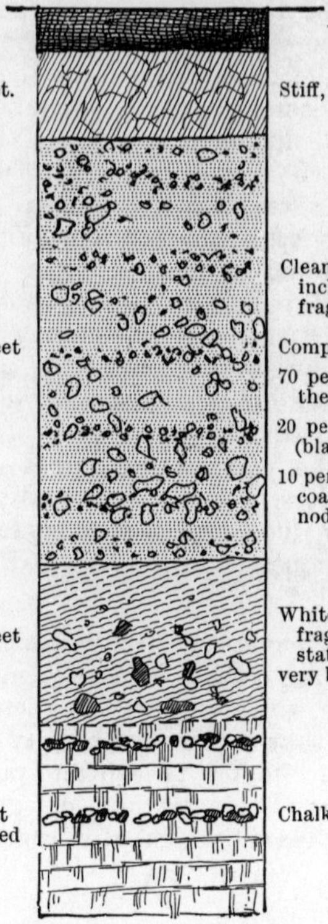

1 foot. — Peaty soil and peat, with Neolithic flint implements.

2 feet. — Stiff, pale yellow, sandy, homogeneous clay.

10½ feet — *The Lower River-Gravel.*
Clean flint-shingle, grey in colour, sarsens up to 12 inches in diameter near the base, and small chalk-fragments intermingled throughout.
Composition:
70 per cent brown flints, most of them well rolled, the rest subangular;
20 per cent. subangular, white-coated, black flints (black where worn);
10 per cent subangular, ferruginous gritstone, green-coated flints, large subangular sarsens, and flint nodules

4 feet — White sandy clay, with black flint-nodules and chalk-fragments, this was only found at the pumping station, and it is probably a confused remnant of the very bottom of the Reading Beds.

5 feet exposed — Chalk with-flints.

The Lower Palaeolithic River-Gravel occupies that portion of the floor of the Kennet Valley lying between the edges of the Upper River-Gravel Terraces already described. At Newbury it rests directly upon the chalk. Fig 3 shews a typical section, obtained when sinking the storage well at the Sewage Pumping Station. This gravel forms the base upon which the Neolithic peat and freshwater-marl have been deposited, and is the lowest found at Newbury. It is a mingling of all the other gravels I have mentioned; the flints are nearly all of large size, especially near the base, where a large percentage of unweathered flints occur that have been directly derived from the chalk. This gravel is very remarkable in appearance, it is greyish in colour, and the flints composing it when not well rounded are abraded to an extraordinary extent. Judging by the battered condition of the large flints and the frequent almost complete absence of any matrix, the currents which dealt with this gravel appear to have been extremely violent; when present, the matrix consists of very coarse and perfectly clean flint sand. Wave action and storm beaches would be inferred if near the coast, for the gravel rises into curious ridges which traverse the valley from side to side, more or less at right angles to the present course of the Kennet, These long mounds shew very little, or not at all, on the surface; (see plate 4) because the basins formed by these old lake barriers are now filled up with the Neolithic peat, clay, and marl. Similar gravel barriers are often found near the mouth of valleys debouching on the sea coast, as at Slapton Sands in Devonshire; but at Newbury no traces of marine shells and organic remains of any kind have been found in this gravel to my knowledge: and there is no geological record of submergence at the period whereof we treat, which turned the Kennet Valley into an estuary. The wave action hypothesis is therefore untenable, and it is probable that ice barriers on a considerable scale—such as occur in some of the Canadian rivers every few years during the annual break-up of the semi-arctic winters—were the true cause of these gravel barriers. The exceptionally abrased condition of the flints is probably due to the heavy current action that would prevail during the summer months of those Pleistocene times.

I possess two large rude but undoubted flint palaeoliths from this Lower River Gravel, both are rather water-worn, but are much less abraded than the flints which surrounded them. From this evidence, and from the fact that a thin bed of clay overlying the Lower River-Gravel has been found to contain palaeolithic implements, it is clear that the age of this gravel is not greatly less than that of the Upper River-Gravel, which also contains very similar implements.

The Prehistoric Lake Series.

[See fig iv and plate 4.]

This is composed generally of the following strata at Newbury, in descending order:—

Neolithic.	Fresh-water Marl, from a few inches to 8 feet in thickness, and rarely missing. Peat, from a few inches to about 10 feet in thickness. Green Loam, 6 inches to 2 feet in thickness ; often absent.
Palæolithic	Stiff dark yellow Clay, 6 inches to 2 feet ; occasionally absent.

Fig. iv.—*Section in Northbrook Street, Newbury.*

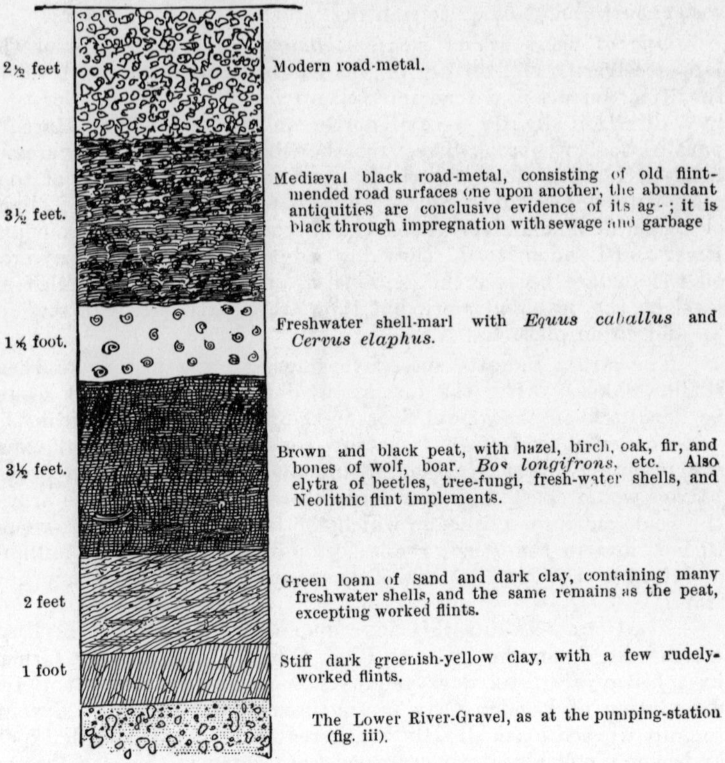

The Peat and Marl—by far the most important of these strata—are undoubtedly of Neolithic age. The Green Loam contains mollusca similar to those found in the Freshwater Marl, and it may therefore be considered Neolithic. The clay is of Palaeolithic age

I have already mentioned the ridges of Lower River-Gravel which here and there cross the floor of the Kennet Valley, and which appear to be due to the action of river-ice at a time near the close of the glacial period, and near the end of Palaeolithic times.

These ridges of gravel dammed the River Kennet up into a series of shallow fresh-water lakes.

The layers of clay, green shelly loam, peat, and fresh-water marl were then gradually deposited and formed, until the lakes were either quite silted up, or the barriers of gravel were ultimately cut through by the river. Local currents and variable depths and conditions have caused these strata to be laid down in a somewhat irregular manner; and occasionally the peat is thick and the fresh-water marl almost or quite wanting, and sometimes vice versâ.

One of these gravel barriers commences at the edge of the Upper River-Gravel terrace in Gas-House Road, at a point where the River-terrace and road intersect each other. The barrier runs in a direction slightly west of north, and traverses the "Marsh" parallel to Northbrook Street; it then bends to the N.E., crosses beneath London Road a little to the west of the junction of that road with the road to Shaw, and finally dies out in the slight elevation of mixed river gravel that occurs between the Lambourn River and London Road. These low ridges are not easily discovered on the surface because the depressions on either side are filled up level by the peat and marl, but they are clearly shewn in sections AB and CD on plate 4.

The strata indicate successive stages in the history of these shallow lakes. After the formation of a barrier, the clay would be deposited on the gravel floor of the pseudo-lake during floods, and render it watertight; marshy conditions would then cause the growth of peat; further silting and puddling of the gravel barrier would cause an increased depth of water sufficient to drown the peat and form a lake, in which the fresh-water mollusca would thrive; and in time their shells accumulated in countless millions and formed the marl on which so many houses in Newbury now stand.

The Clay.—Taking this little lake series in order:—The base, which rests upon the "Lower River-Gravel" is generally formed by a bed of very stiff dark yellow clay, probably the result of the denudation of London Clay in the immediate vicinity. Several roughly worked black slightly-weathered flints of palaeolithic types, and some pieces of water-worn wood were found in this clay, but no bones have been noticed.

The Green Loam lying upon the clay is formed of about equal parts of fine sand and dark greenish clay. Fresh-water shells and rolled logs of birch and oak, with leaves twigs and nuts of the hazel, frequently occur, and are similar to those found in the overlying peat. I obtained a pelvis of roe deer from this bed near the sewage pumping station.

The Peat, next in the series, is of great interest because it is the chief repository at Newbury of the stone weapons and other relics of prehistoric man.

It is composed principally of the remains of bog-moss (or sphagnum) augmented by acquatic plants of many kinds; the trunks and roots of birch oak and fir-trees—nearly all waterworn—are abundant, and large tree fungi have also been found by the author; sedges, hazel-nuts, and bracken are perfectly preserved in the peat of Newbury, and the elytra or wing cases of beetles are numerous. Bones and teeth of the following animals have been found in the peat of Newbury.

1.	Bos longifrons.	An ox. [Nearly extinct in England.]
2.	Cervus elaphus.	Red deer.
3.	Capreolus caprea.	Roe deer.
4.	Equus caballus.	An ancient horse. [Extinct.]
5.	Capra hircus.	A goat. [Extinct species.]
6.	Sus scrofa.	Wild boar.
7.	Ovis.	A sheep.
8.	Canis familiaris.	A dog.
9.	,, lupus.	Wolf. [Extinct in England.]
10.	Mustela martes.	Marten. [Extinct in England.]

The Reindeer was also represented by a piece of drilled and carved antler found in the peat, but this animal was not contemporary with the peat of Newbury; this carved bone of a sub-arctic animal is interesting evidence to shew that Neolithic man in Southern England was probably in communication with the North.

Some of the plant remains, and the presence of marten, indicate a colder climate than that of modern Berkshire. In other parts of the Kennet Valley remains of Beaver, Otter, Badger, Ass, and Bear have been found. The antler of a Great Irish Elk (extinct) is reported to have been obtained from the peat a few miles below Newbury* and Elk has been recently found in Peat near Staines†

The Neolithic relics found in the peat under and in the vicinity of Newbury include numerous flint implements; these have been made chiefly from black kidney-shaped nodules of flint, coated by a thin white oxydised skin. The following types occur:—Fine needle-shaped instruments, hide scrapers, razor-like knives, axes, hammers, arrow heads, and delicate spoon-shaped tools possibly used for extracting marrow from bones; innumerable "wasters" are scattered about in places, and the flint cores from which the flint flakes were struck are by no means uncommon. Two fragments of carved bones, and pieces of badly baked primitive pottery were found by the author, and calcined flints were associated with abundant fragments and layers of charcoal. A portion of a "pile-dwelling" was exposed in 1894 under the roadway opposite the "Coopers Arms" in Bartholomew Street (see plate 4): it was

* Q.J. Geol. Soc., Vol. 59, p 80. † Geol. Mag. 1891, pp. 95 and 480.

constructed of vertical fir-poles about 6 inches in diameter which had been driven into the peat, and there were numerous horizontal poles crossing the tops of the piles. The surface of the platform was level with the surface of the peat, and when the dwelling was inhabited by Neolithic men the surrounding bog would be a natural defence from sudden attack, and would probably be crossed by a single artificial pathway. Most of the implements occurred near the top of the Newbury peat.

The Fresh-Water Marl is composed almost entirely of the shells of about 50 species of mollusca. The majority of these are of modern varieties, but a few are now rare or have nearly disappeared. The climate indicated is similar to our own. Remains of red deer, roe deer, and horse have been found in the marl. These animals were probably drowned in the lake or the river when being hunted by wolves or savage man. There are no authentic records of any human relics being found in the fresh-water marl.

Where the peat is thick the marl is usually thin and vice versâ. I assume the peat where thick to indicate the most stagnant and shallow portions of the ancient lakes; and I consider that areas where the lakes were deeper, or where the water was freshened by the flowing river, are now shewn by thickening of the marl.

The Black Gravel.—Under Northbrook-street, Bartholomew-street and a few of the other ancient roadways of Newbury, there are hard layers of black triturated flint road-metal, the bottom layer resting upon the peat and marl; this "black gravel" is simply a long accumulation of road-mendings, mingled with rubbish and things lost and dropped by the way; it attains a thickness of 7 feet in Bartholomew Street, and is about 4 feet thick in Northbrook Street.

This black gravel is of course "historic" and is enriched with countless antique odds and ends. Much sewage had been thrown out on the roadway during the accumulation of this "macadam," and the phosphates therein have preserved the iron and leather relics in a wonderful manner. The lowest layer has yielded Romano-British and Saxon horse-shoes, Roman tiles, fragments of sandals, a bronze chisel, and a spatula; very large-headed nails of soft iron, having minute fragments of flint imbedded in them are common, and were used to affix the wheel-tyres of vehicles that traversed that old highway across the Kennet, in ancient historic times.

The central portion is mediæval, and articles obtained from this black gravel by the author include a pair of neat small Elizabethan shoes from a girl's slender feet, a stoneware inkpot to be carried in a belt, and a fragment of gilded chain armour. The upper 18 inches contains mementoes of the Civil War, such as cannon balls, once fired from Donnington Castle, and accoutrements, almost rusted away, that tell of—

> "Old unhappy far-off things,
> And battles long ago"

APPENDIX I.

SOME BIBLIOGRAPHY RELATING TO THE GEOLOGY OF NEWBURY AND BERKSHIRE.

Publications of H.M. Geological Survey of England and Wales.

1862 { Bristow, The late, H. W., F.G.S. / Whitaker, W., B.A. LOND., F.R.S., F.G.S. } "The Geology of parts of Berkshire and Hampshire." [Sheet 12, 1862.]

1864 Whitaker, W. "The Geology of parts of Middlesex and Berkshire."

1872 Whitaker, W. "The Geology of the London Basin." [Memoir of Geol. Survey, Vol. IV., 1872.

1889 Whitaker, W. "The Geology of London." [2 vols.]

1902 { Blake, J. H., F.G.S., with contributions by / Whitaker, W. } "The Water Supply of Berkshire."

A list of geological maps, etc., is issued by H.M. Ordnance Survey Department, Southampton, price 1s.

Old series, coloured, sheets 7, 8, 12, 13, 34 and 45, S.W.

New series, coloured, 1898, [Scale, 1 inch = 1 mile.] Nos. 267, 268 and 283.

For Newbury people, the most useful of all these maps is No. 267 of the new series, hand coloured 3s.

Other Literature.

1826 Buckland, Dr. Frank, "The formation of the valley of Kingsclere," etc. Trans. Geol. Soc., Series II, Vol. II., p. 119.

1847 Prestwich, The late Professor Sir Joseph, F.R.S., F.G.S. "On the probable age of the London Clay," Q.J.G.S.* vol. III p. 354.

1847 Prestwich, the late Sir J., "On the main points of structure, and the probable age of the Bagshot Beds, Q.J.G.S., vol. III, p. 378.

1850 " "The Basement Bed of the London Clay." Q.J.G.S., vol. VI, p. 252.

1854 " "The Woolwich and Reading Series." Q.J.G.S., vol. X, p. 75.

1854 " "On the thicknesses of the London Clay," etc., Q.J.G.S., vol. X, p. 401.

1854 Jones, Professor Thomas Rupert, F.R.S., F.G.S. "A lecture on the Geol. History of the vicinity of Newbury, Berks."

* Q.J.G.S. means Quarterly Journal of the Geological Society (of London).

1862 Prestwich, Sir J. "On the Western end of the London Basin," Q.J.G.S., vol. XVII, p. 258.

1869 Adams, The Rev. John, M.A. "Geological Sketch of the Kennet Valley." Wiltshire Archæol. and Nat. Hist. Soc. Mag., vol. 23, p. 122.

1871 Jones, Prof. T. Rupert, "On the Geology of the Kingsclere Valley." Geol. Mag., vol. VIII., p. 511.

1873 Jones, Prof. T. Rupert. "The Geology of the Kennet Valley." Trans. Newbury District Field Club, vol. I, p. 21.

1875 Jones, Prof. T. Rupert, and King, C. Cooper. "On some newly exposed sections of the Woolwich and Reading Beds, at Reading, Berks

1878 Grover, J. W., M.INST.C.E., F.S.A. "Report of the New Water Supply at Newbury." Trans. Newbury District Field Club vol. II, p. 246.

1878 Jones, Prof. T. Rupert, F.R.S., F.G.S. Woodward, B. B., F.R.S., F.G.S. "Excursion to Newbury." Proc. Geol. Association, vol. VI, p. 348.

1883 Monckton, H. W., F.L.S., F.G.S. "The Bagshot Beds of the London Basin." Q.J.G.S., vol. XXXIV, p. 348.

1883 Whitaker, W., M.A., LOND., F.R.S., F.G.S. "List of works on the Geology and Palæontology of Oxfordshire, of Berkshire and of Buckinghamshire." Report to British Association, 1882.

1884 Jones, Prof. T. Bupert. "Some geological notes on the neighbourhood of Newbury, Berks." Geol. Mag. Dec. III, vol I., p. 122.

1886 Jones, Prof. T. Rupert. "History of the Sarsens," with bibliographical list. Wiltshire Archæological and Natural Hist. Soc. Mag., vol. XXII, p. 122.

1886 Irving, A., F.G.S. "The unconformity between the Bagshot Beds and the London Clay." Geol. Mag., Dec. III, vol. III, p. 402.

1886 Monckton, H. W. Herries, R. S., M.A., F.L.S. "The Bagshot Beds of the London Basin." Q.J.G.S., vol. 42, p. 402.

1887 Irving, A., F.G.S. "The Physical History of the Bagshot Beds of the London Basin." Q.J.G.S., vol. XLIII, p. 374.

1890 Prestwich, Sir Joseph. "On the relation of the Westleton Beds," etc., 3 parts, Q.J.G.S., vol. 46, pp. 84, 120 and 155.

1890 Shrubsole, O. A., F.G.S. "Valley Gravels about Reading." Q.J.G.S., vol. 46, p. 582.

1892 Monckton, H. W. "On the Gravels South of the Thames from Guildford to Newbury." Q.J.G.S., vol 48, p. 29.

1893 Monckton, H. W. "On the occurrence of Boulders and Pebbles from the Glacial Drift South of the Thames." Q.J.G.S., vol. 49, p. 308.

1895 White, H. J. O., F.G.S. "Westleton and Glacial Gravels in Oxon and Berks." Proc. Geol. Association, vol. 14, p. 11.

1897 Richards, E. P., F.G.S. "On the Gravels and Associated Deposits of Newbury," (with bibliographic appendix). Q.J.G.S., vol. 53, p. 420 seq.

1897 { Kennard, A. S., Woodward, B. B., F.L.S., F.G.S. } Notes on the Mollusca from the Kennet Valley deposits. Q.J.G.S., vol. 53, p. 434.

1898 Salter, A. E., D.SC., F.G.S "Pebbly and other gravels in Southern England." Proc. Geol. Assoc., vol. 15, p. 264.

1898 Shrubsole, O. A. "High Level Gravels in Berks and Oxon." Q.J.G.S., vol. 54, p. 585.

1900 Blake, J. H., F.G.S. "Excursion to Silchester." Proc. Geol. Assoc., vol. 16, p. 513.

1901 Jones, Professor T. Rupert, F.R.S., "History of the Sarsens" (2 parts). Dec. 4, vol. VIII, pp. 54-59 and 115-125. 1901.

1901 Monckton, H. W. "Origin of the Gravel-flats of Surrey and Berkshire." Geol. Mag. Dec. IV., vol. 8, p. 510.

1902 White, H. J. O. "On a peculiarity in the course of certain streams in the London and Hampshire Basins." Proc. Geol. Assoc., vol. 17, p. 399.

1902 Jukes-Browne, A. J., B.A., F.G.S. "On a deep boring at Lyme Regis." Q.J.G.S., vol. 58, p. 279.

1902 Mackinder, H. J., M.A. "Britain and the British Seas." For notes on river history see under "Berkshire" in index, and at p. 96.

1903 Newton, E. T., F.R.S., F.G.S. "The Elk in the Thames Valley." Q.J.G.S., vol. 59, p. 80.

1905. Salter, A. E., D.SC., F.G.S. "On the Superficial Deposits of Central and Parts of Southern England." Proc. Geol. Assoc., vol. XIX, p. 14 and 15.

The Transactions of the Newbury District Field Club (edited by Walter Money, F.S.A., and others), contain many geological facts and notes relating to the local geology; see vol. I (1871), pp. 21-32, 104-109; vol. II (1878), pp. 2-6, 64, 133-137, 241-250; vol. III (1886), p. 101; vol. IV (1895), pp. 206-210, 257-260.

A list of land and fresh-water Mollusca, from the peat and marl, was compiled by Prof. T. Rupert Jones, and can be found in the Memoir of the Geological Survey, Expl. Sheet No. 12, 1862, p. 48. In the same Memoir Dr. Palmer gives a list of mammalia from the peat of the Kennet Valley.

APPENDIX II.

The following section from a well sunk at Greenham Lodge, about one mile S.E. of Newbury, will be of value to Newbury geologists.

Feet.	ins.			Feet.	ins.
12	0	Soil and Plateau Gravel.		12	0
2	0	Brown loam.	Lower Bagshot Beds.	43	2
4	0	,, sand (little water)			
10	0	,, loam.			
7	0	Blue Clay.			
1	6	Black flint pebbles.			
4	6	Blue sand (little water)			
0	4	Light stone.			
4	8	Dead-blue sand.			
1	2	Hard dark stone.			
3	0	Dark grey sand.			
5	0	Blue sandy Clay.			
35	10	London Clay.	The London Clay.	60	10
0	6	Black flint pebbles.			
24	6	Black sandy clay.			
4	0	Coloured sand and Clay.	Reading Beds.	80	0
12	0	,, sand.			
15	0	Light brown sand (water).			
8	0	Coloured sand and Clay.			
15	0	Mottled Clay.			
13	0	Green sand (water).			
4	0	Black Clay.			
8	6	Hard dark green sand.			
0	6	Flints.			
196	0			196	0

The Chalk was reached at 196 feet from surface.

A BRIEF SKETCH OF THE BOTANY OF THE NEWBURY DISTRICT

BY

G. CLARIDGE DRUCE, M.A., F.L.S.

Author of the "Flora of Berkshire," the "Flora of Oxfordshire," etc.

In the "History and Antiquities of Newbury and its Environs" of 1839, Mrs. Anne Russell published a catalogue of plants seen about Newbury, and more recently Mr. Weaver contributed an interesting list of species observed by him in the neighbourhood to "Hawkins' Guide to Newbury." For a more complete account of plant distribution my "Flora of Berkshire," from which the following account has been taken, should be consulted.

Newbury is especially well situated for the lover of Botany, since a great variety of soils is to be met with in a small area. The irrigated meadows of the Kennet are well known, and from their occasional peaty character give a home to plants which are absent from the meadows of the Upper Thames. The numerous and extensive reed-beds and osier-holts are a pleasing feature, and the river itself is rich in aquatics.

The large Commons of Greenham and Crookham offer a complete change of scene and vegetation, with their noble views of Beacon Hill, Sydmonton, and Highclere, while to the north may be seen the pleasant line of country extending to Snelsmore, Bucklebury, and Cold Ash Commons, and the high ground of Yattendon. The Bramble vegetation is especially luxuriant, and includes many rare species. The Sweet Gale (*Myrica Gale*) and the Black Alder (*Rhamnus Frangula*) still grow there. Among the truly ericetal and uliginal plants are the Ling (*Calluna Erica*), the Heather (*Erica cinerea*), and the Cross-leaved Heath (*E. Tetralix*), the upright Pearl-wort (*Cerastium quaternellum*), the Sand-wort (*Arenaria rubra*), the Bird's Trefoil (*Ornithopus perpusillus*), the Small Gorse (*Ulex nanus*), the Petty Whin (*Genista anglica*), the Pearl Worts *Sagina ciliata*, *S. subulata*, the St. John's Wort (*Hypericum quadrangulum*), the Marsh St. John's Wort (*H. Elodes*), the Bird's-foot Trefoil (*Trigonella purpurascens*), the Hare's-foot

Trefoil (*Trifolium arvense*), the Brambles *Rubus plicatus*, *R. holerythros*, *R. carpinifolius*, *R. Lindleianus*, *R. rhamnifolius*, *R. pulcherrimus*, *R. Selmeri*, *R. Schlechtendalii*, *Rubus Sprengelii*, *R. pyramidalis*, *R. infestus*, *R. Borreri*, *R. Radula*, *R. echinatus*, *R. Newbouldii*, *R. Babingtonii*, *R. Bloxamii*, *R. Mercicus*, *R. Kœhleri*, *R. dasyphyllus*, *R. Marshalli*, *R. diversifolius*, and *R. Balfourianus*, the Hawkweed (*Hieracium rigidum*), the Sheep's-bit Scabious (*Jasione montana*), the Bilberry (*Vaccinium Myrtillus*), the Small Dodder (*Cuscuta Epithymum*), the Spotted Orchid (*Orchis maculata* var. *ericetorum*), the Lancashire Asphodel (*Narthecium ossifragum*), the Pondweed (*Potamogeton polygonifolius*), the Deer's Grass (*Scirpus caespitosus*), the Sedges *Carex pulicaris*, *C. stellulata*, *C. binervis*, *C. flava*, *C. paniculata*, *C. Bœnninghausiana*, *C. remota*, the grasses *Agrostis canina*, *A. pumila*, *Festuca ovina* and var. *tenuifolia*, *F. sciuroides*, *Sieglingia decumbens*, *Molinia varia*, *Kœleria*, *etc.*

Snelsmore Common is almost equally rich, and has also *Rubus nitidus*, *R. nessenssis*, *R. foliosus*, etc. Here, too, as also at Greenham, are the Marsh Violet (*Viola palustris*), the Bog Stitchwort (*Stellaria uliginosa*), the Blinks (*Montia fontana*), the St. John's Worts (*Hypericum humifusum* and *pulchrum*), the All-seed (*Millegrana Radiola*), the Marsh Mallow (*Malva moschata*). the Hemlock-leaved Stork's Bill (*Erodium cicutarium*), the small Crane's Bill (*Geranium pusillum*). the Marsh Lady's fingers (*Lotus uliginosus*), the small Clover (*Trifolium filiforme*), the Broom (*Cytisus scoparius*), the Downy Rose (*Rosa tomentosa*), the Sweet Briers (*Rosa rubiginosa* and *R. micrantha*), the Sun-dews (*Drosera rotundifolia* and *D. longifolia*), *Peplis Portula*, the Marsh Willow herb (*Epilobium palustre*), the Pennywort (*Hydrocotyle vulgaris*), the Marsh Hone-wort (*Apium inundatum*), the Heath Bedstraw (*Galium hercynicum*), the Marsh Bedstraw (*G. uliginosum*), the Cudweed (*Filago minima*), the Heath Cudweed (*Gnaphalium sylvaticum*, the Marsh Thistle (*Cnicus pratensis*), the Golden Rod (*Solidago Virg-aurea*), the Hawkweeds *Hieracium boreale*, *H. sciaphilum*, *H. umbellatum*, the Bog-Pimpernel (*Anagallis tenella*), the Bog-bean (*Menyanthes trifoliata*), the Mouse-ear Scorpion grasses (*Myosotis cespitosa*, *M. versicolor*, *M. collina*), the Marsh Veronica (*V. scutellata*), the Marsh Lousewort (*Pedicularis palustris*), the Heath Lousewort (*P. sylvatica*), the Small Skull-cap (*Scutellaria minor*), the Wood Sage (*Teucrium Scorodonia*), the Buck's-horn Plantain (*Plantago Coronopus*), the Shoreweed (*Littorella juncea*), the Small Willow (*Salix repens*), the Rushes (*Juncus bulbosus* or *supinus*, *J. squarrosus*), the Club Rushes (*Scirpus pauciflorus*, *S. fluitans*, *Schœnus nigricans*), the Cotton grass (*Eriophorum augustifolium*), the Beaked Club rush (*Rynchospora alba*), the Sedges *Carx leporina*, *C. panicea*, *C. rostrata*, *C. flava*, *C. pulicaris*, *C. panicea*, *C. Goodenowii*, *C. remota*, *C. pilulifera*, *C. stellulata*, the grasses *Aira praecox*, *A. caryophyllea*, *Deschampsia fleuxuosa*, *Melica uniflora*, *Nardus*, and many others.

Elsewhere in the neighbourhood, on heathy soil or gravelly ground, have been found the Catchfly (*Silene anglica*), the parasitic Broomrapes (*Orobanche major* and *O. Rapum-genistae*), the small Centaury (*Erythraea pulchella*), the tiny *Centunculus minima*, the Meadow Saxifrage (*Saxifraga granulata*), often in great quantities in gravelly meadows, and a common plant of the Kennet Valley. A variety of the Marsh Mallow, *Malva moschata* var. *Ramondiana*, or to use the earlier name, *integrifolia*, was found by the Author near Theale for the first time in Britain. The woodlands in the neighbourhood afford a home for many interesting species. Among these are the Solomon's Seal *(Polygonatum multiflorum)*, which is quite abundant in many words. A more local plant is the Spiked Star of Bethlehem *(Ornithogalum pyrenaicum)*. There are also the Golden Saxifrage *(Saxifraga oppositifolia)*, the Wood Pimpernel *(Lysimachia nemorum)*, the grass *Poa nemoralis*, and the ferns *Athyrium Filix-fœmina*, *Dryopteris dilatata*, *D. spinulosa*, *D. montana*, *Polystichum aculeatum*, *P. angulare*, *Blechnum Spicant*, the Horse Tails (*Equisetum sylvaticum* and *E. maximum*), the Columbine *(Aquilegia Columbaria)*, the Tutsan *(Hypericum Androsaemum)*, the Peas *Lathyrus montanus* and *L. sylvestris*, the Willow herbs *Epilobium augustifolium* and *E. obscurum*, the Moschatel *(Adoxa Moschatellina)*, the Wall Lettuce *(Lactuca muralis)*, the Cow Wheat *(Melampyrum pratense)*, the Wood Speedwell *(Veronica montana)*, the Toothwort (*Lathrœa Squamaria*) very local, the Yellow Archangel (*Lamium Galeobdolon*), the Bird's Nest Orchid (*Neottia Nidus-avis*), the Hellborine (*Epipactis latifolia*), the Fly Orchis (*Ophrys muscifera*), the Lily of the Valley (*Convallaria majalis*), the Ramsons (*Allium ursinum*), the Gladdion (*Iris foetidissima*), the Daffodil (*Narcissus Pseudo-Narcissus*), the Snowdrop (*Galanthus nivalis*), the Herb Paris (*Paris quadrifolia*), the Wood Rush (*Juncoides sylvaticum*), the Sedges *Carex sylvatica*, *C. pallescens*, *C. laevigata*, and *C. strigosa*.

The Kennet and its tributaries afford the Water-buttercups *Ranunculus peltatus*, *R. fluitans*, etc., the White Water Lily (*Castalia speciosa*), the Yellow Lily (*Nymphœa lutea*), the Cresses *Roripa amphibia*, *R. sylvestris*, the Water Starworts *Callitriche obtusangula*, *C. hamulata*, and *C. stagnalis*, the Water Hemlock (*Œnanthe Phellandrium*), the Milfoils (*Myriophyllum pectinatum* and *M. spicatum*), the Water Violet (*Hottonia palustris*), the Bladderworts (*Utricularia vulgaris* and *U. major*), the Frog-bit (*Hydrocharis Morsus-Ranae*), the Water Honewort (*Ceratophyllum demersus*), the Pondweeds *Potamogeton natans*, *P. lucens*, *P. densum*, *P. crispum*, *P. Friesii*, *P. zosteraefolius*, *P. pectinatum*, *P. pusillum*, *P. interruptus*, *P. perfoliatum*, and the Horned Pondweed (*Zannichellia palustris*), the Club Rushes *Eleocharis acicularis*, *E. palustris*, the Reed Maces *Typha latifolia* and *T. angustifolia*, the Bur-reeds *Sparganium simplex*, *S. erectum*, and

S. neglectum, the Arrow-head (*Sagittaria sagittifolia*), the Bulrush (*Scirpus lacustris*), and the grasses *Phragmites communis, Digraphis arundinacea*; and the sedges *Carex acuta* and *C. paludosa* are abundant, there are also, *C. riparia* and, rarely, *C. vesicaria* and *C. Pseudo-cyperus*, and the Charads, *Chara fœtida* and *C. fragilis*.

The meadows afford the Meadow Rue (*Thalictrum flavum*), the Buttercups *Ranunculus sceleratus, R. Flammula, and R. hederaceus*, the Bitter-cress *Cardamine amara*, the Chickweed (*Stellaria aquatica*), the Knotted Spurey (*Sagina nodosa*), the Meadow Crane's bill (*Geranium pratense*) often in great beauty, the beautiful and local Water Avens (*Geum rivale*), and occasionally the hybrid (*G. intermedium*), the Lady's Mantle (*Alchemilla vulgaris*) is local, the Black and Red Currants *Ribes nigrum* and *R. rubrum*, the Willow herbs *Epilobium hirsutum, E. parviflorum, E. obscurum, E. tetragonum, E. roseum*, the Purple Loosestrife (*Lythrum Salicaria*), the Dropwort (*Spiræa Filipendula*), especially where the soil is calcareous, the Water Dropwort (*Œnanthe fistulosa*), and the very poisonous *Œ. crocata*, the Bur Marigolds (*Bidens cernua* and *B. tripartita*) which prefer the margins of ponds, the Butter bur (*Petasites officinalis*), whose huge leaves are a conspicuous feature of the Kennet vegetation, the Yellow Loosestrife (*Lysimachia vulgaris*), the Forget-me-not (*Myosotis palustris*), the Mints *Mentha aquatica, M. verticillata, M. arvensis*, and *M. Pulegium*, the latter very local, the Orach (*Atriplex deltoidea*), the Bistort (*Polygonum Bistorta*), as well as *P. amphibium, P. Hydropiper, P. mite*, and *P. maculatum*, the Willows *Salix triandra, S. alba, S. viridis, S. fragilis, S. purpurea*—a very characteristic Kennet plant, *S. Smithiana, S cinerea, S. caprea*, and *S. viminalis*, the Alder (*Alnus glutinosa*), the Marsh Orchids *Orchis latifolia* and *O. incarnata*, the Arrow Grass (*Triglochin palustre*); *Scirpus caricis*, and *S. setaceus* are local, the grasses *Glyceria fluitans, G. aquatica, G. plicata, Catabrosa aquatica*, etc., and the Horsetails *Equisetum limosum* and *E. pratense* are common. Two conspicuous plants are now naturalised by the Kennet, namely, the Orange Balsam (*Impatiens biflora*) and the Yellow Monkey-flower (*Mimulus Langsdorfii*), both of American origin, and the Horseradish (*Cochlearia Armoracia*) is not infrequent. The Marsh Valerian (*Valeriana dioica*) is plentiful, and the Water Elder (*Viburnum Opulus*) is frequent, and affords a beautiful feature in the autumn.

The Hedge-rows in the neighbourhood of Newbury afford many Brambles and also, occasionally, the local *Rosa systyla* and *Geranium lucidum*. On clay soils the Hemlock (*Conium maculatum*), the Ragwort (*Senecio erucifolius*), the Flea Bane (*Inula Pulicaria*), and the Teasel (*Dipsacus sylvestris*) are found, and in most gravelly ditches the Hedge Honewort (*Sison Amomum*) abounds. On sunny hedge banks the Chervil (*Cerefolium Anthriscus*), and the Knotted Bur Parsley (*Caucalis nodosa*) will be seen. On stiffer soils, but locally, the Zig-zag Clover (*Trifolium *medium*), the Grass-leaved Vetchling (*Lathyrus Nissolia*), and the Bee Orchis (*Ophrys apifera*) grow. The grasses *Poa nemoralis* and *Melica uniflora* are frequent in old hedgerows. The Wayfaring tree (*Viburnum Lantana*), the Buckthorn (*Rhamnus catharticus*), the Old Man's Beard (*Clematis Vitalba*), the Maple (*Acer campestre*), the Cornel (*Cornus sanguinea*), the Spindle Tree (*Euonymus europæa*) are more frequent on calcareous soil. The range of chalk hills gives quite a distinct flora from that afforded by the Tertiary Commons and Eocene formation of the Kennet valley. On the grassy downs have been gathered the Pasque-flower (*Anemone Pulsatilla*), the Milk-wort (*Polygala calcarea*), the Rock-rose (*Helianthemum Chamæcistus*), the Squinancy wort (*Asperula cynanchica*), the Field Ragwort (*Senecio campestris*), the Field Chickweed (*Cerastium arvense*), the Felwort (*Gentiana Amarella*), the rare and local *G. germanica*, and a hybrid of it with the former which was discovered by the Author and named *G. Pamplinii*, after a well-known Berkshire botanist, the Bastard Toad-flax (*Thesium*), the Musk Orchis (*Herminium Monorchis*), the Frog Orchid (*Habenaria viridis*), the Orchids *Orchis ustulata*, *O. pyramidalis*, *Habenarea conopsea*, the Lady's Fingers (*Anthyllis Vulneraria*), the Horse Shoe Vetch (*Hippocrepis comosa*), the Scabious (*Scabiosa Columbaria*), the Carline Thistle (*Carlina vulgaris*), the Thistles *Carduus nutans*, *Cnicus acaulis*, the Hawksbeard (*Picris Hieracioides*), the Bell-flower (*Campanula glomerata*), the Marjoram (*Origanum vulgare*), the Catmint (*Nepeta Cataria*), the Calamint (*Calamintha Acinos*), the sedge *Carex divulsa*, the grasses *Avena pubescens*, *A. pratensis*, *Trisetum pratense*, *Kœleria cristata*, *Bromus erectus*, etc.

The woodlands on the chalk afford, in addition to many species already noticed, the Butterfly Orchid (*Habenaria chloroleuca* and *H. bifolia*), the Helleborines (*Epipactis violacea*), the Deadly Nightshade (*Atropa Belladonna*). the Ploughman's Spikenard (*Inula Conyza*), the Bellflower (*Campanula Trachelium*), the grass *Milium effusum*. In bushy places the Saw-wort (*Serratula tinctoria*) has been found.

Among other plants of the district round Newbury we may enumerate the Hairy Buttercup (*Ranunculus sardous*), a very rare Berkshire species, the Hoary Cress (*Lepidium Draba*), which is abundantly naturalised on the Lambourn railway, and the very rare grass, *Poa Chaixii*, which may possibly be native near Hungerford. Another grass, *Bromus interruptus*, was discovered by the Author near Pangbourne, and has since been noticed in the Kennet valley. It is a very distinct species, which has not as yet been observed on the Continent. The Hellebores *Helleborus viridis* and *H. fœtidus* exist in the County, and both are probably native. The Grape Hyacinth (*Muscari racemosum*) occurs near Newbury, and there is a field near Inkpen where the Spring Crocus (*Crocus vernus*) is in great quantity. The Lady's Traces (*Spiranthes autumnalis*) has been recorded from Hampstead Marshall. In that Park the Hound's Tongue (*Cynoglossum officinale*) is common. The Misletoe (*Viscum album*) is local and rare. A considerable number of alien plants occur by the railway and near the mills. One of these, *Beta trigyna*, from Hungary, is a conspicuous plant. The American Winter Cress (*Barbarea præcox*) is frequent.

The Cornfields afford the Mouse-tail (*Myosurus minimus*), the Candy-tuft (*Iberis amara*), the Lamb's Lettuce *Valerianella olitoria* and *V. dentata*, the Shepherd's Weather-glass (*Specularia* or *Legousia hybrida*), the Bur Parsley (*Caucalis infesta*), the Hawk's-beard (*Crepis taraxacifolia*), the Blue Cornflower (*Centaurea Cyanus*), the Poppies *Papaver dubium*, *P. Argemone* and, rarely, *P. hybrida*, the Fumitories *Fumaria densiflora* and *F. parviflora*, the Bedstraw (*Galium tricorne*), the Toad flaxes (*Linaria Elatina*, *L. spuria*, and *L. viscida*), the Weasel's Snout (*Antirrhinum Orontium*), the Dodder (*Cuscuta Trifolii*), the Broom Rape (*Orobanche Trifolium pratense*), the Garlic (*Alluin vineale*), etc.

The foregoing is not an exhaustive list, but is only intended to include the salient features of the Newbury flora. Any notes, additions, or queries will always be welcomed by the writer.

118, High Street, Oxford.

Addenda et Corrigenda.

P 17. On the accession of Henry II. to the throne in 1155, he commanded all the castles erected since the death of Henry I. to be demolished, except a few which were retained by the crown on account of their advantageous situation for the defence of the Kingdom, and the protection of maritime towns.

P. 20., line 18 from top, *for* "Fonterraud" *read* "Fontevraud." The famous convent of Fontevrault or Fontevraud, in Anjou, was one in which many royal and noble dames took the veil. Amesbury Abbey was a cell to this foreign monastery.

P. 22. Henry VI. was at Newbury on the 19th of August, 1447, as is shown by a petition granted here of this date. *Archaeologia*, vol. xvi., p. 6.

P. 28. Jack of Newbury was the first manufacturer to introduce *Broad-cloth*, that is cloths of an extra width, into this county.

P. 35, line 21 from top, *for* "Sir Humphrey Foster's" *read* "Forster's"

P. 39. 'Varsity Volunteers. When Oxford became the King's headquarters and most advanced post on the road to London, the students joined the army in large numbers, and the work of education was nearly suspended. Many of the fellows and others became officers and served with distinction in the royal army, such as Matthias Prideaux, Digory Polwhele, William Bew, a native of Newbury, Major of Horse, who became Bishop of Llandaff, and Sir Bevil Grenville, one of the leaders of the Cornish force, which won victory after victory for the King till Grenville fell at the battle of Lansdowne, and with him the westward army lost its onward impulse. Peter Mews, who became Bishop of Bath and Wells, and of Winchester, President of St. John's, also bore arms and was wounded in the Civil War, and in 1685 he was in arms against the rebels headed by the Duke of Monmouth. The learned Chillingworth, and dear friend of Falkland, also took up arms for the king, and served as an engineer at the siege of Gloucester, and elsewhere during the war. John Fell, who became Dean of Christ Church, and Bishop of Oxford, was another 'Varsity Volunteer, and served with the rank of Ensign.

P. 40, line 13 from bottom, *for* "Crookham Heath" *read* "Crockham Heath."

P. 77, Deodand. The Almoner whose business it was to distribute the royal arms, had formerly the disposition of deodands, and the goods of *felo's de se* allowed him by the Crown towards the relief of necessitous persons. Usually the almoner was a Bishop, and "His Majesty's Almoner at Christ Church, Oxford," referred to in the ballad of the "Renowned Shuff" was apparently Dr. John Fell, elected Bishop of Oxford in 1675, and who held the Deanery of Christ Church *in commendam*.

P. 78, "Couragious Soldiers of the West," 1690, is reprinted fully in the *Bagford Ballads*, edited by the Rev. J. W. Ebsworth, F.S.A., (completed in 1880), the broadside being in the Bagford Collection in the British Museum. The stanza referring to Newbury is as follows:—

> "There's not a land in all Christendom
> That can afford men freer to fight;
> Newberrye boyes at hearing the drum,
> Readily come with valour bright."

P. 112. Line 3 from top, *n* omitted in "regiment." Line 13 from top, *for* "commencsd" *read* "commenced."
Military manœuvres also took place in this neighbourhood in 1894, when H.R.H. the late Duke of Cambridge, accompanied by General Sir. Redvers Buller, V.C., Lieut. Gen. Sir W. J. Williams, Maj-Gens. Baker, Russell, and Gore, with Col. Fitz-George and Viscount Downe, aides-de-camp, attended service in Newbury Church, on Sunday, 9th September. In the afternoon the Duke and his staff visited Shaw House.

P. 147 In the Parish Registers there are many names to be found whose descendants were among the first settlers at Newbury in New England, U.S.A.

On the 17th June, 1905, there was inaugurated at this town across the sea a monument in commemoration of its first settlement in the seventeenth century. The base of the memorial is of granite, and on the front is a bronze plaque representing the landing-place on the Parker river, and on the back is another bronze tablet, giving the names of the first settlers. Above the base is a representation of the shallop Mary and John, on which these Pilgrim Fathers are said to have made the voyage across the Atlantic. The monument originated with Mrs. Elizabeth L. Withington, Secretary of the Historical Society of Old Newbury, as the original settlement is now called, and the funds have been principally raised from representatives of old families connected with the town, which has sent forth men and women who have been signally influential in the affairs of state and nation.

P. 152 The only other Dissenting Meeting-houses in the neighbourhood of Newbury, at this time (1669), mentioned in the return, are those of Presbyterian congregations at Lambourn, East Ilsley, and Bradfield; and Quakers at Boxford and Brimpton, where George Fox, the founder of the Society, Joseph Cole, John Burnet, Charles Bacon, Solomon Earle, and other prominent members of the sect are returned as the usual "Teachers."

P. 153, line 2 from top, *for* "Alra." *read* "Alva."

P. 156. Among the plate belonging to the Presbyterian Church authorities is a silver cup, 4/8ins. high, 3/8ins. diameter, with handle. London date letter, 1705-6. Given by Joseph Blandy Bunny, whose initials it bears. Opposite the handle are the arms of the House of Howard, but they are *not* those of the Duke, for the esquire's helmet shows the owner was a *Mr. Howard.* These arms have erroneously been applied to the Bunny family. How the cup came into the possession of Mr. Joseph Blandy Bunny it is impossible to explain—Mr. Bunny was born in 1767, and died in 1834.

P. 187, line 7 from top, replace full stop after Gerbeir by comma.
,, line 14 from bottom, *for* "desceut" *read* "descent."

P. 201. Omit line 1 and 2—repeated.

INDEX.

ADDITIONAL BOOKS BY WALTER MONEY

ALDERMASTON; a topographical and historical account. Newbury, Blacket, 1890

Outline of the history of the Maison Dieu, or hospital of Sir Richard Abberbury, at DONNINGTON, near Newbury. Newbury, Blacket, 1878

Outline of the history of DONNINGTON PRIORY, near Newbury . . . a House of the Maturine Friars. Newbury, Blacket, 1878

Early history of the parish of ENBORNE, in the county of Berks. Newbury, Blacket, 1893.

Collections for a history of the parish of HAMPSTEAD NORRIS. Newbury, Blacket, 1881

Historical sketch of the town of HUNGERFORD, in the county of Berks. Newbury, Blacket, 1894.

History of the ancient town and borough of NEWBURY, in the county of Berks. Oxford, Parker, 1887

The first and second Battles of NEWBURY, and the Siege of Donnington Castle, in the Civil War, A.D. 1643–46. Simpkin Marshall, 1871. 2nd edn. 1874

A Popular history of Newbury, in the county of Berks. . . . accompanied with a memoir on the geology of Newbury by E. P. Richards . . . and a contribution on the botany of the district by G. Claridge Druce. Newbury, Blacket, 1905.

Annals of the Church of St. Mary, SHAW-CUM-DONNINGTON . . . Newbury, Blacket, 1878.

Collections for the history of the parish of SPEEN. . . . Blacket, 1892.

(Ed.) A Perfect Booke of all landes within the hundreds of Evenger, Chutlye, Kingsclere, Pastroe and Overton, reviewed in the year of Our Lord, 1575.

History of Coal-bearing rocks.

PLATE I

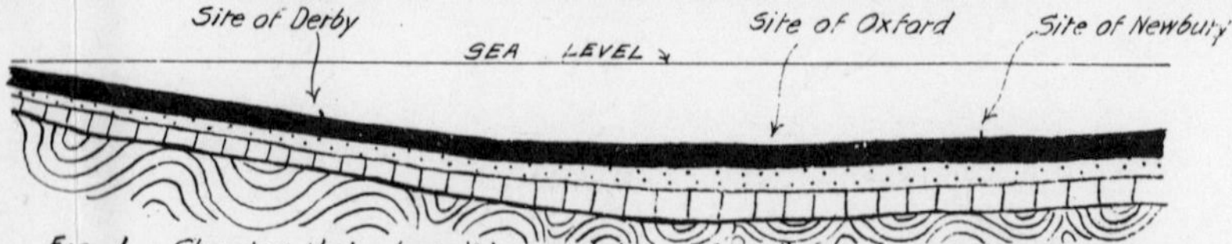

FIG. 1. Shewing their deposition as layers of sediment on the bottom of Ancient Seas, the black stratum contained Coal Seams. The highly contorted rocks forming the sea bottom are similar to those of Wales.

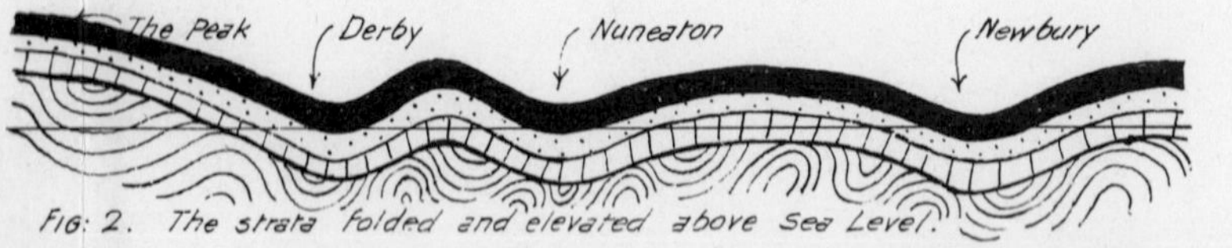

FIG: 2. The strata folded and elevated above Sea Level.

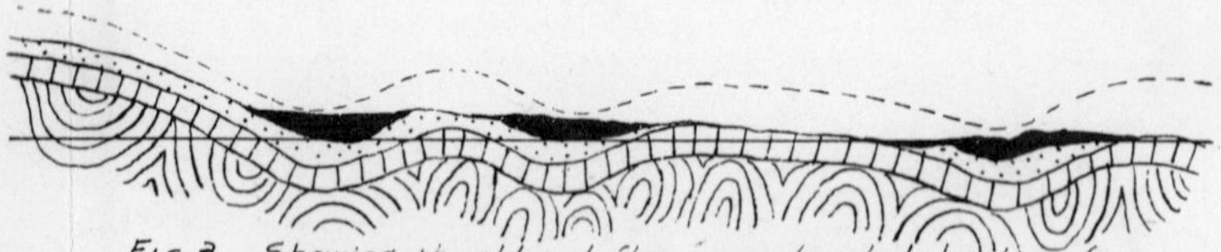

FIG 3. Shewing the old rock floor as a denuded land-surface with the coal seams only preserved in downfolds

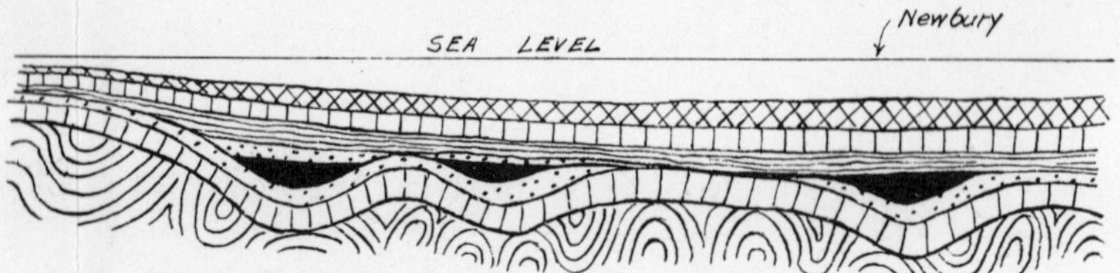

FIG 4. Shewing the deposition of the red sand-stones Jurassic, and Cretaceous on the rock floor after its Subsidence

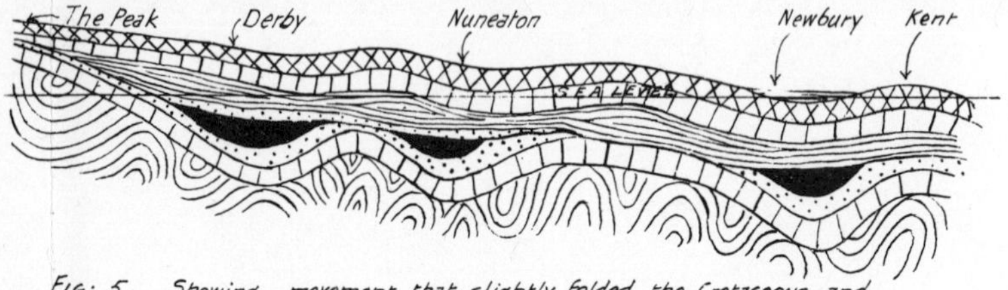

FIG: 5 Shewing movement that slightly folded the Cretaceous and Jurassic Strata and raised them into a new land surface.

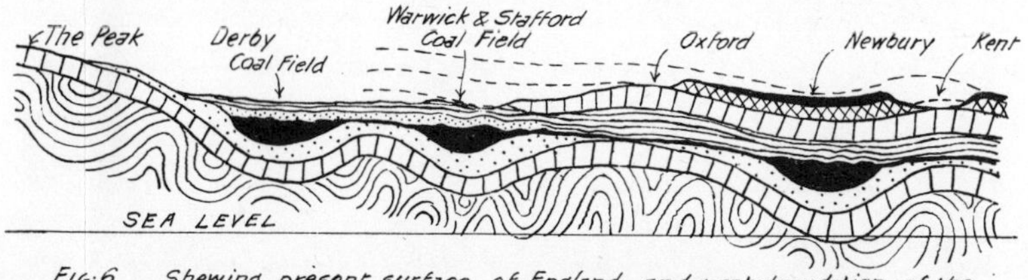

FIG 6. Shewing present surface of England, and great denudation of the Cretaceous and Jurassic that has taken place.

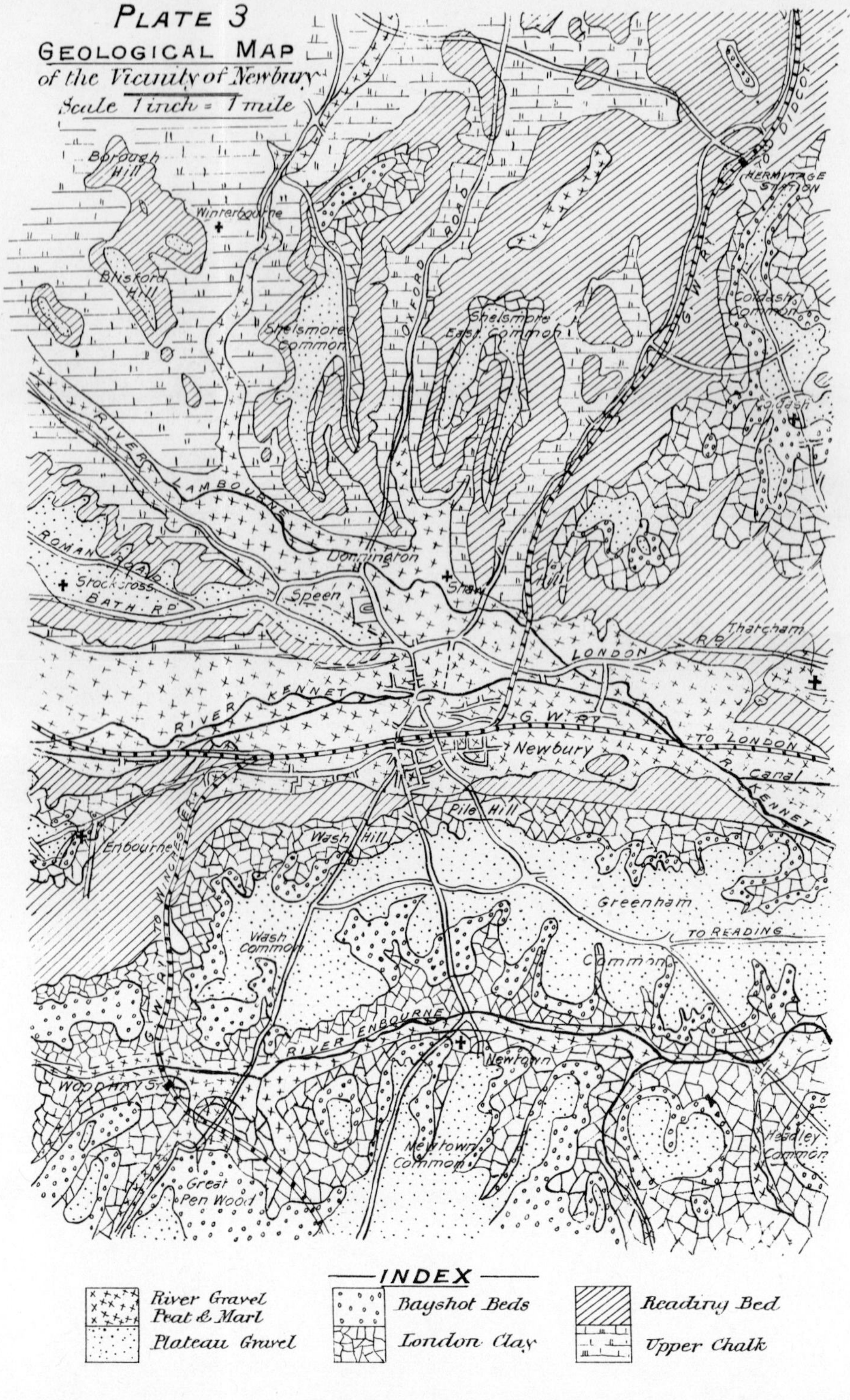

PLATE 3
GEOLOGICAL MAP
of the Vicinity of Newbury
Scale 1 inch = 1 mile
Borough Hill
Winterbourne
Bussford Hill
Shelsmore Common
Shelsmore East Common
OXFORD ROAD
HERMITAGE STATION
DIDCOT
G.W.R.
Coldash Common
Coldash
RIVER LAMBOURNE
ROMAN ROAD
Stockcross
BATH RD
Speen
Donnington
Shaw
Thatcham
LONDON RD
RIVER KENNET
G.W.R.
Newbury
TO LONDON
Canal
R. KENNET
Pile Hill
Wash Hill
Enbourne
Greenham
TO READING
Wash Common
Common
RIVER ENBOURNE
Newtown
WOODHAY STN
Newtown Common
Headley Common
Great Pen Wood
INDEX
River Gravel Peat & Marl
Plateau Gravel
Bagshot Beds
London Clay
Reading Bed
Upper Chalk

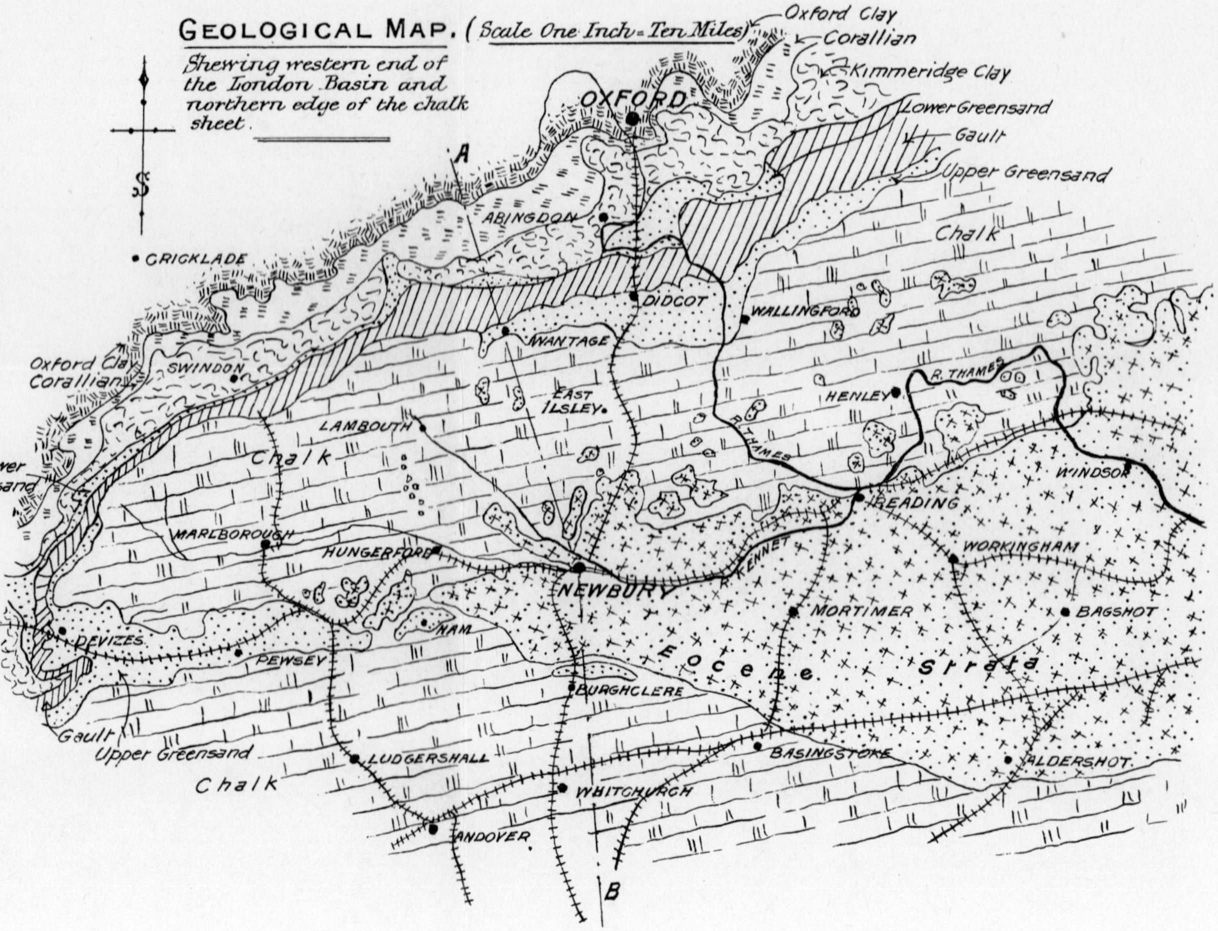

Sketch Section along line A. B.

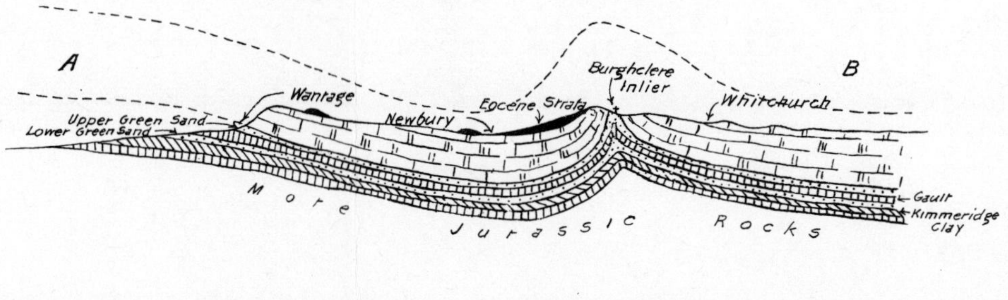